The Italian Language Today

The Italian Language Today

Anna Laura Lepschy
Giulio Lepschy

Hutchinson of London

Hutchinson & Co (Publishers) Ltd
3 Fitzroy Square, London W1

London Melbourne Sydney Auckland
Wellington Johannesburg and agencies
throughout the world

First published 1977
Paperback edition 1979
© Anna Laura Lepschy and Giulio Lepschy 1977

Set in Times New Roman by G. A. Pindar & Son Ltd, Scarborough

Printed in Great Britain by The Anchor Press Ltd,
and bound by Wm Brendon & Son Ltd, both of
Tiptree, Essex.

ISBN 0 09 128020 6 cased
      0 09 128021 4 paper

Contents

Preface

In this work we have tried to describe contemporary Italian and to examine some aspects of its history which have often led people to wonder whether an 'Italian' language really exists.

The first part of the book gives an introduction to the present day linguistic situation in Italy (chapter I) and outlines its origin and its development particularly during the last century (chapter II); it sets out historically the main subdivisions of the Italian dialects (chapter III), and provides information on modern Italian and its varieties (chapter IV).

The second part offers a grammar of Italian, including a detailed examination of special points (chapter V), and a longer discussion of certain questions which present particular problems to students of Italian or are not adequately discussed in current grammars (chapter VI). This part is organized as a reference grammar and not as a progressive grammar, but we hope it may also prove useful for those who are learning the language. Apart from the basic outlines, our coverage is selective: we have concentrated on what seems most interesting to us and have not tried to include the kind of information which is easily found in dictionaries (we have not, for instance, discussed in detail adverbs, conjunctions and prepositions; but as dictionaries do not usually give adequate information on constructions of verb + preposition, we have listed these quite fully). We describe contemporary usage, but mention historical developments wherever we feel they are illuminating.

The first part of the book should clarify and put into the right perspective the assumptions on which the second part is based, particularly with regard to standards of acceptability and correctness. We aim at presenting educated Italian not as it is prescribed in grammars and dictionaries, but as it is actually written and spoken. For those aspects in which there does not seem to be a unitary national standard, we have followed northern usage, which seems to us to enjoy most prestige. We aim at enabling the foreign student to understand a wide range of expressions and to select those which are most suitable for him to use, in speech or writing. Where necessary we have characterized certain usages as formal or informal, colloquial or literary, or typical of certain parts of the country.

Translations are given for all Italian and dialect examples, usually offering only one of the possible meanings, not necessarily the most common, but the one relevant to the point being made. Italics are used for all the examples in traditional spelling in Italian (language or dialects). Where necessary a broad phonetic transcription is given (based on the principles of the International Phonetic Association) between square brackets (see the Table of Symbols, page 240). Only rarely has it been relevant to speak of phonemes (phonological units which are distinctively different); phonemic transcriptions appear between slants. Accent marks are placed directly above the vowel rather than at the beginning of the syllable because syllable divisions do not coincide in all varieties of Italian. Marks for secondary stress appear below the line.

Although this book makes use of many notions of modern linguistics, it is not written for linguists, and it adopts a traditional grammatical framework, accessible to readers who have not studied linguistics. Rules are given in an informal way. The formalism of contemporary linguistics would have made them more precise and explicit, but unusable by the non-linguist. In order to illustrate them we sometimes inevitably make use of sentences which are not likely to appear in everyday conversation.

The data and suggestions offered here, some of which are not available elsewhere, should be of value to the linguist as well as to those for whom this book is intended, students of Italian and others interested in the Italian language.

We are very grateful to the following friends and colleagues whose comments and suggestions on the first draft of this work have enabled us to make many improvements to our text: Guglielmo Cinque, Maria Corti, Denis Devereux, John Hale, John Lindon, Peter Matthews, Luigi Meneghello, John Moores, Andrew Radford, John Scott, Peter Trudgill, Nigel Vincent. We should also like to thank Drina Oldroyd for her helpful reading at proof stage.

Part One
The Linguistic Situation in Italy

I   Italian Today

'The Italian language today': what is it? If one tried to be very 'scientific' and to provide an answer based on observation and verifiable empirically, one would meet with considerable difficulties. A student of linguistics from the University of Mars, sent to the Earth to do some field work, and asked to write a report on the Italian language today, would be faced with a very confusing situation. If he listened to the utterances made by people within the boundaries of the Italian Republic, he would find an extraordinary variety of speech, which could not be interpreted as belonging to one and the same language ('Italian'). Then, if he extended his investigations further he would find that some of the varieties of speech used in Italy are also used by large communities in other parts of the globe, ranging from Australia to the Americas, and in European countries such as France, Switzerland, Germany, and Belgium.

His confusion would be caused not by the speech of the so-called 'linguistic minorities' in the Italian territory (using German for instance in the Alto Adige, and Albanian or Greek in parts of southern Italy), but by the variety of dialects used both in Italy and in the large Italian immigrant communities abroad.

It may be useful at this point to clarify some notions. The Italian situation differs considerably from the English one, where dialects are concerned. English dialects, with grammar, lexis and phonology very different from standard English, are mostly dying out; they survive in the main in isolated or peripheral areas, particularly in the speech of the elderly. Elsewhere, especially in the south of England, the differences between dialects and standard English are less marked. Standard English is spoken with different accents in different parts of the country. There is also a non-regional pronunciation, generally indicated with the abbreviation 'RP' ('received pronunciation'), which is typically used in public schools. During the first half of the twentieth century its diffusion was encouraged by a fairly strict adherence to it on the part of the B B C. It is a flexible standard, in many cases offering a large variety of choices between different pronunciations; and it changes as time passes. This can be seen by looking up in Daniel Jones's *English Pronouncing Dictionary* (which presents R P) the different pronunciations recorded for so many words, and by comparing the changes incorporated in successive editions. This dictionary was meant to be descriptive rather than prescriptive, although it is often used as a model to which foreigners and, when uncertain, some native speakers of English try to conform.

R P, originally based on the speech of the educated in south-east England, is a social rather than a geographical indicator: it characterizes the educated speech of the upper and middle classes. Traditionally, if a speaker uses R P people will not be able to tell from his speech which part of the country he comes from. If he does not use R P not only will he be socially characterized, but to this social characterization will be added a geographical one: people will be able to tell which part of the country he comes from. Eliza Doolittle's speech could be pinned down to Lisson Grove; Professor Higgins, using R P, did not give away his place of origin.

It is against this background that one can understand recent developments and reactions such as the greater use of regional English by the B B C, or the tenacity with which some University students retain their regional accents because of the ideological implications of losing them: using R P would mean not so much substituting a national standard for a regional variety, as substituting the speech of the middle class for the speech of the working class. The class connotations of accent emerge very clearly in the field of politics, trade-unionism, and in the media where it is not uncommon to hear people adapting their accent to the circumstances.

The situation is quite different in Italy. People may of course be characterized socially by the language they use, but it is a question more of their style of speech, of the 'manner' in which they speak, than of their phonological systems. The distinction between Italian and dialect has no firm correlation with social hierarchy, because although ignorance of Italian is limited to the bottom of the scale, the use of dialect is not, and cuts right across class barriers. But it is also true that Italian is inevitably associated with the upper part of the scale and dialect with the lower, and that the attempt to move up from the bottom is often accompanied by rejection of dialect and adoption of Italian.

When people talk of Italian dialects they are not usually referring to different varieties of Italian. Italian dialects differ from literary Italian and among themselves so much that one dialect may be unintelligible to the speaker of another dialect. They may differ among themselves as much as French differs from Spanish, or Portuguese from Rumanian, or for that matter Italian from English. The initial effect of strangeness, foreignness and unintelligibility can be the same. The situation is of course different, because with Italian dialects, which derive from Latin and have had some cultural contact with literary Italian as it developed through the centuries, the establishment of a basis for mutual understanding, the identification of correspondence rules and the beginnings of a translation and of a learning process are obviously so much easier.

Dialects in Italy are far more commonly used and differ from each other and from the national language more radically than dialects in England, and generally one can sharply distinguish between Italian and dialect. The notions of Italian and of dialect, however, both need to be specified.

It has recently been suggested[1] that, for some parts of Italy at least, one needs to distinguish between four strata: besides (a) the national language and (b) the local dialect there is (c) a more inward looking variety of the national language (regional Italian); this is comparable to the phenomenon very much alive in England, of standard English spoken with a local accent; and (d) a more outward looking variety of the local dialect (regional dialect).

Take a simple sentence like 'Go home, boys' as uttered in a village in Venetia. The allegedly standard form in the national language would be [andáte a kkása ragáttsi] and in the local dialect something like [ve káza túzi]. But in the same village people may also use a less local, more regional Venetian form like [nde káza tózi], and a less national, more regional Italian form like [andáte a káza ragási].

In this example the lexical choice (*ragazzo* vs. *toso*) immediately shows the distinction between Italian and dialect, and there are grammatical and phonological differences which allow one to differentiate quite clearly between the two types of dialect (local vs. regional: with and without metaphony (see chapter III, pp. 50–51) and with different forms of *andare*) and the two types of Italian (national vs. regional: with and without double consonants and affricates [ts dz]).

Do these four strata in fact correspond to a fourfold choice offered to the speaker? We deliberately chose a transcription which was broad enough to show up those features which contribute to distinguish the four varieties. But there is no polar opposition between single and double consonants (a novelist with a keen ear for language has noted that a speaker may try to pronounce a double consonant, but succeed only in uttering one and a half)[2], nor between the affricates [ts dz] of the national and the sibilants [s z] of the regional standard. Perhaps one can move between the two varieties of the standard and the two varieties of the dialect with an indefinite number of intermediate stages. Also, even though there is no intermediate stage between *toso* and *ragazzo*, in considering actual utterances, one finds that the various words of one and the same utterance may have been chosen from different varieties. These varieties are more easily definable in terms of the speakers' linguistic situation than in terms of sets to which particular sentences or words can be allotted. One might certainly hear [andáte a káza túzi] and [ve káza ragáttsi]. One should perhaps leave open whether these varieties are more appropriately considered to be distinct entities between which one has to switch, or rather dimensions which allow movements along continuous gradients.

It is doubtful whether the 'top' stratum, the alleged national standard as represented by educated Florentine, ought to appear at all in this example. Florentine features, such as initial voiceless affricates, as in [tsìo], intervocalic voiceless sibilants as in [kása], or syntactic doubling as in [a kkása] are not used in actual fact in northern Italy and do not even constitute a theoretical model which people there try to imitate: they are felt to be either parochial and alien, or affected. In Venetia there may however be a distinction between a more dialectal use of Italian, with [ragási], a less dialectal one, with [ragátsi] and a more national one, with [ragáttsi].

In a village the less local variety of the dialect might conform to a regional standard or might be an attempt to imitate the dialect of the nearest town. In a town like Venice people cannot switch from a local to a regional form of the dialect; the regional standard and the local dialect seem to coincide, and two rather than three or four strata are sufficient to account for the linguistic conditions. The number of strata which are involved ought to be decided instance by instance, rather than once and for all.

In many cases the distinction between these poles may be made more complicated by the presence of another distinction, between a spontaneous and informal vs. a careful and formal style of speech. More complicated, because often (but by no means always or necessarily) the spontaneous and informal is associated with dialect and the careful and formal with Italian. An exclamation like *Guarda che roba!* 'Look at that!' would be [gwȧrda ke rrɔba] in the presumptive standard and [vȧrda ke rɔba] in Venetian; the first word may become [ȧrda] and [ɨda] in both, and may appear as [ȧra] and even [a:] in the dialect. Within the dialect one finds, with decreasing degrees of formality [andė], [nde], [de], and [ne] for 'go!'. A narrower transcription would allow one to capture other pronunciations intermediate between these, and would correspond to the native's intuition that he is here faced more with a continuum than with a set of discrete choices placing him either in the language or in the dialect, either in one variety or in another. As we said, the Martian linguist, trying to be scientific and to ascertain facts rather than opinions, would have no easy task.

A foreigner learning Italian inevitably asks: what variety of Italian shall I adopt, and in particular what sort of pronunciation? Which is the pronunciation that can be considered standard (in some sense 'the best') and used as a model in the same way as RP can be used as a model in British English?

The answer to the latter question is that there is no Italian equivalent to RP. Educated pronunciation is not uniform but varies locally, it is more similar in each region to the uneducated pronunciation of the same region than to the educated pronunciation of other regions. The normal, widely accepted state of affairs in Italy is for a speaker to retain his local accent. This situation is to be expected in the context of Italian history. Italian is no less effective for this (different pronunciations are no real cause for misunderstandings); this variety reflects the different local traditions and cultures which a united Italy has absorbed but not obliterated.

The former question – what pronunciation is a foreigner to adopt? – can perhaps be answered depending on the circumstances, with practical considerations in mind. In chapter V a solution is offered which disregards the phonological oppositions which are treated differently in different parts of Italy (and therefore do not belong to a national standard), and chooses, when a choice has to be made, a northern Italian standard, which has acquired more prestige than other varieties. The choice of this phonological system also facilitates the task of the foreign student as it is more faithfully represented by traditional spelling.

It should be added here that these points are contentious, and that these two questions could receive different answers. In particular there is one position, usually adopted by textbooks and dictionaries, which can be called, for brevity but not inappropriately, puristic, according to which there is only one correct pronunciation of Italian, i.e., educated Florentine, and it is this which ought to be learnt by foreigners – and by Italians.

Cutting across geographical subdivisions (local varieties of Italian) there is another set of partitions into different spheres of linguistic usage (sectional varieties): the language of literature, of bureaucracy, of politics, of journalism, of advertising, of science, of the church, etc. Newspapers, radio and television do not have a clearly definable sectional idiom of their own; they act rather as channels through which idioms of other fields reach a wider public.

The fields from which everyday language borrows most are sport and advertising. Sport is followed with enormous enthusiasm. It has been noted that only with reference to sport do some people who are normally dialect speakers use Italian expressions, learnt from sports commentators. As well as the sports pages in ordinary newspapers, Italy has the privilege of having as many as four dailies devoted entirely to sport. Readers often seem not to realize that the hyperbolic style used by some sports writers corresponds to a very special register, and repeat their baroque images in the wrong key, as if they belonged to a neutral, unmarked stylistic level. Expressions adopted by ordinary language from the field of sport include for instance: *mettere alle corde, seguire a ruota, salvarsi in corner, prendere in contropiede* (roughly translated 'to put into a tight corner', 'to tail', 'to escape by the skin of one's teeth', 'to catch on the wrong foot').

Advertising, in its attempt to persuade, manipulates language in a very elaborate way, making use of the most refined rhetorical techniques. Some advertisements strive to be memorable by their unusual expressions (but mostly they popularize rather than innovate), others try to impress themselves on the public's consciousness (or perhaps on its subconscious) more surreptitiously, through a smooth, colourless message presenting itself as artless rather than drawing attention to its structure. It is very common for fragments of advertisements to become set phrases: e.g., *contro il logorio della vita moderna* 'against the stresses of modern life' (from the advertisement for an apéritif), or *seduce, seduce, seduce* 'it seduces,

seduces, seduces' (from a soap advertisement).

The media are traditionally the butt of puristic complaints: they are accused of polluting the language with their lazy or snobbish use of foreign words and dialectalisms. They have however been among the most important factors in spreading knowledge of Italian. Rather than the use of foreign or dialect words, which may enliven their language, it is their adherence to heavy and opaque formulas that is to be deplored. They are full of the same sort of evasive obscurity which marks the speeches of many Italian politicians, and newspaper articles often appear to be addressed not to the general public but to a highly sophisticated minority capable of reading between the lines and of interpreting convoluted allusions. Even in the more modest reporting of local events the freshness and authenticity of spontaneous expressions is suppressed in favour of a limited and dull inventory of stereotypes, a false idiom which Italo Calvino has called an 'antilanguage', and has exemplified as follows. This is what a witness might say:

Stamattina presto andavo in cantina ad accendere la stufa e ho trovato tutti quei fiaschi di vino dietro la cassa del carbone. Ne ho preso uno per bermelo a cena. Non ne sapevo niente che la bottiglieria di sopra era stata scassinata. 'Early this morning I went into the cellar to light the boiler and I found all those flasks of wine behind the coal-bin. I took one to have with my supper. I didn't know anything about the wineshop above having been broken into.'

This is how an official takes it down on his typewriter: *Il sottoscritto, essendosi recato nelle prime ore antimeridiane nei locali dello scantinato per eseguire l'avviamento dell'impianto termico, dichiara d'essere casualmente incorso nel rinvenimento di un quantitativo di prodotti vinicoli, situati in posizione retrostante al recipiente adibito al contenimento del combustibile e di aver effettuato l'asportazione di uno dei detti articoli nell'intento di consumarlo durante il pasto pomeridiano, non essendo a conoscenza dell'avvenuta effrazione dell'esercizio soprastante.* 'The undersigned having descended in the early hours of the morning to the basement rooms to set in motion the heating installation, declares that he made the fortuitous discovery of a quantity of vinicultural products situated to the rear of the container of combustible material, and that he effected the removal of one of the said articles with the intent of consuming it during his evening meal, not being aware of the burglary which had taken place in the commercial premises above.'[3]

The differences between sectional idioms are mainly apparent in vocabulary, partly in syntax, and minimally in morphology. Phonology is involved through the use of particular intonation patterns which are considered to be appropriate to or typical of, for instance, the reading aloud of poetry, the preaching of a sermon, the presentation of a radio, television or cinema advertisement, or the delivery used in reporting a football match. Usually the geographical subdivisions emerge through the sectional ones, and it is only occasionally that the former are used as a further means of sectional characterization because a southern accent, say, is thought to typify the speech of a policeman or of a bureaucrat, or a Lombard accent a dynamic but philistine industrialist or businessman. For instance in the song *Ma mi* . . . Ornella Vanoni switches from the dialect of the protagonist, a character from the Milanese underworld (*mi son de quei che parlen no* ['I'm one of those who don't talk']), to the Italian, heavily southern in accent and grammar, of the police inspector (*noi li pigliasse . . . ma se parlasse . . .* ['we'll catch them . . . but if you were to talk . . .']). But that is another story, which is interesting for folklore as well as linguistics, i.e., the use of mottoes, often abusive, in which Italians have traditionally incorporated their judgements of the inhabitants of other parts of Italy, making fun of their speech characteristics.

Notes

[1]Cf. PELLEGRINI, G.B., 'Tra lingua e dialetto in Italia', *Studi Mediolatini e Volgari*, 8, 1960, pp. 137–153; 'L'italiano regionale', *Cultura e Scuola*, n.5, 1962, pp. 20–29; 'Dal dialetto alla lingua (Esperienze di un veneto settentrionale)' in *Dal dialetto alla lingua. Atti del IX convegno per gli studi dialettali italiani*, Pisa, 1974, pp. 175–194 (partly reproduced in Id., *Saggi di linguistica Italiana*, Turin, 1975, pp. 11–54). In what follows we shall take examples from the Venetian situation with which we are most closely acquainted.

[2]MENEGHELLO, L., *Libera nos a malo*, Milan, 1975, p. 183.

[3]CALVINO, I., in *Paese Sera*, 3 February 1963; we quote from BALDELLI, I., 'Aspetti della lingua della prosa letteraria contemporanea', *Cultura e Scuola*, n.18, 1966, pp. 15–16.

II   A Historical View

What is the present day linguistic situation in Italy, and how did it originate? During the Middle Ages the written language was Latin; it was a literary language which could of course also be 'spoken', in the Liturgy, in the Universities, on many formal occasions, and would be employed in ordinary conversation by people whose native tongues were different, but who were familiar with Latin and could use it as an auxiliary language. This possibility would only have been open to a tiny minority; most people were illiterate, and hence, by definition one might say, did not know Latin. The majority would use their own native tongue, the vernacular, that is, one of the Italian dialects. These dialects derive from Latin; they are spoken Latin as it evolved naturally, unaffected by schooling and formal education, or, to be more precise, largely unaffected, as some learned influences are in fact found in the development from Latin to Romance.

Why did spoken Latin evolve so differently in different parts of Italy? We do not know for certain. An often accepted explanation uses the notion of *substratum*: the Italian dialects are Latin as spoken by Celts, Veneti, Etruscans, Umbrians, Oscans, etc. In some cases (Tuscan, Venetian, Sardinian) the development appears to show little trace of the languages of the original inhabitants, perhaps because these languages were radically different from Latin; in other cases (most of the central and southern Italian dialects) the substratum languages were less radically different and are alleged to have influenced the development of Latin to a far greater extent. The 'superstratum' is much less important; the Germanic invaders (Goths, Longobards) and the foreign powers (Arab, Norman, Spanish, French, Austrian) which dominated different parts of Italy at various times left little trace on the language, apart from loanwords; this is also the case with 'adstratum' influences, i.e., from foreign linguistic communities with whom there was cultural contact, like English or Slav.

The substratum theory appears tempting because modern dialectal boundaries often basically coincide with the boundaries between the different groups of the inhabitants of Italy before the Roman conquests, and because some linguistic phenomena are the same in the pre-Roman and in the post-Roman period; for instance where Latin has *nd* Oscan has *nn* (Latin *operandam* corresponds to Oscan *úpsannam* 'to be made') and the same applies to the dialects of Campania: Latin *quando* becomes Neapolitan [kwȧnnə] 'when'. There is however the problem that one would have to suppose that some of these substratum influences acted not at the moment (which anyway is difficult to establish with precision) when Latin was adopted, but after intervals, sometimes of centuries, and there is the further problem of how the written documents relate to the language which was actually spoken. The fact is that, in spite of the achievements of comparative historical linguistics, particularly in the field of Indo-European, it is still not known why languages change, why certain changes occur rather than others, and why they occur at a particular time in a particular place.

Another question which cannot be answered with certainty is: when do the Romance languages, in our case the Italian dialects, begin? According to some scholars (e.g., W. v. Wartburg) they derive from different dialects of spoken Latin, and so can be traced back to the first centuries A.D. According to others (e.g., H.F. Muller) they cannot have originated much before their earliest written documents, that is, as late as the eighth century. In this case the birth of Romance would date from the Carolingian renaissance, brilliantly represented by Alcuin, which brought about a greater correctness in the writing of Latin texts; a hiatus was thus introduced between a purified Latin, closer to the classical language, and much more 'vulgar' forms, which were now seen to be very different from it and which precipitated into the vernacular.

What we have here is perhaps not so much a disagreement over facts, as a choice between different points of view: if one looks at individual changes one can trace many of them very far back, but if one is searching for a natural break in the language development, and wants to avoid imposing any artificial subdivision, then one will have to look beyond the examples, to the actual speakers. One will then say that the vernacular begins at the moment in which the speakers become aware of the existence not of two different varieties of the same language (classical vs. vulgar or literary vs.

spoken), but of two different languages, one the vernacular, acquired by all in infancy and used as everyday speech, the other Latin, acquired only as a result of study and used as a literary language. People may have been conscious of a bilingual situation even before the first documents which have come down to us, but we cannot prove it. The first attestations of this awareness come fairly late: the Council of Tours, 813, in its seventeenth deliberation stated '*ut easdem omelias quisque aperte transferre studeat in rusticam romanam linguam aut thiotiscam, quo facilius cuncti possint intellegere quae dicuntur*' (that everyone should try to translate the said homilies into the rustic Roman language or into German, so that everyone may more easily understand what is being said), and the Strasbourg Oaths of 842 are the first document of a Romance language with the French (as well as the German) words of the oath inserted in the Latin narrative.

In Italy evidence of the vernacular emerges later than in France. In the ninth century we find texts which have vernacular characteristics; in the following century we get several references to the use of the vernacular in Italy: the poem *Gesta Berengarii* relates that at the coronation of Berengarius I (915) the senate expressed themselves '*patrio ore*' 'in the language of the fathers' and the people cried '*nativa voce*' 'in their native tongue'. There is a reference to '*nostrae vulgaris linguae quae latinitati vicina est*' 'our vulgar language which is close to Latin' dating from 960; the epitaph of Pope Gregory V (999) states that '*usus francisca vulgari et voce latina instituit populos eloquio triplici*' 'by using French, the vernacular and Latin he instructed the nations in three tongues'. The first dated texts which present the two languages clearly distinguished in one and the same document go back to 960. For the development of a literary vernacular we have to wait until the thirteenth century, when various works are produced in different parts of Italy: Sicilian poetry, Umbrian religious texts, northern Italian didactic poems, Bolognese and then Tuscan verse and prose. Are they written in Italian dialects? The answer is 'yes' only if we accept the use of the term 'dialect' for a period in which there was no standard national language to which the dialect could be opposed, and in spite of the fact that these vernacular writings tended to be 'ennobled' and illustrious and to underplay their more parochial features.

At the beginning of the fourteenth century, Dante provided in the *De Vulgari Eloquentia* a critical survey of vernacular literature in

Italy up to his own day which is still valid now, and at the same time he traced the first outline of Italian dialectology from the point of view of a vernacular writer. The Florentine dialect in which Dante wrote his *Comedy* became the basis of a national literary language partly through the excellence of the literature written in it during the fourteenth century, partly because of general historical developments in Italy at the time (the political, economic and cultural prestige of Florence) and partly on linguistic grounds, as the Tuscan dialects were, not only geographically but also linguistically, intermediate between north and south.

When the vernacular re-emerged, after a period of crisis during the fifteenth century, when many humanists disparaged its use, considering it uncouth, undignified and corrupt compared to Latin, it became the subject of the *questione della lingua*, a controversy which was deeply felt, and far from being an idle rhetorical game, had the most wide-ranging cultural and historical implications. What sort of vernacular was best suited as a medium for literary expression? Modern textbooks present a useful, though too schematic, classification into four positions combining two pairs of contrasting views, modernists vs. archaists, and Tuscanists vs. Italianists: (1) those, like Bembo, who favoured archaic Tuscan, as represented in particular by vernacular classics, Boccaccio for prose and Petrarch for poetry: this language was to be learnt through study, just as Latin was to be learnt through the imitation of such classics as Virgil and Cicero; (2) those, like Machiavelli, Tolomei and Gelli, who favoured modern Tuscan; (3) those, like Muzio, who favoured an archaizing composite literary language; (4) those who favoured a modern composite language, like the 'lingua cortigiana' used by people from different parts of Italy at the main courts in Rome, Urbino, Ferrara, etc.; this preference was expressed among others by Trissino and Castiglione. The first position prevailed, and Bembo's theories, defining a trend which was already implicit in the development of Italian literature, were to mark Italian culture for the next four centuries.

From the sixteenth century on, we find dialect literature proper, in the modern sense. Here 'dialect' has quite a different connotation from the one it had with reference to the thirteenth century. It is now contrasted with a 'standard' literary language, and dialect texts tend to underline, and not to underplay, their parochiality. A new form of bilingualism is introduced into the vernacular, so that during the sixteenth century Italian literature consists of **works** written in three mediums: in Latin, in the national literary language, which is based on early Florentine but has different varieties, and in a dialect, as for example Ruzzante's plays in Old Paduan and Veneziano's poetry in Sicilian.

From then on literature in Italian followed a path of rhetorical preoccupations, of aspiration to formal perfection and of detachment from ordinary life. Authors did not write for the common people, and the common people did not read works of literature, for even if they were not illiterate they would find the style impenetrable. The first great dictionary devoted to any modern language was the Italian *Vocabolario degli Accademici della Crusca* (first edition 1612). Largely through the influence of L. Salviati, the Crusca took its inspiration from Bembo's theories. Its dictionary did not help to make Italian more widely known or to get it adopted as a spoken national language. It was based on a distinction between Tuscan authors, mainly from the past, who were 'pure' and whose words were to be included, and all the rest whose language was 'impure' and so were excluded. The aim of the dictionary was not to present the usage of writers and of cultured people objectively, but to provide the norm to which this minority should conform in their writings.

During the following centuries we find many restatements of puristic principles (from Lionardo di Capua to Antonio Cesari and Basilio Puoti), and rebellions against them, mainly by representatives of new scientific movements and by thinkers open to European ideas, above all French, who wanted to renew Italian culture, as for example the Milanese group of *Il Caffè*, headed by the Verri brothers.[1] It would be wrong to infer from prevailing post-romantic attitudes (still current today) that purists were always reactionary and wrong, and their enemies always progressive and right. Purism might embody a patriotic attitude which in certain circumstances could be progressive.[2]

How could a modern national literature flourish in these conditions? How could one write novels in literary Italian? Manzoni described his predicament with clarity: Italian was like a dead language; he expressed himself spontaneously in the Milanese dialect and found French a rich and versatile literary medium, but he could hardly write a novel addressed to the Italian public either in Milanese or in French. Manzoni turned the *questione della lingua* upside down. He did not want literature to decide what the national language should be, he wanted literature to adopt the language most suited to the conditions of the country. Writers ought not to try to impose on the nation the rhetorical and obsolete language of Italian literature of the past; they ought to use a living idiom, one that could become the national language, both written and spoken. This could only be Florentine. Manzoni wrote his novel three times, trying as best he could the third time (1840) to make it conform to contemporary Florentine. He did not fully succeed, partly because his knowledge of Florentine was insufficient, partly because it is difficult, perhaps impossible, to keep the language of the literary tradition out of a work of literature.

For the first edition of *I promessi sposi* Manzoni used the Milanese dictionary by Francesco Cherubini; but like other dialect dictionaries of the time, Cherubini provided elaborate Crusca renderings for dialect expressions. The juxtaposition of down-to-earth idioms in dialect with the affected and frequently obsolete Crusca turns of phrase often had an unintentionally comic effect, and Manzoni tried in vain to convince Cherubini to adopt contemporary Florentine for the second edition of his dictionary (1839) instead of the language of the Crusca. Manzoni greatly overrated the importance of dictionaries; in a report to the Minister of Education in 1868 (*Dell'unità della lingua e dei mezzi di diffonderla* 'On the Unity of Language and the Means to Propagate it'), arguing for the adoption of contemporary spoken Florentine as the national language, he maintained that the preparation and diffusion of a dictionary of Florentine was the best way of turning his theories into reality. The *Nòvo vocabolario della lingua italiana secondo l'uso di Firenze* 'New dictionary of the Italian language according to Florentine usage' was duly prepared under the editorship of the ex-Minister himself, E. Broglio, and of Manzoni's son-in-law, G.B. Giorgini, and was published between 1870 and 1897.

Perhaps the lasting merit of the *Nòvo vocabolario* is that the publication of its first volume prompted G.I. Ascoli to write his *Proemio* (1873). Ascoli, the greatest linguist Italy has ever had, and one of the leading comparative philologists of his time, established Italian dialectology on a scientific basis, writing and promoting a large number of studies, many still unsurpassed today, which he published in his journal, the *Archivio Glottologico Italiano*. His *Proemio*, i.e., proem or introduction to the first volume of this journal, is a concise and vigorously argued essay – almost a manifesto – on Italy's linguistic problems. After political unification the *questione della lingua* had re-emerged with a new urgency, and with practical implications previously absent.

Against the proposal that contemporary spoken Florentine should be adopted by all Italians and that a main vehicle for its diffusion should be a dictionary, Ascoli pointed out that this was not the way national languages were formed. He drew his examples from the linguistic history of France, England and Germany. In France the dialect of Paris had become the national language, through centuries of political, bureaucratic and cultural centralization. In Germany it was not a local dialect, but the idiom used by Luther in his translation of the Bible, that was the basis of the language adopted by the whole nation, at all social levels, thanks to the advance of literacy and the flowering of cultural and civic activities, which, in spite of the lack of political unity, established close links between all sections of the community. The Italian situation was quite different: there was a literary language, developed by men of letters for men of letters, which had never become truly national and popular; there had been neither political centralization, as in France and England, nor widespread cultural activity as in Germany. Manzoni's choice of modern Florentine was quite arbitrary. It was true of course that literary Italian was based on fourteenth-century Florentine, but it had been shaped in the following centuries by influences from other parts of Italy that had not affected the dialect of Florence, which meanwhile had developed along its own lines, quite differently from the literary language.

Why, asked Ascoli, should one introduce forms with *o* instead of *uo* (such as *Nòvo* in the title of the *Nòvo vocabolario*) when the accepted form in literary Italian had for centuries been the one with the diphthong? The fact that modern Florentine preferred forms without the diphthong was certainly not a good reason. Similarly Florentine used *anello* for 'thimble', while other dialects, both in the north and in the south, used *ditale*, which was accepted as the Italian word, and there was no reason for switching now to a Florentine dialect form. In any case, the linguistic situation of a country could not be changed by decree, nor by giving people a dictionary of the dialect which was being proposed as a standard. The formation of a national language was a complex historical phenomenon which depended on social and cultural forces. Italian was a literary language with elitist and formalistic characteristics deriving from aspects of Italian civilization which Ascoli called 'cult of form' and 'low density of culture'.

Ascoli could clearly see, thanks both to his experience as a linguist and his progressive ideological position, that to try to modify a linguistic situation by making everyone learn the Florentine dialect, in order to change the condition of the country (i.e., to make it a really unified nation, at a deeper level than the political framework of a unified state) was to go about things the wrong way. The formation of a unified language to be used in all parts of the country by all classes, could only be the consequence of deep social and cultural changes.

In accounts of the *questione della lingua*, it is traditional to set Ascoli and Manzoni against each other as representing two extreme positions: the one being that of 'pure science', which does not allow interference with the natural development of language, the other being perhaps over enthusiastic, but more practical, favouring concrete proposals to remedy the linguistic difficulties of the new Italian state; and subsequent developments in the history of the Italian language are presented as corresponding partly to Manzoni's aspirations, partly to Ascoli's forecast.

But this is rather misleading. In the first place Ascoli should not be opposed to Manzoni: in spite of the seeming contrast in their positions, one finds in both the same rejection of a rhetorical approach to literature and culture and the adoption of a much more sober and realistic attitude, which sees questions concerning language and literature in terms of the society in which the language is used and the literature produced, rather than vice versa. (In the *Proemio* Ascoli finely characterized Manzoni's style and the effect it was having on Italian culture: *quel Grande, che è riuscito, con l'infinita potenza di una mano che non pare aver nervi, a estirpare dalle lettere italiane, o dal cervello dell'Italia, l'antichissimo cancro della retorica* 'that great man, who with the infinite power of a hand that seems sinewless, has succeeded in eradicating from Italian letters, or from the brain of Italy, the ancient canker of rhetoric'). In the second place the position upheld in the *Proemio* turned out to be right. The development of the Italian language followed the course opened to it by Italian history, and particularly by the changes which took place in Italian society, and not the course dictated by linguists, or rather *linguaioli* , to use the Italian term indicating people who assume that language ought to conform to their preferences.

The terms 'purist' and '*linguaiolo*' have been used here as labels to cover two outlooks which were in fact very different. For traditional purists the way to achieve correctness lay in imitating a set of texts; according to the *linguaioli* who followed Manzoni,[3] it lay in imitating contemporary Florentine. The opposition between these two standpoints can be seen as a defence of authority versus usage.

Both authority (the classics) and usage (contemporary Florentine) could be fused into a third approach where the subjective personal taste of the writer turned out to be the decisive factor. This is clearly brought out in the preface to the *Lessico della corrotta italianità* (Milan, 1877) 'Lexicon of Corrupt Italian' by Fanfani and Arlía. The argument that bad words may be found in good writers elicits the retort: 'And so what? We respect authority (which helps and strengthens our point) when it does not contrast with good usage, i.e., with reason; but if it does, then, we say frankly, we are not its slaves; we do not follow the *ipse dixit* as a last resort to silence people, because this is true pedantry and may be a cover for abuse.' 'What about the usage of the people? Does it count for nothing?' 'It counts and it doesn't . . . In this context one can only speak of Tuscans, because in Italy one can only speak of the usage of the Tuscan people. Talk a little with the people of Florence, and you will see that in many cases in the midst of the gold which comes out of their mouths, there is much dross, much foreign rubbish.'

This intermediate position, which places the taste of the writer above the authority of the classics and of contemporary Florentine usage, was particularly widespread among Tuscans. Non-Tuscans felt they were on unsure ground and were ready to admit that their usage, however educated, fell short of certain standards of correctness, which were thus assumed to depend not on educated usage but on something quite external to it, i.e., the Tuscan norm. For instance a philologist of the stature of F. D'Ovidio who was also a member of the Crusca Academy, found himself in the ridiculous situation of having to apologize for his Italian. He had used in the title of an essay (*La rimenata di Guido*) the word *rimenata* in the sense of 'scolding'; when it was pointed out to him that this was a southern regionalism, he commented not without irony: 'Now tell me if I have not every reason to feel deeply ashamed. After having spent so many hours of my long life studying our language, in Tuscany, in the classics, in dictionaries, and considering it under the most varied aspects, and preaching against parochialisms – I find as a permanent reproach, printed in a book which I have so carefully polished, such a gross municipalism . . .'[4]

In spite of the differences, these three attitudes share an extrinsic view of language and a mistaken notion that it should be 'pure'. It would be interesting, but would sidetrack us too far, to pinpoint the

precise ideological and political implications of the various positions in these linguistic debates. It seemed to be taken for granted
that the pollution of linguistic purity must come from external
sources; in the case of Italy from below (dialects) and from outside
(foreign languages, particularly French).

The fight against dialects was considered central to the educational process, because schoolchildren (and illiterate adults) in
learning Italian had to suppress the interference of the dialect,
which was their native tongue. Dialect dictionaries were published,
and also handbooks, mostly for the use of schools, which indicated
the main mistakes likely to be made in different regions by dialect
speakers.[5]

Many dialectal usages were collected and criticized at the beginning of this century by the then very popular writer E. De Amicis,
whose *Cuore* was read by generation after generation of Italian
children. In 1905 De Amicis published *L'idioma gentile*, an urbane
and in many ways not unreasonable book, but on the whole superficial and banal in its view of Italian linguistic problems. Although
basically a Florentinist, the author was aware that this position
could be carried to an extreme, as appears from the anecdote which
he introduces into the preface of the second edition (1906), 'in
order to amuse my readers a little' and 'because it may be the object
of useful observations for those who study language'. As the purist
grammarian Raffaello Fornaciari had criticized the word *scrosciare*
('to describe the sound made by freshly baked bread between the
teeth'), De Amicis with the help of some learned friends had tried to
find out in Florence what the right word was, and his field work
produced the following list: *croccare, scricchiolare, scricchiare, cantare, sgrigiolare, crocchiare, sgretolare, scricciolare, sgrigliolare, stridere* (leaving aside *scrogiolare* and *sgricchiolare* 'not heard by
anyone in Florence, but recorded with that meaning by dictionaries
of current usage'). One could certainly make 'useful observations'
on this, although they are likely to be different from those De
Amicis had in mind. Benedetto Croce, in a review of *L'idioma
gentile*, had no difficulty in showing up the silliness of the book,
pointing out how affected it would be if he inserted Tuscan elements
into a piece of writing which, coming from him, was inevitably non-
Tuscan in its conception and whole texture; when talking of non-
Tuscans, Croce noted, 'the word "*toscaneggiare*" itself is mocking',
and he expressed the hope that De Amicis' book would be 'defi-
nitely the last manifestation of the *questione della lingua*'. This hope

was too optimistic.

During the Fascist period there were severe puristic relapses. As early as 1923 a tax was levied on foreign words used in shop signs, and at the beginning of the second world war a law banned such words altogether; a poster appeared with '*Italiani, boicottate le parole straniere*' 'boycott foreign words' (not untypically using the verb *boicottare*, which etymological dictionaries trace back to *c.* 1880, deriving it, through French, from the English 'to boycott', from the name of Captain James Boycott, first victim of this treatment in Ireland). A Fascist law which prohibited the giving of foreign Christian names to Italian children was abolished as late as 1966.[6] In 1938 an official campaign was launched to abolish the *Lei* form of address and instructions were accordingly given to members of the Fascist Party and to all organizations directly and indirectly controlled by the state. The expulsion of *Lei* from the Italian language had been set in motion by an article published in the *Corriere della Sera* of 15 January 1938 by Bruno Cicognani; this writer had the honesty (or the nerve) to reprint it in the sixth volume of his collected works in 1963 in a section called *Amore di lingua Italiana* 'Love for the Italian Language': 'Today – I wrote in 1938 – when Italy is driven towards a deeper consciousness of her true being and a reconquest of her former greatness, let her accomplish this too: the eradication and abolition of a usage which not only clashes with grammatical and logical law, but is a speaking (one can appropriately say) witness of centuries of servitude and abjection'.[7]

Italian purists have long delighted in preparing black lists, or whole dictionaries, of proscribed words. In 1933 the journalist and writer Paolo Monelli published a book, which was to enjoy considerable popularity, with the revealing title *Barbaro dominio. Cinquecento esotismi esaminati, combattuti e banditi dalla lingua con antichi e nuovi argomenti, storia ed etimologia delle parole e aneddoti per svagare il lettore* 'Barbarian Domination. Five hundred foreign expressions examined, attacked and banished from the language with old and new arguments, with the history and etymology of the words and with anecdotes to entertain the reader'. By the second edition, 1943, the '*esotismi*' had grown to 650; in the preface the author explains: 'This campaign was above all a question of pride and dignity. Strong peoples impose their language, their idioms, their abbreviations, they do not pick up foreign rubbish with ridiculous care. The pollution of language is usually the work of people who are ignorant, presumptuous, slavish; this should be enough to provoke reactions against it. There is no place any longer, in a bold and confident Italy, for Balkan-style mumblers of foreign syllables.' After 1945 English replaced French as the butt of the purists. To give one example, the same Paolo Monelli in a interview printed in *L'Espresso* on 13 September 1970 commented on the reporting of a scandal in which 'my newspaper [the *Corriere della Sera*] did nothing but write *killer killer killer*. Then I sent this little telegram to the editor: "May I humbly remind you that one who is hired to kill in Italian is called a *sicario*." The following day the newspaper put *sicario* in the title, but in inverted commas, as if it were a strange word which needed to be explained to someone well acquainted with the word "killer"' (which was no doubt the case).

One could of course reverse the argument: the 'openness' of a language, its ability to absorb foreign elements could be considered a sign of its strength, of the confidence with which it is used. This can apply to one's attitude towards dialects as well. The 'open door' policy has found few explicit supporters where foreign elements are involved, but where dialects are concerned the situation is different. People like Ascoli did not want to pull out *la malerba dialettale* 'the dialect weeds', but stressed the richness of the linguistic and cultural traditions embodied in the dialects and the advantages that could be derived, in the acquisition of the national language, from a comparison between dialect and Italian, underlining that, far from being damaging, it was useful to have a situation of bilingualism, with speakers fully fluent both in their own dialect and in the national language. The educational reform of 1923, known as the *riforma Gentile* from the name of the philosopher Giovanni Gentile, then Minister of Education, harmful though it was in its undermining of the position of grammar in the school system on the basis of a confused notion of language as individual creation, did recognize the importance of dialects as a spontaneous form of expression and as a starting point in the educational process. But even this was of little avail as under the Fascist regime, with its oppressively centralizing attitude, there was a strong tendency to sweep dialects under the carpet as if they were a national disgrace.[8] When, after 1945, characters appeared in films and novels, using a language which bore some resemblance to that actually used in Italy, purists were very vocal in their complaints of 'dialect aggression' against the Italian language. Again, the argument could be reversed. If there was aggression, it was against the dialects. A complaint that can be made against Italian cultural development in the last hundred years is that it has done too little to spread the knowledge of Italian, and that the little it has done cost an unnecessarily heavy price in terms of the destruction of dialects and local cultures. It failed to bring about the situation which some of the most progressive minds looked forward to at the time of unification: a situation whereby the acquisition of a national language both authentically popular and common to the whole nation might be achieved not at the expense of the dialects, but through their survival and fuller development.

In the cinema and in literature dialectal features are mostly used for deliberate stylistic effects. One may recall the striking flavour of reality in the succession of dialects as the Allies travel up from Sicily in the six episodes of Rossellini's *Paisà*, the uncompromising, sombre Sicilian of Visconti's *La terra trema* (which was unintelligible on the mainland and had to be given an Italian commentary), and the moderate Roman colouring of De Sica's *Bicycle Thieves*. In the vulgar post-neorealist films the 'vernacular' is used for purposes of characterization, for a narrow portrayal of Italian provincial life. Fellini uses Romagnolo and Roman in his films as a powerful source of evocation in the process of exploring his memories (even the title *Amarcord* is effective; it means simply 'I remember' in Romagnolo, but to an Italian audience it suggests the idea of bitterness, as well as that of the heart, and has the sound of a mysterious formula like the magic abracadabra). Pasolini makes original use of dialectal background in his *Gospel according to Matthew*, in which the disciples speak with a southern accent, Caiphas speaks Tuscan, Salome speaks like a little servant girl from the Veneto, and Christ speaks with a polished 'non identifiable' stage accent, i.e., in a language which, for Italy, is rather out of this world.

In literature it is rare to find an authentic picture of a dialectal situation in all its complex cultural and psychological implications, but a successful example is *Libera nos a malo* by L. Meneghello, where the linguistic usages and attitudes of a Venetian mainland village are presented with a mixture of affectionate participation and ironically detached observation. It is more common to find experiments such as those by Gadda and Pasolini (at opposite ends of the spectrum), the former using an expressionist mixture of technical, literary and obsolete Italian, with elements culled from different dialects, in an attempt to produce extreme effects and reach a heightened stylistic tension, and the latter aiming to reproduce, with sometimes misleading precision and objectivity, the violent language of boys who have grown up in the general deprivation and linguistic Babel of the Roman outskirts. In the course of the last ten years Pasolini discovered that he did not need to use the stark dialectal mixture of *Ragazzi di vita* (1955) and *Una vita violenta* (1959) because something new had happened: 'in these last few years' he announced in 1964 'Italian as a real national language has come into being'. Its mewlings could be heard, he said, in the 'industrial triangle' (Turin–Milan–Genoa) and its model was the usage of technocrats and bureaucrats (as exemplified, for instance, in the speeches of the southern politician Aldo Moro); it is a thin, bloodless language, well suited to the squalid neo-capitalist society that uses it. I do not like it, said Pasolini, but there it is: Italy, for the first time in its history, has a national language, and not just a literary language confined to a minority.

These statements by Pasolini were widely discussed. A collection of pieces variously related to them was published by O. Parlangèli under the title *La nuova questione della lingua*.

This may be related to a wider debate, mainly cultural and ideological (centred round the so-called *avant-garde* movements, *le avanguardie*) in which linguistic questions are on the whole used as pretexts or examples. Those who maintain the need for a revolutionary struggle against language, which as part of the system is in the service of the ruling class, claim for instance that repressive freedom gives people the illusion that they can say whatever they want, thus restricting the field of what they may want to say, to what can in fact be said, and making them believe that what cannot be said in their language, they do not want to say. But their point is not very clear. Is language taken as a human faculty (stunted perhaps in the interests of the preservation of existing social structures), whose powers have to be increased by rendering it capable of expressing the inexpressible (in the sense, one imagines, of the student protest slogan 'be realistic, ask for the impossible')? Or are they objecting to a particular language of culture with its unnecessarily complex rules, '*una lingua mandarina*', a Mandarin language serving to prevent those who do not master it (i.e., the working class) from raising themselves socially and reaching positions of power? In the first case the objection involves dialects as well as the national language; in the second case there are two views: one held by those who consider dialects the embodiment of an authentically popular working-class culture and hence more suited than the national language to express revolutionary feelings and ideals; the other by those who see the dialects as the necessary counterpart of the standard lan-

guage, as belonging to the same oppressive system: a Mandarin language for the bourgeoisie and a second-class, primitive dialect for
the common people. In practical terms, the problem might be
whether a trade unionist should use the standard language to make
his point effectively at national level, or whether by doing so he
would inevitably be selling out, separating himself from the workers
he represents and playing the class enemy's game on the enemy's
terms.

All this however is more often discussed from the point of view of
literary experiments or of an abstract ideological debate. The isola-
tion of intellectuals from wider questions affecting the cultural
conditions of the whole nation has roots, as we have seen, going far
back in Italian history, and in its present form originates in the
thwarted social and political development which immediately followed unification. The problems which both Manzoni and Ascoli
had seen in social terms rapidly sank to the level of rhetoric and
became once more the concern of a handful of authors whose only
public (the reading public) was a small minority of the Italian
population. In poetry we find the classical accents of Carducci's
rhetoric, and the affectations of D'Annunzio, drawn from French
decadents and early Italian authors. Major Italian prose writers
after Manzoni, like Verga, Svevo and Pirandello, still had to work in
a language which was not their everyday language and which they
had some difficulty in mastering; their writings reflect not so much
Italian usage as the problems inevitably faced by authors trying to
write Italian (but it is also true that the individual manner in which
each of them grappled with language is an essential element of their
achievement as writers). Most of the Italian literary movements of
the twentieth century, from the Futurists down to the Hermeticists,
the Neo-realists, the Neo-experimentalists and the Neo-*avant-
garde* of our own day are characterized by being minority
phenomena, ineffectual on the level of popular culture. De Mauro
sees the first ten years of this century (when there was considerable
social and political progress under Giolitti's administration) as a
turning point in the evolution of the Italian literary language,
marked in poetry by Pascoli's *Canti di Castelvecchio* and in prose by
Croce's *Estetica*. The change mainly concerns the attitude of writers
towards the national language; a strong awareness that the language
of literature should draw closer to the language of everyday speech
is conveyed by Gozzano in tones which are still fresh today, when
much of the work of his contemporaries is irretrievably dated. But

the Italian at the disposal of these writers was inadequate as an everyday language, and in this they were the victims of a situation which they had not themselves created.

How much do we know about the linguistic situation as a whole rather than just the literary language? How much did it change after unification? It is difficult to answer these questions. The most important attempt at an answer was made by De Mauro in his *Storia linguistica dell'Italia unita*, from which we shall draw documentation for what follows.

There is no reliable information for the present day concerning the number of people who can understand and/or speak (a) varieties of a dialect, (b) varieties of Italian, or (c) both, and in the last case in which circumstances they use one or the other. For what it is worth, our impression of the linguistic usage of urban speakers in northern Italy is that most people can understand both Italian and dialect, and that people who only speak dialect are mostly limited to the older generation, whilst more and more of the younger generation can only speak Italian. The data would be difficult to collect and would have to be broken down region by region, taking into account at least the differences between town and countryside, between one town and another according to size, and between the sexes, age groups and cultural conditions. Although there are no works which attempt to provide this kind of information for the whole of Italy, there are some pilot studies on individual communities, which try to capture the relationship between the standard language, the local dialect and the dialects of the immigrants.[9]

For the past any computation is bound to be even more problematic. De Mauro stresses how misleading it is to identify speakers of Italian with Italians. But the identification was in any case never complete because on the one hand the existence of large Italian communities in North and South America, France, Belgium, Germany, etc., was taken into account, as well as those in Corsica and in Switzerland and on the other one was aware of the linguistic minorities, the communities in Italy using a 'foreign' language as their native tongue.[10]

One may assume that at the time of unification, outside Tuscany and Rome, only people who were literate were able to use Italian. The illiterates were all confined to their dialects. The census figures give about 75 per cent illiterates in 1861, but it would be rash to assume that the 25 per cent who were nominally literate could speak

Italian proficiently. From what one gathers about elementary schooling from the main reports on the Italian educational system (those by Carlo Matteucci of 1867 and Camillo Corradini of 1910) it would seem that a large proportion of those who had received some schooling and were classified as literate could in fact not read or write and were certainly also unable to speak Italian. According to De Mauro's estimate it is more realistic to assume that in 1861 the number of those able to use Italian could not have amounted to many more than 600 000 (400 000 Tuscans, 70 000 Romans, and about 160 000 from the rest of Italy) i.e., 2.5 per cent of the total population.

But the situation gradually changed. The percentage of illiterates dropped from 75 per cent in 1861 to almost 50 per cent at the beginning of this century, and to 40 per cent in 1911, 20.9 per cent in 1931, 12.9 per cent in 1951, 8.4 per cent in 1961. De Mauro reports that in 1951 18.5 per cent of the Italians used only the national language, and 13 per cent used only a dialect, but even if those who could use Italian amounted to 87 per cent, the percentage of those who normally used their dialect in most circumstances was still 63.5 per cent.

Leaving aside schooling, a variety of factors contributed to the spread of literacy and the use of Italian. Among these one should mention mass emigration which, between 1871 and 1951, involved about twenty-one million people, of whom fourteen million returned to Italy in the end. One of the side effects of emigration was that it reduced the number of illiterates at home, and made both those who had stayed behind and those who returned with more advanced ideas, aware of how important it was to be educated and to be able to use the national language as a weapon in the fight to improve their conditions; other factors were industrialization, and connected with it, urbanization and the consequent progressive abandonment of the countryside and of agriculture in favour of industrial work in the cities, and internal migration, with large numbers moving from the south to the north, particularly to Lombardy, Piedmont and Liguria, after the second world war. These phenomena naturally had an effect on the linguistic as well as the cultural situation, but it is difficult to define it exactly. The general trend of these developments was undoubtedly to weaken the dialects and to strengthen the use of Italian; but De Mauro, generalizing from the attitude in Rome, which seems to be exceptionally receptive, perhaps overestimates the extent of osmosis, of linguistic fusion working towards an Italian model. As C. Grassi pointed out, with regard to urbanization one must not overlook movements to a town from the neighbouring countryside, or to a regional capital from the region, which are likely to strengthen rather than weaken the urban dialect. As far as internal migration is concerned, Grassi continues, there has certainly not been a phenomenon of linguistic mixture in the case of southerners immigrating to the industrial north; on the contrary, adaptation has been totally one-sided, linguistic conformity being accepted by the southerners as one of the means of trying to overcome the prejudices of the northerners against them (prejudices of the '*polentoni*' against the '*terroni*'; these terms, far from having only the dubiously comic connotations of skits and regional farces, reflect attitudes often verging on racialism). Linguistic mimetism entailed the attempt on the part of the immigrants themselves, or, if they did not succeed, of their children, to adopt the language used by the proletariat, i.e., usually the dialect, but more recently Italian, the poorly controlled Italian of the lower middle class, taken as an ideal by the native working class and thus constituting for the immigrants **a model one remove further away**.[11]

Other important factors advancing linguistic unification were bureaucracy, which from the centre imposed on the whole country a uniform mixture of literary pomposity and technical administrative jargon, with a sprinkling of regionalisms (like *incartamento* 'file', *disguido* 'hitch'), and the army, which drew young men together from all parts of the country sending them to regions other than their own. De Mauro sees in the experience of the first world war, when hundreds of thousands of soldiers were concentrated in Venetia, the beginnings of a spoken national language, the '*italiano popolare*', which found its expression in songs, stories, and letters exchanged between the soldiers and their families, where the efforts of people who in many cases were semiliterate seem to have given birth to a new idiom, a graceless and ungrammatical but vigorous mixture of stark dialectal expressions and of literary clichés from official rhetoric, relating to the army, the fatherland and the war. Another linguist, M. Cortelazzo, has a more puristic view than De Mauro of this *italiano popolare*, which he defines as a 'type of Italian imperfectly acquired by people who have a dialect as their mother **tongue**'.[12] **He sympathetically analyses in detail, however, many of** these popular texts and concludes that they have common features which are different from those of literary Italian, but cannot be explained on the basis of the authors' native dialects. Some features of this kind of Italian are in fact now found in the colloquial language, for instance the agreements *ad sensum* (*la commissione hanno deciso*: singular noun, plural verb, as in the English 'the committee have decided'); the multipurpose *che* (see chapter V. 10(c)); the expressive or redundant repetition of pronouns (*a me mi piace* 'me I like it'); the generalized dative *gli* 'to him' for feminine and plural as well (see chapter IV. 2(c)); the use of the indicative instead of the subjunctive (*spero che viene* 'I hope he comes' (see chapter IV. 2(g) (v)). In the authors' intentions these texts are clearly Italian, and not local, as is indicated by the prevalence of hypercorrect forms over dialectal ones.

Mass media have of course played a role in the unification of the language: from newspapers (which predictably, however, given their limited readership, could not have much effect on the spoken language), to radio, and lastly to television, the introduction of which is generally considered to have constituted a turning point in the diffusion of Italian throughout the country and in the decline of the dialects.[13]

There is another context in which dialect speakers have been brought into contact with Italian: Mass is now celebrated in the vernacular, following the Second Vatican Council (1962–1965).

In chapter IV we shall try to give more examples of the developments mentioned above, when discussing different varieties of Italian. The considerations in this chapter have been largely external, which is inevitable since modifications over the last century present themselves less as an internal evolution of Italian or of the Italian dialects than as a change in their respective positions, dialects being progressively italianized and gradually disappearing. Italian is known and used more and more widely in Italy, not only as a written language but also as a spoken one. As a spoken language it appears in the form of many regional, or rather 'local' varieties, characterized above all by their pronunciation. Given these circumstances it would be misleading to try to outline the history of Italian as if it were a homogeneous entity evolving in time. Different communities in different parts of Italy have used their own dialects and the Italian literary tradition to elaborate systems of rules which allow the individual to conform, as a speaker, to the usage of the local community, and to accept, as a hearer, usages characteristic of communities other than his own. These different systems are thus integrated into a general framework which is homogeneous enough to guarantee reciprocal comprehension within the national community and to safeguard its linguistic cohesion, and differentiated enough to allow people to identify themselves in their speech with their local community and to preserve their solidarity with what still remains of regional traditions. In their interplay these are not opposed to but constitute national culture.

Notes

[1] VERRI, ALESSANDRO, 'Rinunzia avanti nodaro degli autori del presente foglio periodico al Vocabolario della Crusca' ('Renunciation before a Notary, by the Authors of the Present Periodical News-Sheet of the Crusca Dictionary'), in *Il Caffè* No. 4 1764 (Brescia, 1765, pp 30–31; modern edition, Milan, 1960, pp. 39–41). But the renunciation could not have been so radical if Pietro Verri felt obliged to observe in No. 30 of *Il Caffè* that *'nodaro'* was a misprint for *'notajo'* (cf. 1765 edn, pp. 237–240; 1960 edn, pp. 239–242).

[2] On this point see TIMPANARO, S., *Classicismo e illuminismo nell'Ottocento italiano*, Pisa, 1969 (2nd enlarged edn).

[3] Manzoni was neither a *linguaiolo* nor a purist. When the priest Michele Ponza in his journal *L'Annotatore Piemontese* (2, 1835, pp. 75–80) criticized Tommaso Grossi for having used the expression *sentir messa* in his novel *Marco Visconti:* '*"Sentire la messa" è modo di dialetto: la messa si ode, si ascolta, alla messa si assiste*' (*Sentire la messa* [to hear mass] is a dialectal idiom. What you do when you go to mass is *udire, ascoltare, assistere* [to hear, listen, be present at. Both *sentire* and *udire* mean to hear, but Ponza is here objecting to the use of *sentire* with 'mass']), Manzoni planned to reply, together with Grossi, and a draft of his answer was published by D. Bulferetti under the title *Sentir Messa* (Milan, 1923). Ponza continues: *scenata* 'scene': 'This word is not given in Italian dictionaries, nor by Cherubini [the author of a Milanese dictionary]; it is used by Milanese scullions: could one not have used *commedia, scena* ['play', 'scene']? Does our language need these novelties? *sorseggiare* ['to sip'] is not Italian, it should be *sorsare*'; Italians 'when they want to entertain their brothers, from the valley of Usseglio [in Piedmont] down to the last stone of Lilibeo [in Sicily] speak one language, the only common heritage left to us. Should a good Italian defile this too? I know that Grossi, and before him Manzoni, and all their followers reply that that's nature – letting people speak according to their character and education. Nonsense! Then one might as well write in dialect and renounce the honour of being part of Italian literature, then it's like being born and dying on the same crossroads; but if one is gifted enough to join the sacred family of Italian writers, it is a crime against the

fatherland to defile them with the barbarity of dialects, it is a corruption of youth, who believe and swear by the authority of a few names, in sum it is a cruel vituperation of the fatherland'. (For analogous expressions in our own day cf. BONFANTE, G., in *L'Italia Dialettale,* 21, 1967, pp. 181 ff.)

[4] D'OVIDIO, F., in a letter to Raffaello Fornaciari printed in *Il Marzocco,* 2 June 1901; we quote from D'OVIDIO, F., *Opere,* vol. 10 (*Varietà filologiche*), Naples, n. d., pp. 273–274.

[5] A systematic examination of these texts has never been attempted, but it would be rewarding, as is clear from those we have been able to study.

[6] Cf. *Lingua Nostra,* 28, 1967, p. 61.

[7] One is reminded here of a predecessor neglected by our purists (and one can see why), Count Ferdinando dal Pozzo, who in Paris in 1833 published a book with the following title: *Della felicità che gli Italiani possono e debbono dal governo austriaco procacciarsi, col piano di un'associazione per tutta Italia, avente per oggetto la diffusione della pura lingua italiana, e la contemporanea soppressione de' dialetti che si parlano ne' vari paesi della penisola. Si fa altresì cenno in questo piano della inelegante e goffa maniera d'indirizzare il discorso a qualcuno in terza persona così scrivendo come parlando, la qual maniera si dovrebbe, generalizzandosi il 'voi', abolirsi affatto.* 'Of the happiness which Italians can and must obtain from the Austrian government, together with a proposal for an association for the whole of Italy, having as its object the diffusion of pure Italian language and the simultaneous suppression of the dialects which are spoken in the various parts of the peninsula. In this proposal mention is also made of the inelegant and clumsy habit of addressing people in the third person, both in speech and writing, a habit which as *voi* becomes more widespread, should be abolished altogether.' In the book he suggests (p. 172) that the government should impose good Italian 'with the powerful influence which it can exert on public and private education, on forms of worship, on all corporations, on all employees, on public offices, both administrative and judiciary, by distributing or withdrawing prizes, promotions and honorific distinctions.' He was a true precursor of the modern *linguaioli* who invoke the arm of the Constitution and the law to impose their linguistic views, and would like all school teachers who do not conform to them to be debarred from a job (cf. PIERACCIONI, D., in *Belfagor,* 20, 1965, pp. 587–95; TAGLIAVINI, C., *La corretta pronuncia italiana,* Bologna, 1965, pp. viii–ix).

[8] Cf. for more information FLORA, F., *Ritratto di un ventennio. Appello al Re. Stampa dell'era fascista,* Bologna, 1965.

[9] Cf. PAUTASSO, M., *Dialetto, lingua e integrazione linguistica a Pettinengo,* Turin, 1969.

[10] In 1861 we find about 104 000 speakers of French, Provençal and Franco-Provençal in Piedmont, almost 100 000 Albanian speakers in small communities in southern Italy and Sicily going back to fifteenth-century immigration, and about 30 000 speakers of other languages: Greek linguistic islands in Salento and Calabria: Bova, Condofuri, Palizzi, Roccaforte and Roghudi, going back according to some linguists (e.g., Rohlfs) to classical colonization, according to others (e.g., Battisti) to Byzantine; Catalan at Alghero, dating from 1354; Slav in the Molise, dating from the arrival of Croatian refugees escaping from the Turks in the fifteenth century; Franco-Provençal in the province of Foggia and Provençal at Guardia Piemontese in Calabria. We also find Gallo-Italian colonies in Sicily: at Piazza Armerina, San Fratello, Nicosia, Francavilla and Novara di Sicilia, which are 'foreign' in respect of Sicily, but not of Italy. These 'foreign language' communities made up less than 1 per cent of the twenty-five million inhabitants of Italy. In 1866 after the annexation of Venetia there were some German linguistic islands in the provinces of Vicenza and Verona and in 1919 after the annexation of Trentino and Venezia Giulia there were about 255 000 speakers of Slovenian, 200 000 speakers of German, 95 000 speakers of Serbocroat and 1500 speakers of Istro-Rumanian. The linguistic minorities then amounted to about 800 000 speakers, i.e., 2.1 per cent of a total of almost thirty-eight million.

[11] Cf. GRASSI, C., in *Archivio Glottologico Italiano,* 49, 1964, pp. 58-67; DE MAURO, T., in *Il Veltro,* 9, 1965, pp. 3-21.

[12] CORTELAZZO, M., *Avviamento critico allo studio della dialettologia italiana,* vol. 3, *Lineamenti di italiano popolare,* Pisa, 1972, p. 11. For De Mauro's position see DE MAURO, T., 'Per lo studio dell'italiano popolare unitario', in ROSSI, A., *Lettere da una tarantata,* Bari, 1970.

[13] Cf. DE MAURO, T., 'Lingua parlata e TV', in *Televisione e vita italiana,* Turin, 1968, pp. 247-294; 'Mass media, televisione e lingua parlata negli anni sessanta', in *Storia linguistica dell'Italia unita,* Bari, 1972, pp. 430-459.

III Italian Dialects

The following discussion of Italian dialects aims both at presenting the main dialect subdivisions and at providing background information for the description of local varieties of Italian (chapter IV). By its very nature this chapter is more suitable for reference or for reading at a much slower pace than the rest of the first part of this book. The adoption of a diachronic point of view (connecting Latin to the present day stages of the dialects) seems appropriate, for it offers a net with a mesh much finer than the one provided by synchronic analysis (short of making the latter so elaborate that it would be unreadable for anyone not versed in linguistics) with which to extract such features as can help identify the dialect of a text. The word [sùo] 'his' can be both Italian and Venetian; [sùo] with the meaning 'I sweat' is Venetian but not Italian. This makes sense diachronically when one considers a series like Latin SŪDŌ 'I sweat', NŪDŬM 'naked', CRŪDŬM 'raw', Italian *sudo, nudo, crudo*, Venetian [sùo], [nùo], [krùo], where D is preserved in Italian but falls in Venetian.[1] If we compare the Italian words [fìlo] 'thread', [nève] 'snow', [vèro] 'true' with the corresponding Sardinian ones [fìlu], [nìve], [vèru], we find an apparently unsystematic situation: in the stressed syllable Italian [e] corresponds to either Sardinian [i] or [ɛ], and Sardinian [i] corresponds to either Italian [i] or [e]; but in diachronic terms everything immediately falls into place: the three Latin vowels ī, ĭ, Ē (in FĪLŬM, NĬVĔM, VĒRŬM) are reduced to two both in Italian and in Sardinian, but those which lose their distinction are ĭ and Ē in Italian (both becoming [e]), and ĭ and ī in Sardinian (both becoming [i]).

Italian dialects are usually classified as follows:

1. **Northern**, among which one distinguishes Venetian from the Gallo-Italian dialects (Piedmontese, Ligurian, Lombard and Emilian);

2. **Tuscan**, subdivided into central (Florence), western (Lucca,

Pisa, Livorno), southern (Siena, Arezzo);
3.   **Central**, northern Latium, parts of Umbria and the Marches;
4.   **Southern**, a Neapolitan type (southern Latium, Abruzzi, Campania, part of Lucania, northern Puglia), and a Sicilian type (Salentine peninsula, Calabria, Sicily).

A separate place is usually given to Sardinian, Ladinian and Istriote. There is a gradual transition from Tuscan to central, and from central to southern dialects; a fairly well defined boundary separates the Gallo-Italian from the Tuscan dialects, along the La Spezia-Rimini line, particularly on the watershed of the Appennines between Emilia and Tuscany, less sharply in the west (in the Lunigiana) and in the east, where certain northern isoglosses[2] reach as far south as Rome, through the northern Marches and Umbria (for instance *adesso* 'now' <ĂD (ĬD) ĬPSŬM vs. the Tuscan *ora*<HŌRĀ and the southern *mo*<MŎDŌ). Certain southern isoglosses (e.g., ND>[nn]) reach as far north as the Grosseto-Ancona line.

Some lexical items are particularly widespread in certain regions: for instance for 'killing' (a pig) northern and central Italy prefer *ammazzare*, Venice *copar*, the south *accidere*, and Sicily *scannari*; certain words are generally known as being typical of certain regions, and as such are sometimes used in Italian, for instance the terms for 'boy' and 'girl': Piedmontese *cit* and *tota*, Lombard *bagai*, Venetian *toso* and *putelo*, Friulan *frut*, Emilian *burdèl*, Tuscan *bimbo*, Abruzzese *quataro* (mentioned by Dante in the *De Vulgari Eloquentia*), Neapolitan *guaglione*, Sicilian *picciotto* and *caruso*. There are many other typical terms which are considered to capture local colour, like Ligurian *mugugno* 'grumble', Venetian *ostrega*, *ostregheta* 'goodness!', Roman *pennichella* 'nap', Neapolitan *sfizio* 'fancy', Sicilian *intrallazzo* 'racket'.

The vowel system

In Classical Latin vowel quantity (or length) was phonemic, that is sufficient to distinguish systematically one vowel from another. This can be shown with many minimal pairs (couples of words in which the two terms are identical apart from one phoneme, in this case the short vs. long vowel).

Here are some examples: PĪLŬM 'javelin' vs. PĬLŬM 'hair'; VĒNĬT 'he came' vs. VĔNĬT 'he comes'; MĀLŬM 'apple' vs. MĂLŬM 'bad'; CŎLŌ 'I cultivate' vs. CŌLŌ 'I filter'; PŬTĔT 'may he think' vs. PŪTĔT 'he smells'.

There were five vowel timbres or qualities: I (high, front), E (mid, front), A (low, central: i.e., when a vowel is low there is no opposition between front and back), O (mid, back), U (high, back), and as for each one there could be a long or a short phoneme, there were ten vowel phonemes: Ī Ĭ Ē Ĕ Ā Ă Ŏ Ō Ŭ Ū (in the fourth and fifth pairs the short vowels are put first because this allows a neater pattern later in the diachronic tables; the order is obviously conventional).

It is useful to remember that the terms 'long' and 'short' are also used for Latin metre, but there they refer to syllables and not to vowels. To avoid confusion we shall use the terms 'light' instead of 'short', and 'heavy' instead of 'long' when referring to syllables.

The most schematic account of the situation is as follows: a distinction is made between checked (or closed) and free (or open) syllables. A checked syllable ends in a consonant, a free syllable ends in a vowel. A single consonant is considered to go with the following syllable, leaving the preceding one free. When there is a consonant cluster (or a long consonant, which for this purpose can be treated as a cluster of two adjacent occurrences of the same consonant) the syllable boundary falls within the consonant cluster and its first consonant belongs to the preceding syllable, making it checked. This does not necessarily apply to the clusters which Latin grammarians called *muta cum liquida*, consisting of a stop ([p t k b d g]) followed by a liquid ([l r]). It would seem that in the spoken language these clusters belonged to the following syllable, making the preceding one free (but not, in early and late Latin, in words like ĬNTĔGRŬM 'whole'), while in the literary language they could be split and so make the preceding syllable checked.

A light syllable is a free syllable ending in a short vowel; all other sorts of syllables are heavy (they may be free ending in a long vowel, or checked containing either a long or a short vowel).[3]

If we use V to represent any vowel and C to represent any consonant, and we ignore as irrelevant what comes before the vowel, we have the following possibilities (with reference to the first syllable of each example):

(1) V̆ as in PĬ-LŬM 'hair' (light syllable: free, ending in a short vowel);

(2) V̄ as in FĪ-LŬM 'thread' (heavy syllable: free, ending in a long vowel);

(3) V̆C as in CŎR-PŬS 'body' (heavy syllable: checked, containing a short vowel);

(4) V̄C as in SCRĪP-TŬM 'written' (heavy syllable: checked, containing a long vowel).

The distinction between heavy and light syllables in Classical Latin was independent of the position of the accent (both accented and unaccented syllables could be either heavy or light), and only partially dependent on the quantity of the vowel: a syllable with a long vowel was necessarily heavy, as in (2) and (4) above; a syllable with a short vowel could be either light, if it was free, as in (1) above, or heavy, if it was checked, as in (3) above.

The position of the accent was determined by the phonological structure of the word. In monosyllables there was obviously no choice. In polysyllables the accent was on the penultimate syllable if this was heavy (or in any case if the word had two syllables only), on the antepenultimate (in words of more than two syllables) if the penultimate was light; the quantity of the antepenultimate was irrelevant.

Examples: DĒCĪDŌ 'I cut off', with the accent on the -CĪ- because the penultimate is heavy; DĒCĬDŌ 'I fall off', with the accent on the DĒ- because the penultimate is light; the antepenultimate happens to be heavy, but this is irrelevant; in SŬPĔRŌ 'I overcome' the penultimate is light and consequently the accent is on the antepenultimate even though this too happens to be light.

This system undergoes fundamental changes in Vulgar Latin. A difference in quality (timbre) comes to be associated with the difference in quantity, long vowels becoming closed, short vowels becoming open (with the exception of the most open vowel, A, in which the quantity distinction does not give origin to a quality distinction): ī>[i:], ĭ>[ɪ], ē>[e:], ĕ>[ɛ], ŏ>[ɔ], ō>[o:], ŭ>[ʊ], ū>[u:]. Then the distinction between long and short ceases to be phonemic and becomes allophonic, conditioned by the structure of the syllable. In stressed syllables vowels become long if the syllable is free, short if the syllable is checked. The quality distinction between closed and open, which was originally secondary, now becomes paramount and takes on the function of a phonemic opposition.

The phonemic quantity of Classical Latin vowels disappears, and in the Romance vowels we find a new quantity conditioned synchronically by syllable structure and diachronically independent of Classical Latin quantity. The open or closed quality of Romance vowels depends on the quality of Vulgar Latin vowels, which in turn depends on the quantity of their sources in Classical Latin. Romance quality depends, indirectly, on Classical Latin quantity. In other words, knowing the quantity of Classical Latin vowels may help to predict the quality, not the quantity of the Romance vowels deriving from them. In some Italian dialects we find quantitative oppositions (short vs. long vowels) with a phonemic value. These are new developments, independent of Classical Latin quantity. There is for instance in Milanese [vestÍ] 'to dress' vs. [vestÍ:] 'dress', [redý] 'to reduce' vs. [redý:] 'laughed' (past participle), [dit] 'said' (past participle) vs. [dÍ:t] 'finger'.

The four syllable structures listed above for Classical Latin are reduced to two in Vulgar Latin and Italian, according to a rule often called 'lex Ten Brink' after the nineteenth-century Dutch philologist Bernhard Ten Brink, (1) and (2) giving V̄ and (3) and (4) giving V̆C: the Tuscan outcomes are [pé:lo] (<PĬLŬM) and [fÍ:lo] (<FĪLŬM), both with V̄; [kɔ́rpo] (<CŎRPŬS) and [skrÍtto] (<SCRĪPTŬM) both with V̆C.[4]

For brevity we shall indicate in the following pages the Classical Latin stage and its present-day Romance outcome, omitting the intermediate stages, but we hope that what has been said so far will help to clarify the developments. In our tables we start from the ten Classical Latin vowels (reduced to nine because we do not distinguish between long and short A). It would also be possible to start from a list of five Classical Latin vowels, preserved in Sardinian (table 5), which develop through an opposition between close and open timbres for E and O in Sicily (table 4), for I but not for U in part of Lucania (table 7) and for E, O, I, U in the rest of Italy (tables 1–3, 6, 8, 9).

Table 1

Ī	Ĭ	Ē	Ĕ	Ā̆	Ŏ	Ō	Ŭ	Ū
i	e		ε	a	ɔ	o		u

This is the **Tuscan** system. The same system, preserving the Vulgar Latin distinctions, apart from [ɪ] being fused with [e] and [ʊ] with [o], can be postulated as the starting point for northern and central Italian and for some southern Italian dialects. Examples for Tuscan (left to right, as also below): FĪLŬM>[fÍlo] 'thread', PĬLŬM>[pélo] 'hair', TĒLĂM>[téla] 'cloth', SĔPTĔM>[sɛ́tte] 'seven', MĀTRĔM>[mádre] 'mother', PĂTRĔM>[pádre] 'father', ŎCTŌ>[ɔ́tto] 'eight', vōcĕm>[vòtʃe] 'voice', crŭcĕm>[kròtʃe] 'cross', mūrŭm>[mùro] 'wall'.

One phenomenon typical of Florentine as against other Tuscan dialects is 'anaphonesis': in front of a nasal followed by a velar [ŋk ŋg] (and in front of certain clusters containing palatal consonants [tʃ dʒ ʃ ɲ ʎ]) [i] is found instead of the expected [e], and [u] instead of the expected [o], as in [vìŋko] 'I win'<vĭncō, [famìʎʎa] 'family'<fămĭlĭăm, [ùŋgja] 'nail'<ŭngŭlăm, [pùɲɲo] 'fist' <pŭgnŭm. According to some scholars (e.g., G. Devoto) we have here a preservation of the Latin timbres ɪ, ʊ and not a development [e]>[i], [o]>[u]: 'anaphonesis', suggesting a movement from lower to higher vowels, would then be an inappropriate term. The fact that these are the standard Italian forms (*vinco, famiglia, unghia, pugno*) can be used to show that Italian phonology is based specifically on Florentine and not on Tuscan in general.

In Tuscan in stressed penultimate free syllables ĕ and ŏ do not give [ɛ] and [ɔ] but the diphthongs [jɛ] and [wɔ]: pĕdĕm>[pjɛ̇de] 'foot', bŏnŭm>[bwɔ̇no] 'good'. The distinction between the outcomes of Latin free and checked syllables is much more visible in other dialects, for instance in **Bolognese,** where the two following developments are found in syllables which were free in Latin (Table 2) and in syllables which were checked in Latin (Table 3):

Table 2

Table 3

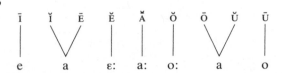

Examples: Table 2: ămīcŭm>[amì:g] 'friend', pĭlŭm>[pajl] 'hair', tēlăm>[tȧjla] 'cloth', mĕtĭt>[me:d] 'he reaps', pācĕm>[pɛ:z] 'peace', rŏtăm>[rȯ:da] 'wheel', ămōrĕm>[amȧwr] 'love', crŭcĕm>[krawz] 'cross', lūcĕm>[lu:z] 'light'; Table 3: dīxĭt >[dess] 'he said', pĭscĕm>[pass] 'fish', crēscĭt>[krass] 'he grows',

SĔPTĔM>[sɛ:t] 'seven', GĂTTŬM>[ga:t] 'cat', ŏSSŬM>[o:s]'bone', ŌLLĂM>[àlla] 'pot', RŬSSŬM>[rass] 'red', ĒXSŪCTŬM>[sott] 'dry'.

Other patterns are as follows (examples are given only for those developments which differentiate each system from the others):

Table 4

This is the **Sicilian** system; it is found not only in Sicily but also in southern Calabria, in southern Cilento (in the province of Salerno), in Salento (southern Puglia), and in a part of Lucania. Examples in Sicilian: FĪLŬM>[fìlu] 'thread', NĬVĔM>[nìvi] 'snow', TĒLĂM>[tìla] 'cloth', VŌCĔM>[vùtʃi] 'voice', NŬCĔM>[nùtʃi] 'nut', LŪNĂM>[lùna] 'moon'. Final vowels are reduced to three, [a i u], with -E>[i] and -O>[u]. This system should be familiar to students of Italian literature who will have met it in connection with the language of the thirteenth-century Sicilian school of poetry.

Table 5

This is the **Sardinian** system; it is found not only in Sardinia, but also in southern Corsica (in northern Corsica the system is basically Tuscan; the official language of the island is French), and in a zone at the boundary between Lucania and Calabria, from Maratea and Diamante to Castrovillari and Cassano. Examples in Sardinian: FĪLŬM>[fìlu] 'thread', NĬVĔM>[nìve] 'snow', VĒRŬM>[vèru] 'true', FĔLĔ>[fèle] 'gall', RŎTĂM>[ròda] 'wheel', SŌLĔM>[sòle] 'sun', CRŬCĔM>[rùke] 'cross', MŪRŬM>[mùru] 'wall'.

Table 6

This is called the **Apulian** system; it is found in parts of Puglia, northern Abruzzi, part of Cilento, northern and eastern Lucania. Examples from Avetrana (in the province of Taranto): PĬPĔR>[pɛ́pə] 'pepper', CRĒTĂM>[krɛ́ta] 'clay', SĔPTĔM>[sɛ́ttə] 'seven', CŎRĔ>[kɔ́ri] 'heart', SŌLĔM>[sɔ́li] 'sun', NŬCĔM>[nɔ́tʃi] 'nut'.

Table 7

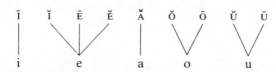

This asymmetric system is found in a small part of **Lucania**, southeast of Potenza. Examples from Castelmezzano (in the province of Potenza): NĬVĔM>[nɛ́və] 'snow', TĒLĂM>[tɛ́la] 'cloth', PĔDĔM >[pɛ́də] 'foot', CŎRĔ>[kɔ́rə] 'heart', SŌLĔM>[sɔ́lə] 'sun', CRŬCĔM>[krútʃə] 'cross', MŪRŬM>[múrə] 'wall'.

There are cases which appear even more asymmetric, such as the following ones in **Northern Abruzzi** and **Southern Marches**:

Table 8

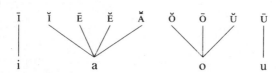

Examples from the province of Teramo: PĬLŬM>[pálə] 'hair', MĒNSĔM>[másə] 'month', MĔTĬT>[mátə] 'he reaps'.

Table 9

Examples from the province of Ascoli Piceno: LĬNGŬĂM>[láŋgwa] 'tongue', TĒLĂM>[tálə] 'cloth', ŎCTŌ>[áttə] 'eight', SŌLĔM>[sálə] 'sun', CRŬCĔM>[krátʃə] 'cross'.

In Gallo-Italian dialects there is a tendency to palatalize vowels, in varying conditions: Ă>[æ ɛ e], particularly in Emilia (in Bolognese NĀSŬM>[nɛ:z] 'nose'), but also in dialects of the Marches, Abruzzi, Umbria and southern Tuscany (cf. Aretine -ĀRĔ>−[ɛr]), and in the south (RĀMŬM>[rɛ̇mə] 'branch' at Martina Franca); Ū>[y], Ŏ>[ø] in parts of Piedmont, Liguria, Lombardy (cf. in Milanese MŪRŬM>[myr] 'wall', RŎTĀM>[rɸda] 'wheel'); the two mixed vowels [y] and [ø] often appear together in the same dialect, but in many cases there is one of the two only: for instance in Parma and Piacenza there is [ø] but not [y]; Ē, Ĭ and Ō, Ŭ often give [ɛj] [i] and [ɔw] [u] respectively: Ligurian NĬVĚM>[nɛ̇jve] 'snow', Piedmontese TĒLĂM>[tɛ̇jla] 'cloth', Lombard SĒRĂM>[slra] 'evening', MĒNSĔM >[mis] 'month', Emilian SŌLĚM>[sɔwl] 'sun', Lombard, Piedmontese, Emilian FLŌRĚM>[fjur] 'flower'.

Unstressed vowels tend to fall in Piedmontese, Lombard, Emilian, but not in Ligurian; final unstressed vowels, apart from A, systematically fall. This causes the appearance of many consonant clusters which do not exist in Tuscan and give the word a character very different from the generally accepted idea of what Italian sounds like: cf. for instance in Bolognese [stamg] 'stomach' <STŎMĂCHŬM, [dmȧndga] 'Sunday'<DŎMĬNĬCĂM, [sbdɛ:l] 'hospital' <HŎSPĬTĀLĔM, [pordg] 'arcade'<PŎRTĬCŬM.

Northern dialects are in their combinations of phonemes nearer than Tuscan to a European model, allowing a richer syllable structure and greater economy of usage, i.e., the production of a greater number of syllables using the same number of phonemes. The opposite happens in the south, where not only do unstressed vowels rarely fall, but vowels are often introduced to break consonant clusters (this phenomenon is called epenthesis or anaptyxis): cf. for instance Abruzzese [sȯlekə] vs. Italian *solco* 'furrow', Sicilian [mȧgiru] vs. Italian *magro* 'thin', Salentine [ȧmpulu] vs. Italian *ampio* 'wide'. In the north the Venetian vowel system developed in a way more similar to the Tuscan one than to the Gallo-Italian one.

The main southern Italian vowel systems have been exemplified in the tables above. A feature which affects dialects of the Neapolitan type (in Campania, Abruzzi, Puglia in particular) is a general weakening of unstressed vowels, and the reduction of final vowels to -[ə] or, sometimes, their disappearance. This does not happen in dialects of the Sicilian and Sardinian type.

We also find developments conspicuously different from the ones given in the above tables, for the high and mid-high vowels, particularly in the dialects of the Marches, Abruzzi and Puglia. For instance from ī we get [e] (DĪCŌ>[dɛ̇kə] 'I say' at Massignano in the province of Ascoli Piceno), [ej] (FĪLŬM>[fɛ̇jlə] 'thread' at Alberobello in the province of Bari), [ɛj] ([fɛ́jlə] at Spinazzola in the province of Bari), [aj] (SPĪCĂM>[spájkə] 'ear of corn' at Gessopalena in the province of Chieti), [oj] (VĪTĂM>[vójtə] 'life' at Bitonto in the province of Bari), [ɔj] ([fɔ́jlə] at Canosa in the province of Bari), [øj] ([fǿjlə] at Fara San Martino in the province of Chieti),[uj] (VĪTĔM>[vújtə] 'vine' at Tocco in the province of Pescara); from ū we get [o] (FŪMŬM>[fómə] 'smoke' at Massignano), [ow] (LŪNĂM>[lównə] 'moon' at Alberobello), [aw] ([láwnə] at Vico del Gargano in the province of Foggia), [ew] ([léwnə] at Spinazzola), [iw] (FŪSŬM>[fɨ́wsə] 'spindle' at Vasto in the province of Chieti), [øw] ([fǿwsə] at Trani in the province of Bari); from ē, ĭ we get [ɛj] (TĒLĂM>[tɛ́jlə] 'cloth', NĬVĔM>[nɛ́jvə] 'snow' at Lucera in the province of Foggia), [aj] ([tájlə], [nájvə] at Alberobello), [ɔj] ([tɔ́jlə], [nɔjf] at Fara San Martino); from ō, ŭ we get [ɔw] (SŌLĔM>[sɔ́wlə] 'sun' at Martina Franca in the province of Taranto), [aw] ([sáwlə] at Canosa), [ɛw] ([sɛ́wlə] at Agnone in the province of Campobasso), [a] ([sálə] at Bellante in the province of Teramo).

Other changes, conditioned by the phonological context, appear in the important phenomenon called **metaphony** or metaphonesis. This is a change in the stressed vowel caused by the presence of certain following (usually final) vowels. In Indo-European comparative grammar it is traditional to talk of apophony or Ablaut when a change in grammatical function (meaning) is manifested by a change in the vowel of the root: for instance in Latin FĂCĬT 'he does' vs. FĒCĬT 'he did', or VĔNĬT 'he comes' vs. VĒNĬT 'he came', or in English *sing, sang, sung*. Changes which do not have a grammatical function but are determined by certain vowels in the syllables which follow, as in German *Fuss* vs. *Füsse* 'foot' vs. 'feet', *Hand* vs. *Hände* 'hand' vs. 'hands', are called metaphony or Umlaut (in these examples the plural is indicated by the final –*e*, whose presence causes the Umlaut).

An attempt has been made to interpret Ablaut as resulting from an earlier Umlaut in Proto-Indo-European; this derivation is inevitably hypothetical, but a similar one appears in the historic stages of Indo-European languages: for instance the opposition between *foot* and *feet* in English appears synchronically as a case of Ablaut, but it derives from an earlier Umlaut phenomenon: in the plural of [fo:t] a final -[i] caused the [o:] to change to [e:], and then disappeared, leaving the difference between singular and plural to be shown by the difference of vowel in *foot* vs. *feet*. An analogous phenomenon is found in Italian dialects, where the disappearance, or the weakening to –[ə], of final vowels changes what was originally Umlaut into a case of Ablaut.

The final vowels which cause metaphony (to use the term preferred in Italian dialectology) are generally both ī and ŭ in southern Italy (with the consequence that masculine, with metaphony, is opposed to feminine, without metaphony), and only ī in northern Italy (with the consequence that the masculine plural, with metaphony, is opposed to the masculine singular, without metaphony, whereas the feminine, both singular and plural, is without metaphony).

For instance in Campania [nέrə]<NĬGRĂM, NĬGRAE vs. [nìrə]<NĬGRŬM, NĬGRĪ 'black'; [róssə]<RŬSSĂM, RŬSSAE vs. [rùssə]<RŬSSŬM, RŬSSĪ 'red'; [bέllə]<BĔLLĂM, BĔLLAE vs. [bjέllə] <BĔLLŬM, BĔLLĪ 'beautiful'; [bɔ́nə] <BŎNĂM, BŎNAE vs. [bwónə]<BŎNŬM, BŎNĪ 'good': in all these examples we find feminine singular and plural without metaphony vs. masculine singular and plural with metaphony.

In southern Italy it is also possible to find a metaphonic opposition between singular and plural: for instance at Bellante, in the province of Teramo, [ɛp]<ĂPĔM vs. [ip]<ĂPĒS 'bee' vs. 'bees', [ɣɛll]<GĂLLŬM vs. [ɣill]<GĂLLĪ 'cock' vs. 'cocks', [ɣatt]<GĂTTŬM vs. [ɣitt]<GĂTTĪ 'cat' vs. 'cats', [kɛn]<CĂNĔM vs. [kin]<CĂNĒS 'dog' vs. 'dogs'. This is the function which metaphony normally has in the north, as in Venetian [tózo]<TŌNSŬM vs. [tùzi]<TŌNSĪ 'boy' vs. 'boys', or, with fall of final vowels, in Lombard [kwɛst]<ĔCCŬ+ĬSTŬM vs. [kwist]<ĔCCŬ+ĬSTĪ 'this' vs. 'these', Ligurian [kaŋ] <CĂNĔM vs. [keŋ] <CĂNĒS 'dog' vs. 'dogs', Emilian [pa]<PĔDĔM vs. [pi:]<PĔDĒS 'foot' vs. 'feet'.

Metaphony may cause different changes in the vowels affected. Most frequently we find a closure of mid-high into high vowels and a breaking of mid-low vowels into diphthongs: [e]>[i], [o]>[u], [ɛ]>[je], [ɔ]>[wo].

The consonant system

For Classical Latin the following consonants may be listed (omitting problems which are not relevant for our present purpose): stops [p t k b d g], fricatives [f s h], nasals [m n], lateral [l], vibrant [r]; to these the semiconsonants [w] and [j] have to be added. It will be noticed that there are no palatals, no affricates, no voiced counter-

parts of [f] and [s]. Among the main changes, we should mention:
(1) early disappearance of [h];
(2) tendency to eliminate final consonants;
(3) tendency to preserve initial consonants;
(4) sonorization or voicing; this affects voiceless intervocalic consonants in Tuscan in a very capricious manner: [rĭva] 'shore'<RĪPĂM, [strȧda] 'street'<STRĀTĂM, [ȧgo] 'needle'<ĀCŬM, but [ȧpe] 'bee'<ĀPĔM, [atʃéto] 'vinegar'<ĂCĒTŬM, [amĭko] 'friend'<ĂMĪCŬM. Many vain attempts have been made to explain why this phenomenon occurs so erratically, either by looking for a phonological or a grammatical explanation (Meyer-Lübke, Ascoli), or by having recourse to a subdivision in vocabulary between native words and words influenced by some external factor. Merlo thought that voicing was the spontaneous Tuscan development and that the voiceless consonant was preserved in Latinisms; Rohlfs suggested that Tuscan preserved the voiceless (see the past participles –[ȧto], -[ŭto], -[ĭto], which must belong to popular everyday speech) and that words with sonorization were loanwords from the north (he tried to prove this by showing that in many cases the borrowing can be explained on cultural grounds). In northern Italy sonorization takes place systematically.

Sonorization, or lenition as it is sometimes called, being in Italy a change from voiceless and tense to voiced and lax, is considered a form of weakening and it is related to spirantization (as in [p]>[v]) and to complete disappearance (particularly for [t]>[d]>Ø): cf. ĂMĬTĂM>Lombard [mɛ́da], Venetian [ȧmja] 'aunt'. For the three examples given above without sonorization in Tuscan cf. Venetian [ȧva], [azéo], [amĭgo], Bolognese [ɛ:v], [azȧ], [amĭ:g].

In southern Italy we often find sonorization in clusters of [s]+consonant, and always in clusters of [n]+consonant: cf. in Bari [zdaŋgȧtə] for *stancato* 'tired', in Naples [móndə] for *monte* 'mountain'; in many southern dialects there is a laxing of articulation which makes northerners interpret a word like *napoletano*, in a Neapolitan pronunciation, as [nabuledȧnə].
(5) palatalization: in Tuscany and central Italy velar stops [k g] followed by a front vowel develop into [tʃ dʒ], and these often further into [ʃ ʒ]: VĪCĪNŬM>[vitʃĭno] [viʃĭno] 'near', ĂGĬLĔM>[ȧdʒile] [ȧʒile] 'agile'.[5]

In northern Italy the development is to [ts dz] and often further to [s z]; in Venetia there are many cases of [θ ð] ([θénto] 'a hundred'<CĔNTŬM, [θéna] 'supper'<CĒNĂM, [θĭma] 'summit'

<CŸMĂM, [ðenɔtʃo] 'knee'<GĔNŬCŬLŬM, [ðɛ́naro] 'son-in-law'<GĔNĔRŬM, [ðelår] 'to freeze'<GĔLĀRĔ vs. *cento, cena, cima, ginocchio, genero, gelare*); in parts of Piedmont and Lombardy there is [dʒ] and not [dz]: [dʒɛ́ner] 'son-in-law'<GĔNĔRŬM, [dʒelɛ́] 'to freeze'<GĔLĀRĔ; the chronology of the disappearance of the initial stop element (i.e., of the change of the affricates [ts dz tʃ dʒ] into sibilants [s z ʃ ʒ]) varies according to the dialect. In Friulan [k g] are palatalized before [a]: CĂSĂM>[tʃåze] 'house', GĂLLŬM>[dʒal] 'cock'.

In southern Italy, before front vowels, [k]>[tʃ], [g]>[j] and [ʃ]: Sicilian [krútʃi] 'cross'<CRŬCĔM, Neapolitan [jəlå] 'freeze' <GĔLĀRĔ, Pugliese [lɛ́ʃə] 'read'<LĔGĔRĔ.

In a central, linguistically more conservative, part of Sardinia [k g] preserve their velar sound even before front vowels: [kɛ́rtu] 'certain'<CĔRTŬM, [kɛ́ntu] 'a hundred'<CĔNTŬM, [kɛ́ra] 'wax' <CĒRĂM, [dɛ́ke] 'ten'<DĔCĔM, [akɛ́tu] 'vinegar'<ĂCĒTŬM, [giråre] 'to turn'<GŸRĀRĔ, [gelåre] 'to freeze'<GĔLĀRĔ, [lɛ́gere] 'to read' <LĔGĔRĔ;

(6) the development of [j] and of clusters of consonant +[j] is rather complex.

In Tuscan in intervocalic position we find [j dj gj]>[ddʒ]: MAĬŬM>[måddʒo] 'May', HŌDĬĒ>[ɔ́ddʒi] 'today', RĒGĬĂM>[rɛ́ddʒa] 'royal palace';[6] [tj]>[tts]: VĬTĬŬM>[vɛ́ttso] 'habit';[7] [kj]>[ttʃ]: BRĂCHĬŬM>[bråttʃo] 'arm'; when a consonant precedes the cluster we find analogous developments, except for consonant+[dj] which gives consonant+[dz] (PRĂNDĬŬM>[pråndzo] 'meal', HŎRDĔŬM >[ɔ́rdzo] 'barley'); this is not surprising, as -[dj]- reduces to -[j]- (and then undergoes the same changes as [j]) when it is intervocalic, but not when it is preceded by a consonant.

There are also words which present different developments from these, such as consonant+[tj]>consonant+[tʃ] as in CŬMĬNĬTĬĀRĔ >[komintʃåre] 'to begin' (perhaps owing to hypercorrection); [tj]>[ʒ] and [dʒ] in words like *ragione* 'reason', *stagione* 'season', *pregio* 'value', etc., probably owing to the influence of Gallo-Italian dialects where -TĬŌNĔM>-[zón]: the [z] pronounced with some degree of palatalization (as many Gallo-Italian sibilants still are) may have been interpreted as [ʒ] and identified with the Tuscan [ʒ] which freely alternates with [dʒ] in words such as *agile* 'agile'; hence forms like *ragione* pronounced as [raʒóne] and [radʒóne].

[kj]>[ts] (as in *CĂLCĔĂM>[kåltsa] 'stocking'), and [j dj gj]>[ddz] (as in GAĬĂM>[gåddza] 'magpie', MĔDĬŬM>[mɛ́ddzo] 'half',

*GRĔGĬŬM>[grĕddzo][8] 'rough') show the same development which we find in northern dialects (where one may also find [ts]>[s], [dz]>[z], as has been seen above for the palatalization of [k g]; cf. Venetian [bråso] [mĕzo]).

In southern dialects we get [j dj gj] > [j] (Calabrian [jɔ́ku] 'play'<JŎCŬM, [måju] 'May'<MĀĬŬM), but in Puglia and eastern Lucania frequently [ʃ] (Apulian [ʃinnåru] 'January'<JĀNŬĀRĬŬM, [måʃu] 'May'<MĀĬŬM), [tj kj]>[tts] (Calabrian [kjåttsa] 'square' <PLĂTĔĂM, [vråttsu] 'arm'<BRĂCHĬŬM).

Other clusters with [j] also offer useful criteria for distinguishing between dialects:

(1) -[rj]- is simplified to -[j]- in Tuscany and to -[r]- in the rest of Italy: cf. the suffix -ĀRIUM giving -[åjo] in Tuscan and -[åro år ɛr], etc., in other dialects;

(2) -[sj]->-[ʃ]- in Tuscany and central Italy (BĀSĬŬM>[båʃo] 'kiss', CĂMĪSĬĂM>[kamíʃa] 'shirt', CĀSĔŬM>[kåʃo] 'cheese', CŌNSŬŌ >*COSIO>[kúʃo] 'sew', *BRŪSĬĀRĔ>[bruʃåre] 'to burn') and [s], or with sonorization [z], in other parts of Italy (Neapolitan [våsə], Venetian [båzo]<BĀSĬŬM).

The pronunciation with [tʃ] instead of [ʃ] in these words (cf. the spellings *bacio, camicia, cacio, cucio, bruciare*) must have originated on the model of words like *vicino*, with [k]>[tʃ]>[ʃ], where the two stages [tʃ] and [ʃ] both survived and the two sounds were considered alternants; similarly they must have been considered alternants in the series *bacio, camicia*, etc., where there was originally no [k] and consequently no [tʃ].

There is a series of words with sonorization in Tuscan such as [tʃiljɛ́ʒa] 'cherry'<CĔRĔSĔĂM, [faʒɔlo] 'bean'<PHĂSĔŌLŬM, [kaʒóne] 'cause'<ŎCCĀSĬŌNĔM, [priʒóne] 'prison'<PRĒNSĬŌNĔM where [ʒ] similarly alternates with [dʒ] (cf. the group of words mentioned above with [tj]>[ʒ] alternating with [dʒ]: *ragione, stagione, pregio*, etc.);

(3) -[lj]->-[ʎʎ]- in Tuscan, as in FĪLĬŬM>[fiʎʎo] 'son', MŬLĬĔR>[móʎʎe] 'wife', but it has different outcomes in other dialects: -[j]- in the north (Lombard [påja] 'straw'<PĂLĔĂM) (also [dʒ] in Venetian and Ligurian, [ådʒo], [ådʒu] 'garlic'<ĀLĬŬM), -[jj]- in central Italy (Roman [fíjjo] 'son'<FĪLĬŬM), -[jj]- or -[ȷȷ]- in the south (Abruzzese [fíjjə], Sicilian [fíȷȷu]);

(4) -[pj]- > -[ppj]-; -[bj]-, -[vj]- > -[bbj]- in Tuscan (SĂPĬĂT >[såppja] 'may he know', HĂBĔĂT>[åbbja] 'may he have', CĂVĔĂM >[gåbbja] 'cage'), but -[ttʃ]- and -[ddʒ]- in the south (Neapolitan

[såttʃə], [ådd3ə]); *piccione* 'pigeon'<PĪPĬŌNĔM must have been borrowed by Standard Italian from the south as its [ttʃ] instead of [ppj] indicates;

(5) -[mj]->-[mmj]- in Tuscan, but -[mj ɲ m]- in the north, and -[ɲɲ]- in the south (VĬNDĒMĬAM>Tuscan [vendėmmja], Lombard [vendėmja], Ligurian [vendɛ́ɲa], Venetian [vendėma], Campanian [vennɛ́ɲɲa] 'grape harvest').

There are other consonant clusters whose development may be used to differentiate between the dialects:

(1) PL>[pj] in Tuscany and the north (but [tʃ] in Ligurian: PLĀNŬM>[tʃån] 'flat', PLĂTĔAM>[tʃåsa] 'square'), and [kj] in the south: PLŪS>Tuscan [pju], Neapolitan [kju] 'more', PLĀNŬM >Tuscan [pjåno], Neapolitan [kjånə] 'flat', PLŎVĬT>Tuscan [pjȯve], Neapolitan [kjȯvə] 'it rains'; PL is preserved in Ladinian ([plaŋ]) (as well as other clusters with L: Germanic *blank*>*BLANCUM>[blaŋk] 'white', CLĀMĂT>[klåma] 'he calls', ĔCCLĔSĬAM>[glėzje] 'church'), and in parts of Abruzzi (PLĀNŬM>[plėnə] 'flat'), or the L may change to [r] as in Sardinia (PLĒNŬM>[prėnu] 'full') and in parts of Abruzzi (PLĬCĀRĔ>[prəkå] 'fold');

(2) BL>[bj] in Tuscan and in the north (but [d3] in Ligurian: Germanic *blank*>*BLANCUM>[d3åŋku] 'white'), and [j] or [d3] in the south: Tuscan [bjåŋko], Neapolitan [jåŋkə] 'white';

(3) KL>[kj] or [c] in Tuscan and in the south, but [tʃ] in the north: CLĀMĂT>Tuscan [kjåma], [cåma], Neapolitan [kjåma], Venetian [tʃåma] 'he calls'; in an internal position it may become [j] or [d3] in the north-west and [tʃ] in the north-east: AURĬCŬLĂM>Piedmontese [urija], Lombard [urėd3a], Venetian [rėtʃa] 'ear';

(4) GL>[gj] or [ɟ] in Tuscan, [d3] in the north, [j ɟ ʎ] in the south: *GLĂNDĂM>Tuscan [gjånda], [jånda], Venetian [d3ånda], Abruzzese [jånna], Neapolitan [ʎånna], Sicilian [ɟɟånna] 'acorn';

(5) FL>[fj] in Tuscan and in the north, but [ʃ] in the south: FLŪMĔN>Tuscan [fjůme], Neapolitan [ʃůmmə] 'river'.

Other consonant clusters undergo assimilation in Tuscany and in the south: PT>[tt] (SCRĪPTŬM>Tuscan [skrĭtto] 'written'), BT>[tt] (SŬBTŬS>Tuscan [sȯtto] 'under'), KT>[tt] (ŎCTŌ>Tuscan [ȯtto] 'eight'), PS>[ss] (SCRĪPSĬT>Tuscan [skrĭsse] 'he wrote'), KS>[ss] (DĪXĬT>Tuscan [dĭsse] 'he said'), etc.

In the north the double (or long) consonants of Latin are systematically reduced to single consonants, as in GĂTTŬM>[gåt(o)] 'cat', ĂNNŬM>[ån(o)] 'year', etc.

This applies also to Romance double consonants resulting from the assimilation of clusters of two different Latin consonants. But in some cases these clusters have altogether different outcomes in the north, e.g., KT>Piedmontese and Ligurian [jt], Lombard [tʃ], Emilian and Venetian [t]: LĂCTĔ, FĂCTŬM>Tuscan [làtte], [fàtto], Piedmontese and Ligurian [lajt], [fajt], Lombard [latʃ], [fatʃ], Emilian [lat], [fat], Venetian [làte], [fàto] 'milk', 'done'.

The clusters ND, MB remain as [nd], [mb] in Tuscany and in the north, but are assimilated into [nn], [mm] in the south: QUĂNDŌ>Tuscan [kwàndo], Neapolitan [kwànnə] 'when', PLŬMBŬM>Tuscan [pjómbo], Neapolitan [kjùmmə] 'lead'; the clusters [nd], [mb] exist in southern dialects as outcomes not of ND, MB, but of NT, MP, as we have seen above: CĂNTĀRĔ>[kandà] 'to sing', CĂMPĀNĂM>[kambàna] 'bell'.

Other characteristic phenomena found in many parts of the south are LL>[dd] or [ɖɖ]: BĔLLŬM>Sicilian [bèɖɖu] 'beautiful', and a development called 'betacism' consisting of the fusion of [b] and [v] both resulting in [v] when the consonant is single, and in [bb] when the consonant is double: in Neapolitan BŬCCĂM>[vòkka] 'mouth', ĂDVĔNTĀRĔ>[abbentà] 'to rest', and cf. [a vèna] 'the vein' vs. [e bbènə] 'the veins', because the plural feminine article causes the doubling of the initial consonant of the following word.

In front of a consonant L>[w] in Piedmont (ĂLTŬM>[awt] 'high', CĂLĬDŬM>[kawd] 'hot', FĂLSŬM>[faws] 'false'), and in parts of central and southern Italy ([àwtu] at Velletri in the province of Rome; FĂLCĔM>[fàwtʃe] 'scythe' at Sora in the province of Frosinone); LD>[ll] in parts of central and southern Italy (CĂLĬDŬM>[kàllo] 'hot' in the Marches); L in front of a consonant may also become [r]: in Roman ĂLTŬM>[àrto] 'high', ĬL(LŬM) CĂNĔM>[er kàne] 'the dog'; D>[r] in some Southern dialects: in Neapolitan DĬGĬTŬM>[rìtə] 'finger', DŬŎDĔCĬM>[rùrətʃə] 'twelve'; in Sicilian DĔCĔM>[rètʃi] 'ten', CRĒDĔRĔ>[krìriri] 'to believe'.

One cannot delve here into points of grammar, but it is clear that the study of dialects reveals many interesting features not found in the literary language.

For instance in dialects of central and southern Italy one finds the survival of a distinction between masculine and neuter, the neuter form of the article coming from ĬLLŬD, and the masculine from ĬLLŬM, as in (1) [u mmèlə] 'honey' vs. [u kànə] 'dog' in Bari, the neuter causing syntactic doubling; (2) [lo làtte] vs. [lu kàne] in Rieti, or [o låtte] vs. [u kåne] at Nemi in the province of Rome, the neuter issuing from a more open and the masculine from a more closed ŭ; for the same reason there is a neuter (and feminine) [kwėʃtə] 'this' without metaphony and a masculine [kwiʃtə] with metaphony in Abruzzese, and one distinguishes [lo pėʃʃo] 'fish' (collective) vs. [lu pėʃʃu] 'fish' (individual) at Servigliano in the province of Ascoli Piceno; and similarly in Neapolitan [o ffjėrrə] 'iron', as substance, vs. [o fjėrrə] 'the iron', as a tool, and with pronouns [o bbėkə] 'I see it', with reference to a mass noun vs. [o vėkə] 'I see it', with reference to a countable noun. Features such as this may emerge in the use of the standard language and be quite inexplicable if one is not aware of the conditions prevailing in the dialect.

Many other points could be discussed, such as the postposition of the possessives in the south (Campanian [fråtətə] vs. Lombard [to fradėl] 'your brother'); the first person plural endings in the verb, where standard Italian has generalized -[jåmo], but in Piedmontese we find -[ùma] ([kantùma] 'we sing', [venùma] 'we come'), and in other northern dialects -[ėmo], -[imo] (Venetian [kantėmo] 'we sing', [dormimo] 'we sleep'); the third person plural which in some dialects is identical to the third person singular (for instance in Venetian [el bėve] 'he drinks' and [i bėve] 'they drink'); the gradual elimination of the past historic and the generalization of the compound past in the north; the substitution for the conditional of the imperfect indicative in Puglia, of the imperfect subjunctive in Abruzzi and parts of Campania, or of forms deriving from the Latin pluperfect, like Sicilian [kantåra], Calabrian [kantårra]<CÅNTĂ-VĔRĂT 'he would sing' (cf. the literary Italian *fora* 'he would be'<FŬĔRĂT). Many dialects have a conditional in –[ia], from the imperfect of HĂBĒRĔ, instead of –[ėi] from its past historic (the –*ia* conditionals of the literary language probably originate from the Sicilian school). Many southern dialects have substituted various periphrastic expressions for the future and for the infinitive. Many northern dialects have eliminated the stressed forms of the personal pronouns in the nominative, and use obligatory proclitic forms of the pronouns with the verb, as in French.

We give overleaf (disregarding the use of pronouns) the present indicative of a verb ('to say') in Latin, in Italian, and in six dialects, three from the north and three from the south: it offers a telling picture of the varied development of the Italian dialects:

Latin	Italian	Milanese	Bolognese
DĪCŌ	[dǐko]	[dǐ:zi]	[deg]
DĪCĪS	[dǐtʃi]	[dǐ:zet]	[di:]
DĪCĬT	[dǐtʃe]	[di:s]	[di:z]
DĪCĬMŬS	[ditʃámo]	[dǐ:zum]	[dʒaŋ]
DĪCĬTĬS	[dǐte]	[dizé]	[dʒi:]
DĪCŬNT	[dǐkono]	[dǐ:zen]	[dǐ:zen]

Venetian	Abruzzese (Bellante)	Apulian (Canosa)	Sardinian (Sassari)
[dǐgo]	[dǝk]	[dɔjkǝ]	[dǐggu]
[dǐzi]	[dǝtʃ]	[dɔjtʃ]	[di]
[dǐze]	[dǝtʃ]	[dɔjtʃ]	[dǐdzi]
[dizémo]	[ditʃámǝ]	[dǝtʃɔjmǝ]	[dǐmmu]
[dizé]	[ditʃátǝ]	[dǝtʃɔjtǝ]	[dǐddi]
[dǐze]	[dǝtʃ]	[dǐkǝnǝ]	[dǐdzini]

To show what dialectal texts look like, in traditional spelling rather than in phonetic transcription, we quote some popular verses (from the *Canzoniere Italiano*, edited by P. P. Pasolini, Milan, 1972) with their literal Italian translation, and also an English rendering.

From Piedmont: *O mama mia, cuntentèmi 'l cori,*
Dè-mi cul giuvinin ch'a j'ò amicissia,
Tütti me dizu che l'è ün rumpacolli:
Dè-m-li, mama, ch'a i farò cambiè vita.

O mamma mia, contentatemi il cuore,	O mother, satisfy my heart,
datemi quel ragazzo che c'ho amicizia.	Give me the boy I am friends with.
Tutti mi dicono che è un rompicollo: datemelo, mamma, gli farò cambiare vita.	Everyone tells me he is a madcap, Give him to me, mother, I'll make him change his ways.

From Liguria: *Passu de s'tu caruggiu tantu növu:*
Ra lün-na a mesa nöcce a nun lüxiva,
U 'n j' era nè ra lün-na, nè lu sule,
I' occhi dra bella ch'i mnava' s'sprendure.

Passo per questo vicolo tanto nuovo: la luna a mezzanotte non splendeva,	I go down this alley which is so new: The moon was not shining at midnight,

non c'era nè la luna nè il sole,

There was neither the moon nor the sun,

c'erano gli occhi della bella a far splendore.

There were the eyes of my fair one shedding their light.

From Romagna: *Lavora, cuntadèn, lavora fört,*
Quando ti vé a partì, e' gran l'è pöc;
Lavora, cuntadèn, a la sicura,
Patron e' gran, e' cuntadèn la pula.

Lavora, contadino, lavora forte,
quando vai a spartire, poco è il grano;
lavora, contadino, lavora sicuro,
al padrone il grano, al contadino la pula.

Work, peasant, work hard,
When you go to share it out, there's little corn;
Work, peasant, work confidently,
The corn goes to the owner, to the peasant the chaff.

From Venetia: *Tuti sti marineri a 'na galera,*
Ma Toni belo fusselo picà:
E fusselo picà perchè l'è belo,
Perchè la vita sua me dà martelo.

Tutti questi marinai a una galera,

Let all these sailors be sent to a galley,

ma Toni bello fosse impiccato:

But fair Toni, I would see him hanged,

e fosse impiccato perchè è bello,

I'd like him hanged because he's fair,

perchè la vita sua mi dà martello.

Because his life torments me.

From Friuli: *O ce bièl lusôr di lune*
Che il Signôr nus ha mandàt!
A bussà fantatis bielis
No l'è frègul di peçhat.

O che bel chiaro di luna
che il Signore ci ha mandato!
A baciare ragazze belle
non c'è briciola di peccato.

What beautiful moonlight
The Lord has sent us!
In kissing beautiful girls,
There's not a scrap of sin.

From Rome: *Ve possino dà tante cortellate*
Pe' quante messe ha ddetto l'arciprete
Pe' quante vorte ha ddetto: Orate frate.

Vi possano dar tante coltellate   May you be stabbed as many times
per quante messe ha detto l'arciprete   As are the masses the priest has said
per quante volte ha detto: Orate   As many times as he has said: Orate
fratres.   fratres.

From Abruzzi: *Bbella, chell'altra notte me te 'nzunnaje*
             Parè ch'a lu mio late te teneve.
             Me revutaje, ca nen fu lu vere!
             Pianze 'na nott'e 'na ggiurnata 'ndiere.

Bella, l'altra notte ti sognai: Fair one, the other night I dreamt of you:
mi pareva che al mio fianco ti tenevo.   I felt I had you at my side.
Mi rivoltai, e non era vero.   I turned, it was not true.
Piansi una notte ed un giorno intero.   I wept a whole night and day.

From Naples: *La notte è lu repuose de la gente,*
            E i' mescheniello nu' repose maie:
            Reposa l'acqua e reposa lu viento,
            Lu viento abente, e i' n'abento maie.

La notte è il riposo della gente,   Night is when people rest,
e io, meschinello, non riposo mai.   But I, wretched one, never rest.
Riposa l'acqua, riposa il vento,   Water rests, the wind rests,
il vento ha pace, io non ho pace mai.   The wind finds peace, I never find peace.

From Sicily: *Calu di sta vanedda lentu lentu,*
           Pri vidiri cu' m'ama 'nta stu cantu;
           Arrivu unn'era lu mè caru 'ntentu,
           L'occhiu mi calu e moru di lu chiantu.
           Idda rispusi: 'Ora statti cuntentu,
           Picciottu, cchiu nun fari tantu chiantu.'

Scendo da questo vicolo lento lento,   I go down this alley slowly slowly
per vedere chi m'ama in questo luogo.   To see someone who loves me in this place.
Arrivo dov'era il mio caro amore,   I come to the spot where my dear love was,
l'occhio mi si abbassa, muoio per il pianto.   I lower my eyes, I die weeping.
Ella rispose: 'Ora sta contento,   She replied: 'Be glad now,
ragazzo, più non fare tanto pianto.'   Boy, do not cry so any more.'

From Sardinia: *In s'oru 'e su mare*
            Canta' su rissignolu
            Cun boghe dolentìa.
              No minde podìa ilthare
              In sa campagna solu
              Ca a tie non bidìa.

Nell'oro del mare	In the gold of the sea
canta l'usignolo	The nightingale sings
con voce addolorata.	With a sorrowful voice.
Non potevo restare	I could not stay
nella campagna solo	In the countryside alone
senza vedere te.	Without seeing you.

Notes

[1] We transcribe with the symbols of the International Phonetic Association. For many Italian dialects there are several conflicting traditional spelling systems. As is customary we use small capitals for Latin; long vowels are marked above with a macron (¯), short vowels with a breve (˘). A preceding * indicates a form which is reconstructed and not documented.

[2] An isogloss is a line on a map marking the boundary of a linguistic phenomenon.

[3] In the schematic representation of feet with the symbols of macron and breve, one marks the 'quantity' of the syllables even though it may conflict with that of the vowel. The word TĔRRĀS 'lands' in metre is represented as a spondee, i.e., $- -$. It is inexact to state, as some Latin grammars do, that a short vowel may become long 'by position'. The second syllable of LĔGĬT is light (short) in LĔGĬT ĔPĬSTŬLĂM 'he reads a letter', and heavy (long) in LĔGĬT SCRĪPTŬM 'he reads a text', but the vowel it contains obviously does not change its quantity and remains short. As word boundaries do not affect syllables, for metrical purposes we have in the first case a free (GĬ–TĔ) and in the second a checked (GĬT–SCRĪP–) syllable.

[4] In our phonetic transcriptions vowel quantity is marked when it is distinctive or, as here, when it is relevant to the point being made.

[5] But *agile* is a learned word; in popular words one has [ddʒ] in intervocalic position: FŪGĬT>[fùddʒe] 'he flees'.

[6] From Ē one would expect [e] and not [ε], but one often finds [ε], [ɔ] instead of [e], [o] in learned, literary words which did not undergo ordinary, popular development.

[7] Another, more learned outcome, is [vìttsjo]. Forms like *vezzo* and *vizio*, deriving from the same Latin source through different developments, are usually called 'allotropes' (the term was borrowed from chemistry by the philologist U. A. Canello in 1878).

[8] The presence of [e] in this example is not satisfactorily explained.

IV   Varieties of Italian

1

As we have said (chapters I and II), it is more realistic to talk about varieties of Italian (regional or sectional) than about an alleged standard, which not only does not exist in actual usage, but is not even an ideal to which existing varieties strive to conform.

Local varieties are not substandard forms of Italian living in the shadow of a national standard form: they are what Italian consists of. The differences between them are most conspicuous in the field of phonology, they are still noticeable in syntax and lexis, but practically non existent in morphology.

First of all there is intonation in the sense of the general musical movement of discourse (Italian has several terms for it, such as *cantilena, cadenza, calata*), a cadence which makes the speech of certain regions (like Liguria, Venetia, Abruzzi, Puglia) clearly recognizable. There may also be some variation from one part of Italy to another in the use of intonational systems as part of grammar.

(a) It is easier to pinpoint differences which concern **phonology** proper, although too little satisfactory work has been done on the description of local varieties of Italian, and this makes it difficult to give a coherent account region by region. A disservice which puristic studies have done, in order to prove their point, is to compare educated Florentine, given as the model, with uneducated non-Florentine varieties (to provide examples of 'mistakes'), so that there is very little information about uneducated Florentine, and even less about educated non-Florentine varieties. The way in which local pronunciations are usually discussed and transcribed gives the impression that, outside Florence, one Florentine phoneme is being mistakenly used for another. The reader should be on his guard against this misinterpretation.

We shall present Florentine phonology (which is best known)

first, and then indicate the main points in which other local varieties differ from Florentine.[1]

(i) The Florentine system generally adopted by handbooks and dictionaries of Italian includes seven vowels, twenty-one consonants, and two semiconsonants (for the classificatory labels see the table on p. 240).

i			u	p	t	ts	tʃ	k
e		o		b	d	dz	dʒ	g
	ɛ	ɔ		f	s		ʃ	
	a			v	z			
				m	n		ɲ	
					l		ʎ	
					r			
			w				j	

For fifteen out of twenty-one consonants there is an opposition between double and single,[2] as exemplified by the following minimal pairs: [p] vs. [pp] *rupe* 'rock' vs. *ruppe* 'he broke'; [b] vs. [bb] *libra* 'he poises' vs. *libbra* 'pound'; [t] vs. [tt] *grato* 'grateful' vs. *gratto* 'I scratch'; [d] vs. [dd] *cade* 'he falls' vs. *cadde* 'he fell'; [tʃ] vs. [ttʃ] *luci* 'lights' vs. *lucci* 'pikes'; [dʒ] vs. [ddʒ] *mogio* 'downcast' vs. *moggio* 'bushel'; [k] vs. [kk] *eco* 'echo' vs. *ecco* 'here is'; [g] vs. [gg] *fuga* 'flight' vs. *fugga* 'may he flee'; [f] vs. [ff] *tufo* 'tufa' vs. *tuffo* 'plunge'; [v] vs. [vv] *avito* 'ancestral' vs. *avvito* 'I screw'; [s] vs. [ss] *casa* 'house' vs. *cassa* 'box'; [m] vs. [mm] *gramo* 'wretched' vs. *grammo* 'gram'; [n] vs. [nn] *cane* 'dog' vs. *canne* 'reeds'; [l] vs. [ll] *mole* 'mass' vs *molle* 'soft'; [r] vs. [rr] *caro* 'dear' vs. *carro* 'cart'.

The six consonants to which this opposition does not apply are [ts] [dz] [ʃ] [ɲ] [ʎ] (which are always double in intervocalic position) and [z] which is always single; for example *vizio* 'vice' [vìttsjo]; *vizi* 'vices' and *vizzi* 'withered' are both [vìttsi];[3] when the consonant is not intervocalic one has *alza* 'he lifts' [àltsa], *zio* 'uncle' [tsìo] (but *lo zio* 'the uncle' [lo ttsìo] because the word-initial [ts], being preceded by [lo], becomes intervocalic); *mezzo* 'half' [mèddzo], *ozono* 'ozone' [oddzóno], *orzo* 'barley' [órdzo], *zero* 'zero' [dzèro], *lo zero* [lo ddzèro]; *ascia* 'axe' [àʃʃa]; *conscio* 'conscious' [kónʃo]; *scemo* 'stupid' [ʃèmo], *lo scemo* [lo ʃʃèmo]; *ogni* 'each' [óɲɲi]; *gnocco* 'a kind of noodle' [ɲòkko], *gli gnocchi* [ʎi ɲɲòkki]); *foglia* 'leaf' [fòʎʎa], *fargli* 'to do to him' [fàrʎi], *gli* 'the' [ʎi], *anche gli zii* 'also the uncles' [àŋke ʎʎi ttsìi];[4] *rosa* 'rose' [ròza].

If the fifteen double consonants are considered to be independent phonological units (rather than adjacent occurrences of the single ones) we have an inventory of thirty-six consonants instead of twenty-one.

In Florentine there is a phonological opposition between [e] and [ɛ], [o] and [ɔ], [ts] and [dz], [s] and [z]; each couple, however, is represented in traditional spelling by one letter only: *e, o, z* (or *zz*) and *s* respectively. There are in each case minimal pairs, fairly numerous for the vowels, fewer for the consonants.

Consider for instance the following homographs, for which we give the meaning of the words with the closed vowel first, and the meaning of the words with the open vowel second:
accetta 'hatchet' vs. 'he accepts'; *affetta* 'he slices' vs. 'he affects'; *corresse* 'that he ran' vs. 'he corrected'; *credo* 'I believe' vs. 'credo'; *esse* 'they' (feminine) vs. 'the name of the letter *s*'; *legge* 'law' vs. 'he reads'; *lessi* 'boiled' vs. 'I read' (past); *pesca* 'fishing' vs. 'peach'; *premetti* 'you premise' vs. 'I pressed'; *re* 'king' vs. 'the note D'; *venti* 'twenty' vs. 'winds';
botte 'barrel' vs. 'blows'; *colto* 'learned' vs. 'caught'; *fosse* 'that he were' vs. 'holes'; *imposto* 'imposed' vs. 'I post'; *indotto* 'induced' vs. 'unlearned'; *porci* 'to put there' vs. 'pigs'; *porsi* 'to put oneself' vs. 'I handed'; *porti* 'to put you' vs. 'you bring'; *pose* 'he put' vs. 'postures'; *posta* 'placed' (feminine singular) vs. 'mail'; *riposi* 'I put away' (past) vs. 'you rest'; *scopo* 'I sweep' vs. 'aim'; *scorsi* 'I glided' vs. 'I glimpsed'; *sorte* 'arisen' (feminine plural) vs. 'destiny'; *volgo* 'populace' vs. 'I turn'; *volto* 'face' vs. 'I turn';
and, giving the meaning of the words with the voiceless consonant first, with the voiced second: *zannata* 'a bite' (with fangs: *zanne*) vs. 'clowning' (as of a *Zanni*); *razza* 'race' vs. 'ray' (fish); *fuso* 'spindle' vs. 'fused'; *chiese* 'he asked' vs. 'churches'.

The number of minimal pairs may be fairly small, but this of course does not mean that, when one of the two terms of a phonological opposition occurs, it can be exchanged for the other if there is no minimal pair. There is still a phonological choice to be made between, e.g., [e] in *metto* 'I put', *pelo* 'hair', *neve* 'snow', and [ɛ] in *sette* 'seven', *bello* 'beautiful', *bene* 'well'; [o] in *rotto* 'broken', *come* 'how', *sole* 'sun', and [ɔ] in *otto* 'eight', *cosa* 'thing', *nuovo* 'new'; between [ts] in *zio* 'uncle', *zucchero* 'sugar', *zampa* 'paw', *zecca* 'mint', *zitto* 'silent', *zoccolo* 'clog', *zolfo* 'sulphur', *zoppo* 'lame', *zucca* 'pumpkin', *pazzo* 'mad', *alzo* 'I lift', *marzo* 'March', *anzi* 'rather', and [dz] in *zero* 'zero', *zebra* 'zebra', *zelo* 'zeal', *zona* 'zone', *mezzo* 'half', *orzo* 'barley', *pranzo* 'meal', *razzo* 'rocket', *gar-zone* 'delivery boy'; between [s] in *asino* 'donkey', *casa* 'house', *così* 'thus', *riso* 'rice', *naso* 'nose', *cosa* 'thing', *inglese* 'English', *chiuso* 'closed', *peso* 'weight', and [z] in *caso* 'case', *vaso* 'vase', *viso* 'face', *francese* 'French', *uso* 'use', *quasi* 'almost'.

Note also the following phenomena:

(A) In intervocalic position (not just within the word, but in the spoken chain with words adjoining each other) we find [h] or even Ø for [k], [φ] for [p], and [θ] for [t]. This spirantization, often called *gorgia* or *aspirazione*, presents itself differently according to (I) which of the consonants is affected, and to what extent: the area (with Florence, Pistoia and Siena) in which [p] and [t] are spirantized being included in a larger area (with Lucca, Pisa, Livorno, Grosseto as well) in which [k] is spirantized (or, frequently, elided, in the provinces of Lucca, Pisa, Livorno); (II) social class and level of formality, the *gorgia* as a whole being more widespread and more marked in uneducated and informal speech; but a spirantization of intervocalic [k] is a constant characteristic of Florentine speech for all social classes and at all levels of formality.

(B) Similarly [tʃ] and [dʒ] in intervocalic position are spirantized to [ʃ] and [ʒ]. There have been many discussions on the relationship between the [ʃ] resulting from the spirantization of [tʃ], as in *pece*, and the intervocalic double [ʃʃ] as in *pesce*. The double consonant is more *fortis* than the single one and has a more pronounced degree of lip rounding, but for practical purposes the same symbol is used here for the two sounds, repeated twice for the double consonant; spirantized [tʃ] (i.e., [ʃ]) can only occur in intervocalic position, where a [ʃ] which is not a spirantized [tʃ] is always double ([ʃʃ]): the distinction is therefore systematically represented in our transcription.

(C) Syntactic doubling. Certain words cause a doubling of the initial consonant of the following word. The semiconsonants [j] and [w] are not doubled, and doubling does not occur when it would produce an unacceptable cluster: *a sapere* [a ssapére] 'to know' but *a stare* [a stáre] 'to stay'; *è tradotto* [ɛ ttradótto] 'it is translated' but *è spostato* [ɛ spostáto] 'it is moved'. Syntactic doubling is caused by (I) all words ending with a stressed vowel (here we can include so-called strong monosyllables, i.e., monosyllables which can carry sentence stress); if they are polysyllabic they have an accent mark in traditional spelling, if they are monosyllabic they may or may not have an accent mark. For instance: *andò* 'he went', *cantò* 'he sang', *perchè* 'because', *così* 'thus', *però* 'however', etc.; *è* 'he is', *più* 'more', *può* 'he can', *do* 'I give', *gru* 'crane', *re* 'king', *blu* 'blue', *tre* 'three', *me* 'me', *te* 'you', *sè* 'himself', *ciò* 'that', *no* 'no', *sì* 'yes', *già* 'already', *giù* 'down', *là* 'there', *lì* 'there', *qua* 'here', *qui* 'here', *nè* 'neither', etc.;

(II) a series of so-called weak monosyllables (i.e., monosyllables which are always unstressed; emphatic stress is of course not relevant here) such as *e* 'and', *o* 'or', *a* 'to', *da* 'from', *fra* 'between', *che* 'that', *se* 'if', *ma* 'but', etc., and a few polysyllables which are not stressed finally: *come* 'like', *dove* 'where', *qualche* 'some', *sopra* 'on', *sovra* 'on'.

There are two reasons for syntactic doubling: (*a*) synchronic: final stressed vowels are short, but syllabic structure does not admit stressed short vowels followed by single consonants (V̆C); of the two possible structures, V̆C̄ and V̄C̄, the former is selected in the cases of syntactic doubling; (*b*) diachronic: syntactic doubling represents the assimilation of a final Latin consonant (*e*<ĔT, *a*<ĂD, *o*<AUT, etc.) to the initial consonant of the following word. The first reason (or the first and the second concurrently) apply to the cases in (I), the second to the cases in (II). It is generally accepted that some words, such as *se*<SĪ, cause doubling by analogy with other words which cause it for etymological reasons.

As a result of the phenomena mentioned in (A), (B) and (C) we have the following variations between [h] [k] [kk], [ʒ] [dʒ] [ddʒ], [ʃ] [tʃ] [ttʃ] [ʃʃ]: in words like *casa* 'house', *giorno* 'day', *cena* 'supper', *scena* 'scene':

di casa [di hȧsa]	*per casa* [per kȧsa]	*a casa* [a kkȧsa]
di giorno [di ʒȯrno]	*per giorno* [per dʒȯrno]	*a giorno* [a ddʒȯrno]
di cena [di ʃėna]	*per cena* [per tʃėna]	*a cena* [a ttʃėna]
di scena [di ʃʃėna]	*per scena* [per ʃėna]	*a scena* [a ʃʃėna]

Note that [ʃ] may represent the initial of *cena* in *di cena* and of *scena* in *per scena*. In intervocalic position we find [ʃʃ] both in *di scena* and in *a scena*: this is why some handbooks state that syntactic doubling does not apply to [ʃ], [ʎ], [ɲ], [ts], [dz], i.e., to the consonants which in intervocalic position are always double anyway.

Syntactic doubling is not usually represented in traditional spelling, but etymologically the same phenomenon is at work in *a prendere* 'to take' [a pprėndere] and *apprendere* 'to learn' [apprėndere] (D+P>[pp]), *e bene* 'and well' [e bbėne] and *ebbene* 'well' [ebbėne] (T+B>[bb]), etc. (The two items in each pair are homophonous: word separation in our transcription is only conventional).

Some distinctions must be noted: *te lo porta* [te lo pɔ́rta] 'he brings it to you' vs. *a te lo porta* [a tte llo pɔ́rta] 'it is to you that he brings it', with [l] in the first case because *te* is weak, and [ll] in the second case because *te* is strong; *se lo prende* [se lo prɛ́nde] 'he takes it' with [l] because *se* is weak, *per sè lo prende* [per se llo prɛ́nde] 'he takes it for himself' with [ll] because *sè* is strong, and *se lo prende* [se llo prɛ́nde] 'if he takes it' with [ll] because *se* 'if' causes doubling; *come, dove, sopra* cause doubling when they are used as prepositions: *sopra la tavola* [sɔ́pra lla tȧvola] 'on the table', but not as adverbs: *di sopra c'è la soffitta* [di sɔ́pra tʃɛ lla soffítta] 'upstairs there is the attic'. The imperatives of *dare* 'to give', *fare* 'to do', *stare* 'to stay', *andare* 'to go' may or may not cause doubling: *sta calmo* [sta kȧlmo] or [sta kkȧlmo]: they do not cause doubling when they are derived from the imperatives *dai, fai, stai, vai* reduced to *da', fa', sta', va'*; they do cause it when they are the original *dà, fa, sta, va*; similarly for *dire* 'to say' the imperative may (*dì*) or may not (*di'*) cause doubling; the third person singular of the present indicative causes the doubling: so [va vvía] may mean either 'he goes away' or 'go away!' but [va vía] can only mean 'go away!'.

Doubling may be inhibited by a syntactic boundary or it may be introduced if a weak monosyllable becomes stressed. This explains some often quoted examples which appear to be self-contradictory, such as: *'qualche' raddoppia, 'di' non raddoppia* [kwȧlke raddóppja di nnon raddóppja] *'qualche* doubles, *di* does not double', without the normally required doubling after *qualche*, because it does not combine with the following word to form a noun phrase, and with a normally refused doubling after *di*, because, being quoted, the word acquires a stress, thus ending in a stressed vowel.

Some words behave idiosyncratically: *Dio* 'God' doubles its initial consonant after any preceding vowel: not only [a ddío] 'to God', but also [di ddío] 'of God'; this is apparent also in the obligatory use of the article *gli* in the plural: *gli* does not occur in front of single consonants, and *gli dei* is [ʎi ddɛ́i] 'the gods'. Also unexpectedly the initial of *Cristo* 'Christ' does not double after *Gesù* 'Jesus': [dʒezú krísto], and the initial of *santo* doubles in *Spirito Santo* [spírito ssȧnto] 'Holy Ghost' and *Ognissanti* [oɲɲissȧnti] 'All Saints'.

Many other characteristics could be mentioned, such as (D) the use of [ɔ] instead of a diphthong, in words like [bɔ́no] 'good', [nɔ́vo] 'new', etc.

(E) the tendency to avoid consonant endings, particularly if the final syllable is stressed: hence [rùmme] for *rum* 'rum', [tràmme] for *tram* 'tram', [spòrte] for *sport* 'sport', [koɲɲàkke] for *cognac* 'brandy', [gàsse] for *gas* 'gas'. In front of a vowel (at the beginning of a suffix or of a following word) there is a sort of counterpart of syntactic doubling: *cognacchino* [koɲɲakkìno] 'a small brandy', *cognac invecchiato* [koɲɲàkk invekkjàto] 'aged brandy', *gassoso* [gassóso] 'gaseous', *gas asfissiante* [gass asfissjànte] 'poison gas'. This does not apply to proclitics: *non importa* [non impòrta] 'it does not matter', *son andati* [son andàti] 'they have gone'.

(F) One can also mention a Tuscan, but not Florentine, pronunciation with the palatal stops [c] and [ɟ] instead of [kj] [gj], which is at the origin of spellings such as *mastio* (cf. *maschio*) 'donjon', *diaccio* (cf. *ghiaccio*) 'icy'. This is also widely used in central and southern Italy. Purists accept it as a correct alternative, although admitting that it is not common.

(ii) We shall now discuss some phonological differences between other varieties of Italian and Florentine.

In many varieties of Italian points (i) (A)–(F) listed above are not found. The situation is very complex as regards [e] vs. [ɛ] and [o] vs. [ɔ]. There are varieties of Italian in which there is only one mid-front and one mid-back vowel, e.g., in Sicily, Sardinia, parts of Venetia. In other varieties the phonological opposition between open and closed applies only to the front or only to the back vowel. For instance in Turin there is only [ɔ] but both [e] and [ɛ]; the opposition between the latter two however is only possible in a stressed, word final position, otherwise they are in complementary distribution, with [e] in a free syllable or in a syllable checked by a double consonant, and [ɛ] in other checked syllables.[5]

In most varieties of Italian the opposition exists for both vowels, but it may be neutralized in many positions; for instance, in some northern varieties in syllables checked by double consonants, or in final stressed free syllables there is only [ɛ] and not [e], as in *bicicletta* [bitʃiklɛtta] 'bicycle', *stella* [stɛlla] 'star', *re* [rɛ] 'king'.

Corresponding to Florentine [ɛ] one often finds [e], as in *piede* [pjéde] 'foot', *breve* [brève] 'short', *bene* [bène] 'well' in northern Italy and in parts of southern Italy (Naples, Salento, Sicily, Sardinia); corresponding to Florentine [o] one often finds [ɔ], as in *sole* [sòle] 'sun', *colpa* [kòlpa] 'guilt' in Piedmont, Liguria, and in parts of southern Italy (e.g., in Puglia).

What makes the situation particularly complicated is that even those varieties which have phonological oppositions between [e] and [ɛ], [o] and [ɔ], often use them differently from Florentine. Puristic handbooks devote a lot of attention to the words (there are a couple of hundred) in which Rome (e.g., with *lettera* [léttera] 'letter', *bistecca* [bistɛ́kka] 'steak', *colonna* [kolónna] 'column', *dimora* [dimóra] 'residence') differs from Florence (with [léttera], [bistɛ́kka], [kolónna], [dimɔ́ra]). In other varieties, where a comparison with the local dialect is possible, it is clear that no simple correlation can be found between the local variety of Italian and either the local dialect or the Florentine variety. For instance in Venice in the local variety of Italian one has *bene* [bɛ́ne] 'well', *re* [rɛ] 'king', *bosco* [bósko] 'wood', *ogni* [ɔ́ɲi] 'each', and in the dialect [beŋ], [rɛ], [bósko], [ɔ́ɲi] vs. Florentine [bɛ́ne], [re], [bɔ́sko], [óɲɲi]; but for *posto* [pɔ́sto] 'place', *vengo* [véŋgo] 'I come' the dialect, with [pósto], [vɛ́no] has the same vowels as Florentine [pósto], [véŋgo]; on the other hand in *piove* [pjɔ́ve] 'it rains', *sporco* [spɔ́rko] 'dirty', *poco* [pɔ́ko] 'a little' one has the same vowels in the Venetian and in the Florentine varieties of Italian, as against the Venetian dialect [pjóve], [spórko], [póko].

As far as double consonants are concerned, in northern Italy there is a tendency to reduce them. In educated pronunciation this tendency (owing to the manner in which Italian was originally learnt and used, mainly as a written, literary medium) has been checked in those cases where doubling is represented by spelling, but it has prevailed where spelling was no guide, i.e., for [ɲ] [ʎ] [ʃ], and for those [ts] and [dz] which are represented in spelling by a single *z*: so there is *pugno* [púɲo] 'fist', *figlio* [fiʎo] 'son', *uscio* [úʃo] 'door', *vizi* [vítsi] 'vices', *Gaza* [gádza], but *vizzi* [víttsi] 'withered', *gazza* [gáddza] 'jay'. There is of course no syntactic doubling (except in cases in which it survives fossilized in spelling: *ebbene* 'well', *chicchessia*, 'anyone', etc.).

In central and southern Italy different conditions apply. Double consonants are usually the same as in Tuscan, and in some cases they are used where Tuscan has a single consonant. But one also finds single instead of double: in Rome (as in northern Latium, the Marches, and western and southern Tuscany) there is a tendency to reduce [rr] to [r]: [fɛ́ro] for *ferro* 'iron', [tɛ́ra] for *terra* 'earth', [a róma] for *a Roma* 'to Rome', but [a nnápoli] for *a Napoli* 'to Naples'. There are parts of central and southern Italy where a distinction is made between single [ts]<TI, as in *nazione* [natsjóne]

'nation', and double [tts]<cti, pti, as in *azione* [attsjóne] 'action', *concezione* [kontʃettsjóne] 'conception'; in the extreme south in learned words, which do not follow popular development, there is a single [ts], which is voiced to [dz], as in *vizio* [vídzjo] 'vice'.

Generally in central and southern Italy intervocalic, and sometimes initial, [b] [dʒ] and [j] are doubled: *roba* [róbba] 'stuff', *agile* [áddʒile] 'agile', *la bella gente* [la bbɛ́lla ddʒɛ́nte] 'the fine people', *era buio* [ɛ́ra bbújjo] 'it was dark'. Other doubling phenomena are more limited, e.g., initial [d] in Calabria: *la danza* [la ddándza] 'the dance', initial [r] in Sicily and Sardinia: *la riva* [la rríva] 'the shore', and sporadically in other cases: *stomaco* [stómmako] 'stomach'.

The opposition of [ts] vs. [dz] in northern Italy is neutralized in an initial position, where we only find [dz]; the use of [dz] and not [ts] initially is also found in Sicily, Sardinia, and parts of the south. It is gaining ground in the rest of Italy, including Tuscany. In parts of southern Italy there is a tendency to sonorize the affricate in a postconsonantal position: *alzare* [aldzáre] 'to lift', *calza* [káldza] 'stocking', *marzo* [márdzo] 'March'; in the extreme south we find voicing of the single affricate, in intervocalic position as well: *grazie* [grádzje] 'thank you', *nazione* [nadzjóne] 'nation'.

Even in Florentine the opposition between [s] and [z] exists only in an intervocalic position; in a preconsonantal position there is [s] in front of a voiceless consonant and [z] in front of a voiced one; in a prevocalic initial position there is [s], in a postconsonantal position there is [s] as in *falso* [fálso] 'false', but assimilation to a following consonant prevails: *disbrigo* [dizbrígo] 'dispatch', *dislocare* [dizlo-káre] 'to dislocate', *transvolare* [tranzvoláre] 'to fly across'. In northern Italy we find only [z], and in central and southern Italy only [s] in an intervocalic position: so [s] and [z] are allophones in complementary distribution: they are phonologically opposed only in Tuscan. But from the point of view of surface oppositions there are cases of [s] contrasting with [z] in northern Italy, in intervocalic position, as in *presento*, with [s] meaning 'I forebode', and with [z] 'I present'. This happens because a morpheme-initial [s] may be preserved as voiceless in an intervocalic position as in *ventisei* 'twenty-six', *ventisette* 'twenty-seven', *risentito* 'resentful', *risolvere* 'to resolve', *proseguire* 'to proceed', *presidente* 'president', *risalire* 'to go up again', *riserva* 'reserve', *risorgere* 'to rise again', *trasognato* 'dreamy'. But there are many cases where it is no longer felt to be morpheme-initial and northern Italian usually has [z] as against Florentine [s]: *disegno* 'drawing', *designato* 'designated', *desiderare* 'to desire', *resistere* 'to resist', *risarcire* 'to reimburse', *risaltare* 'to show up', *risultare* 'to result', and with *trans-: transalpino* 'transalpine', *transatlantico* 'transatlantic', *transazione* 'transaction', *transigere* 'to compromise', *transitivo* 'transitive', *transito* 'transit', *transitorio* 'transitory', *transizione* 'transition'.

These are the main phonemic differences. But there are many phonetic ones, some typically and permanently characterizing the local variety in which they appear, some dependent on the degree of education and formality.

Considering vowels first: one finds a palatalized [æ] instead of [a] particularly in Emilia-Romagna and Puglia (the inhabitants of Parma and Bari pronounce the names of their towns in a way which is teasingly represented by other Italians as *Perma* and *Beri*). A velarized variety of [a] verging towards [ɔ] is found in Piedmont and Liguria, particularly before [l]+ consonant, in words like *alto* 'high', *caldo* 'hot', where the [l] is also velarized. In Emilia one finds [æ] for [ɛ] in words like *martello* 'hammer', [ɪ] for [i] and [ʊ] for [u] in words like *fitto* 'thick', *tutto* 'all'. In Sicily one finds [ɪ] for [i] (hence a jocular spelling like *seceleano* to refer to the local pronunciation), and in many parts of southern Italy [ə] for unstressed vowels (particularly for [i] [e] [o]); this is most noticeably marked in the case of final vowels, which may disappear altogether in Abruzzi, Puglia, Lucania and Campania. In parts of northern Italy final stressed vowels are long, as in *perchè* [perkɛ:] 'why', *te* [tɛ:] 'you'.

As far as semiconsonants are concerned, in Emilia [w] tends to lose its semiconsonantal character and to become a [v]: one hears [vɔmo] for *uomo* 'man', [evrɔpa] for *Europa* 'Europe', [lȧvra] for *Laura*, [aftomɔbile] for *automobile* 'car' (with [v] being devoiced in front of a voiceless consonant). The opposite is found in parts of southern Italy where [j] and [w] become fully vocalized, as in [buȯno] for *buono* 'good', [iɛ̇ri] for *ieri* 'yesterday', each with three syllables: [j] or [i] are often heard between a palatal and the following sound in the south: [tʃiɛ̇ko] for *cieco* 'blind', [ʃiɛ̇ndza] for *scienza* 'science'.[6]

Proceeding to consonants: one notes that an intervocalic voiceless stop in northern Italy (except Venetia) and Sardinia is usually more *fortis* than in Florence, as in [pȧp·a] for *papa* 'pope', [pat·ȧt·a] for *patata* 'potato', [amɪk·a] for *amica* 'friend'. In parts of central and southern Italy (Latium, Umbria, the Marches, Abruzzi, Campania) it is *lenis*, as in [i b̥ȧb̥i] for *i papi* 'the popes', [la b̥ad̥ȧd̥a] for *la patata*, [amɪ̥ga] for *amica*; and may spirantize to [β] [ð] [ɣ] in informal speech. These consonants may be interpreted by speakers of other varieties of Italian as voiced (because voiced consonants are *lenes*). Actual sonorization is often found in the south after nasals, as in [kwȧndo] for *quanto* 'how much', [ȧŋge] for *anche* 'also', [kȧmbo] for *campo* 'field', [mȧndʒa] for *mancia* 'tip', [avandzȧre] for *avanzare* 'to advance'. Also in central and southern Italy [s] preceded by [n] [r] [l] tends to become [ts] (and, as we have seen, particularly after [n], may be voiced to [dz]): [fȯrtse] for *forse* 'perhaps', [tɔ́ltse] for *tolse* 'he removed', [kontsέntso] and [kondzέndzo] for *consenso* 'consent'. In the north [nz] for [ns] is used in the Trentino-Alto Adige: [penzjóne] for *pensione* 'boarding-house'. In front of a consonant [s] is often palatalized in southern Italy, and in Piedmont and Emilia: [bɔ́ʃko] for *bosco* 'wood', [ʃkȧla] for *scala* 'stairs'.

Intervocalic [tʃ] is reduced to [ʃ] not only in Tuscany but also in central Italy and in many parts of the south; but the parallel Tuscan reduction of [dʒ] to [ʒ] is not found in central and southern Italy because, as we have seen, [dʒ] is here always double.

In northern Italy the sibilants are usually more retracted than in Florentine: one finds [sȧnto] for *santo* 'saint', [kȧṣṣa] for *cassa* 'box', [kȧẓa] for *casa* 'house'; instead of palato-alveolar sibilants one may find [ṣ] or [ṣj], as in [ṣέmo] for *scemo* 'fool', [lȧṣja] for *lascia* 'leave'. The Bolognese in particular are made fun of by other Italians for 'interchanging' the alveolar sibilant, e.g., of *sì* 'yes', and the palato-alveolar sibilant, e.g., of *sci* 'ski'. In uneducated speech instead of affricates one may find sibilants, as in [grȧsje] for *grazie* 'thank you', or, in Emilia, dental fricatives, as in [pȧθθo] for *pazzo* 'mad', [mέððo] for *mezzo* 'middle'. In the Veneto palatal stops are found in words like [amȧci] for *amici* 'friends', [aɟto] for *agito* 'acted', where [tʃ] and [dʒ] are used in other varieties.

Parallel to [ṣj] instead of [ʃ] in northern Italy one may find [nj] where Florentine has [ɲ] and [lj] where Florentine has [ʎ]. But northern varieties of Italian may also employ a distinction between a short vowel followed by [lj] [nj] [sj] and a long vowel followed by [ʎ] [ɲ] [ʃ] (these being single and not double as in Florentine): [l itȧlja] for *l'Italia* 'Italy' vs. [li tȧ:ʎa] for *li taglia* 'he cuts them'. As this goes against the rules of Tuscan syllabic structure, northerners are teased by Florentines for saying *l'Itaglia* instead of *l'Italia* and *li talia* instead of *li taglia*.

In central and southern Italy we may find [ʎ] for [lj] and [ɲ] for [nj], thus introducing an opposition of single vs. double, as in [ɔ́ʎo] for *olio* 'oil' vs. [fɔʎʎo] for *foglio* 'sheet', [krȧɲo] for *cranio* 'skull' vs. [stȧɲɲo] for *stagno* 'pond'.

In the north, particularly in Venetia, a nasal tends not to assimilate to a following consonant, but to appear in front of any consonant as a velar [ŋ], with strong nasalization of the preceding vowel: [kåŋpo] (or even [kåpo]) for *campo* 'field', [såŋto] for *santo* 'saint', [påŋtʃa] for *pancia* 'belly' (this is the reason for common misspellings like *canpo, anpio,* etc., for *campo, ampio,* etc.). This happens also in word final position ([sāŋ mȧrko] for *San Marco* 'Saint Mark', [ūŋ pȧdre] for *un padre* 'a father'), even in front of a vowel: [kōŋ affḙtto] for *con affetto* 'with love', [nōŋ aŋkȯra] for *non ancora* 'not yet').

In Tuscan after a final -[n] or -[r] there is a tendency to introduce a prosthetic [i] in front of a word beginning with [s]+consonant; this may even be represented in traditional spelling, *per ischerzo* 'as a joke', *in Isvizzera* 'in Switzerland'.

Consonant clusters are sometimes eliminated by the introduction of weak epenthetic vowels, particularly in the south ([probbᵉlḙma] for *problema* 'problem') and in Emilia ([pȧdᵉre] for *padre* 'father'). In Florentine there are frequent assimilations: [i rre] for *il re* 'the king', [i kkȧne] for *il cane* 'the dog', [tḙnniko] for *tecnico* 'technical' vs. southern [tḙkkᵉniko]. Vowel clusters are avoided in parts of the south (particularly in Abruzzi) by the introduction of a glottal stop or voiced fricative: [alleʔȧto] or [allefiȧto] for *alleato* 'ally'.

Many other local features could be added: for instance the pre-palatal [r] used in Piedmont and Liguria, or the retroflex [ʈʈ] [ɖʈ] used in Sicily and south Calabria, as in [tʈḙno] for *treno* 'train'.

Syntactic doubling, which, as we have said, is absent in the north, in central and southern Italy follows rules somewhat different from the Florentine ones. For instance in Rome *da* 'from', *dove* 'where' and the names of the musical notes do not cause doubling; *come* 'like' does, but only in comparative expressions ([kȯme tte] *come te* 'like you', vs. [kȯme va] *come va?* 'how are you?'); *lo, la, li, le* only double their initial consonants if their vowels are elided in front of a stressed vowel: [ɛ ll ȧnima] *è l'anima* 'it is the soul' vs. [ɛ l animȧle] *è l'animale* 'it is the animal', [ɛ la dȯnna] *è la donna* 'it is the woman'; *di* 'of', *da* 'from', *ne* 'about it', *nel* 'in the', *non* 'not' never double their initial consonants; and *chiesa* 'church', *così* 'thus', *là* 'there', *lì* 'there', *malattia* 'illness', *maledetto* 'damned', *maschera* 'mask', *più* 'more', *qua* 'here', *qui* 'here', *sedia* 'chair' always do. In southern

Italy there is no syntactic doubling after polysyllables ending in a stressed vowel, nor after *ha* 'he has', *chi* 'who', *da* 'from', *o* 'or', *sta* 'he stays', *va* 'he goes'.

(b) In the field of **syntax** and **morphology** the following features can be mentioned, at various levels of informality:

(i) in northern varieties of Italian (A) the use of the perfect at the expense of the past historic; (B) the suppression of the article in expressions like *mia mamma* 'my mother', *mio papà* 'my father'; (C) the use of the object instead of the subject form of personal pronouns, as in the title *Il padrone sono me* 'The master is me' (for the third person the forms *lui, lei, loro* are now commonly used as subjects in literary Italian, see chapter V. 8(a)(ii)); (D) constructions like *sono dietro a fare* 'I am doing', *non stare a fare* 'do not do', *quando che* 'when', *mentre che* 'while', etc.

(ii) in Tuscan (A) the use of the object instead of the subject form of the pronoun, as in *te sei* 'you are'; (B) the use of unstressed subject pronouns as in *e' dice* 'he says', *gli è* 'it is', *la parla* 'she speaks'; (C) a very frequent[7] use of *noi si* + third person singular verb at the expense of the first person plural (this construction also belongs to other local varieties in which the first person plural form of the verb is more vital than in Tuscan); (D) forms like *vedano* for *vedono* 'they see', *dasti* for *desti* 'you gave', *se io dassi* for *se io dessi* 'if I gave'.

(iii) in central and southern Italian (A) frequent interchanges of conditional and subjunctive, so that one finds all combinations: *se direi farei, se direi facessi, se dicessi farei, se dicessi facessi* 'if I said, I would do'; (B) the indicative is used where the literary tradition would require the subjunctive, as in *spero che viene* 'I hope he comes', more frequently than in ordinary colloquial usage, where the same tendency however is present; (C) a very frequent use of the present instead of the future; (D) the extension of the passive to constructions like *voglio essere spiegato questo, desidero essere imparato questo* 'I want this to be explained to me', 'I wish to be taught this'; (E) the construction with *a* of animate direct objects: *vedo a Ugo* 'I see Ugo', and a frequent use of the type *amico a* 'friend of', *figlio a* 'son of', with *a* instead of *di*; (F) in the Sicilian variety the order *siciliano sono* 'I am Sicilian' is found, used not for expressiveness but as the unmarked construction.

(c) **Lexis** In 1956 R. Rüegg published the results of a linguistic inquiry he had carried out in Italy;[8] 124 speakers from 54 Italian provinces had been asked which words they used for 242 common notions. What emerged appeared to be rather dramatic: only for one notion 'a strong coffee, drunk at a bar' did all speakers use the same word, *espresso*. For most notions on the list there was no single word common to all 54 provinces. But it would be wrong to conclude from this that people from different parts of Italy have only the word *espresso* in common.

It is natural that words adopted in recent years in connection with new technological developments should be the same throughout the country, and that in fields administered by a central state authority terminology should be unified. But for objects produced locally there are often still no terms common to all regions. The small piece of thick cloth used to grip the handles of pots and pans just off the stove ('kettle holder', 'oven cloth') has no national Italian term: it is called *presa*, *presina* in Tuscan, but these words are not used in other regions which have *patta*, *pattina*, *chiappino*, *pugnetta*, *cuscinetto*, etc.; similarly for 'shoe laces' we find not only *stringhe* but also *lacci*, *laccetti*, *laccioli*, *legacci*, *legaccioli*, *aghetti*, etc.; the 'plumber' is called *idraulico*, but also *fontaniere*, *lanternaio*, *lattoniere*, *stagnaio*, *stagnaro*, *stagnino*, *trombaio*, etc. *Lavandino*, *acquaio*, *secchiaio*, *lavabo*, *lavello*, *scafa*, *sciacquatore* are used in different parts of Italy for 'sink' and/or 'basin'; a coat hanger is often called *ometto* in northern Italy, *gruccia* in central Italy and *stampella* in southern Italy (*attaccapanni* is a more supraregional word, also meaning 'coat hook'). For *marinare la scuola* 'to play truant', *bucare* is used in Piedmont, *fare la manca* in Venetia, *far forca* in Tuscany, *far sega* in central Italy.

In many cases the terms preferred in different parts of Italy, like *formaggio* in the north and *cacio* in Tuscany 'cheese', can be considered supraregional and may be used indifferently. In other cases terms are limited to a more local usage; we list some according to their geographical origin:

In the north one finds *braghe* for *calzoni* 'trousers', *vera* for *fede* 'wedding ring', and Piedmontese *arrivare* for *capitare* 'happen', *chiamare* for *domandare* 'ask', Lombard *michetta* for *panino* 'bread roll', *bauscia* for *sciocco* 'silly', Venetian *altana* for *terrazza* (a kind of roof garden), *balcone* for *finestra* 'window'.

Tuscan dialectalisms are *albero* for *pioppo* 'poplar', *anello* for *ditale* 'thimble', *anno* for *l'anno scorso* 'last year', *balocco* for *giocattolo* 'toy', *chicche* for *dolci* 'sweets', *gota* for *guancia* 'cheek', *granata* for *scopa* 'broom', *infreddatura* for *raffreddore* 'cold', *mota* for *fango* 'mud'.

Southern dialectalisms are *buttare* for *versare* 'to spill', *carnezzeria* for *macelleria* 'butcher's', *controra* for *siesta* 'siesta', *coppola* for *berretto* 'cap', *scorno* for *vergogna* 'shame', *stare* for *essere*, as in *sta contento* 'he is pleased', *tenere* for *avere*, as in *tiene fame* 'he is hungry', *trovare* for *cercare* 'to look for'.

2

So far some of the differences between local varieties of Italian have been discussed. To conclude this chapter some features will be listed which are common to many local varieties and can be said to characterize a chronological rather than a geographical variety, i.e., contemporary Italian as against earlier stages documented by the literary language of previous centuries.

(a) There is an enlargement of the range of acceptable phonological structures, in particular with regard to consonantal endings. Words of foreign origin like *sport*, and abbreviations like *MEC* 'Common Market', are not treated as extraneous items clashing with the rules of Italian phonology. This development must have been facilitated in northern Italy by the fact that in Gallo-Italian dialects complex consonantal clusters can occur in all positions.

(b) There is a tendency to eliminate or reduce the difference between the various shapes traditionally taken by words depending on their respective positions in the sentence: (i) there are fewer prosthetic vowels: *per scherzo* 'as a joke' rather than *per ischerzo*; (ii) there is a less frequent fall of final vowels: *la amica* 'the friend', *una opera* 'a work', *gli italiani* 'the Italians', *andare bene* 'to go well', *fare adagio* 'to go slowly', etc., without elision or truncation, are becoming more and more common; *le energie* 'the energies' is now the norm, and *l'energie* is felt to be rather odd; (iii) forms like *quelli* 'those' and *belli* 'beautiful' are frequently used where the traditional norm requires *quei, bei*, or *quegli, begli*; for other words this process is now complete and forms like *capei* and *capegli* for *capelli* 'hair', *tai* or *tagli* for *tali* 'such', *gli* for *li* 'them' (as in *gli ascolta* 'he listens to them') are so archaic as to be excluded from modern usage; (iv) the fused forms of preposition + article are more and more frequently substituted by the separate forms: *con il, con la* 'with the' rather than *col, colla*; with *per* the fused forms *pel, pella* 'for the', etc., are obsolete.

(c) In the field of morphology the old ending in *-a* of the first person singular of the imperfect indicative has disappeared altogether from current usage, and has been replaced by an analogical *-o*. We can see the process in action when Manzoni changes the imperfect endings from *-a* to *-o* in his revision of *I promessi sposi*; but the tenacity of the literary ending in *-a* is such that one of the best Italian grammars written in English still gives *-a* in its verb tables (Grandgent and Wilkins). Forms like *siano* 'let them be', *stiano* 'let them stay', have definitively overcome *sieno*, *stieno* which now sound old-fashioned; there is a tendency for *-ei* to prevail over *-etti* in the past historic (*temei* rather than *temetti* 'I feared'). An invariable dative *gli* 'to him, to her, to it, to them', is becoming increasingly common also for the feminine (instead of *le*) and even more so for the plural (instead of *(a) loro*).

(d) In the sphere of word formation we find:

(i) a tendency to shorten words, as in *cine*, or *cinema* for *cinematografo* 'cinema', *moto* for *motocicletta* 'motorcycle', *auto* for *automobile* 'car', etc.; in teenage slang *matusa* for *matusalemme* 'Methuselah', to indicate someone no longer a teenager;

(ii) a more frequent use of abbreviations made up of initial letters or parts of words (*sigle*). Some of these are pronounceable as individual words like *UDI* [údi] *Unione Donne Italiane*, *CIGA* [tʃíga] *Compagnia italiana grandi alberghi*, *UTET* [útet] *Unione tipografico-editrice torinese*; they may be punning abbreviations as in *FIAT* [fíat] *Fabbrica italiana automobili Torino* which is also the Latin word popularly known from the formulas of Catholic liturgy (as in *fiat voluntas Dei*). Other abbreviations are not pronounceable as individual words, and are then modified, as *MSI* pronounced [mis] *Movimento sociale italiano*, or pronounced letter by letter as *DC* [ditʃí] *Democrazia cristiana*,[9] *PCI* [pitʃíi] *Partito comunista italiano* (also [pitʃí] for *Partito comunista*). Abbreviations made up of parts of words are sometimes called *parole macedonia* ('cocktail words'), for instance *Confindustria: Confederazione generale dell'industria italiana*, *Polfer: Polizia ferroviaria*. Abbreviations are used, like other nouns, with the article; the gender and number of the abbreviation normally depend on the full form: *la DC, il PCI, le ACLI* [ákli] *Associazioni cristiane dei lavoratori italiani*. In many cases abbreviations such as *NATO* [náto], *CIA* [tʃía], *DDT* [didití], *DNA* [dienneá] are commonly used although most people who use them are unable to give the full expressions which they stand for;

(iii) the frequent formation of nouns from verbs through zero suffixation, as in *ammanco* 'deficit', *blocco* 'block', *bonifica* 'land reclamation', *convalida* 'ratification', *decollo* 'take-off', *qualifica* 'qualification', *rettifica* 'correction', *scontento* 'discontent', *verifica* 'verification';

(iv) verbs deriving from nouns, with the suffixes *-are*, *-eggiare* 'to be like -', *-izzare* 'to make like -': *contattare* 'to contact', *presenziare* 'to attend', *revisionare* 'to overhaul', *sovvenzionare* 'to subsidize'; *maramaldeggiare* (often with a direct object) 'to act like Maramaldo', i.e., to strike a man who is down, *comunisteggiare* 'to act like a communist' vs. *comunistizzare* 'to make something communist'; *ipotizzare* 'to hypothesize', *nazionalizzare* 'to nationalize', *strumentalizzare* 'to instrumentalize', 'to exploit';

(v) the use of adjectives in *-ale*, often to replace a noun complement: *stato confusionale* 'state of confusion', *condizione conflittuale* 'condition of conflict', *potere decisionale* 'power of decision', *iniziativa direzionale* 'managerial initiative';

(vi) the use of prefixes like *a-* as in *apartitico* 'non party', *inter-* as in *interdisciplinare* 'interdisciplinary', *para-* with the value of 'quasi-', as in *parastatale* 'government controlled' and not as in the more traditional compounds like *parafulmine* 'lightening conductor', *pre-* as in *prescolare* 'pre-school', *post-* as in *postbellico* 'postwar', *super-* as in *supertestimone* 'key witness'; particularly striking is the use of prefixoids, i.e., elements halfway between prefixes and nouns occupying the first place in a compound, for instance *aero-*, *auto-*, *avio-*, *mini-*, *moto-*, *radio-*, *tele-*, etc.; these may develop until one of the meanings they acquire in a particular compound becomes primary and reappears in different compounds: *autoscuola* is not 'self-schooling' as the original meaning of *auto* (as in *automobile* 'car') suggests, but a 'driving school'; *telespettatore* is not a viewer from far away, but a 'television viewer';

(e) many adjectives are used as nouns, originally through omission of the noun they accompanied: *la (squadra) celere* 'flying squad', *un (treno) accelerato* 'a stopping train', *il (comitato) direttivo* 'management committee', *la (polizia) stradale* 'traffic police'; many other expressions are similarly shortened, as in *un rigore* (for *calcio di rigore*) 'penalty kick'; *un vertice* (for *un incontro al vertice*) 'a summit meeting';

(f) a very productive use of juxtapositions, probably on the model of English compound words, but always following the Italian pattern of modified first, modifier second: *borsa valori* 'stock exchange', *cassa integrazione* 'supplementary payment fund', *donna tipo* 'typical woman', *trasmissioni radio* (and then, with *radio* used as a prefixoid, *radiotrasmissioni*) 'radio broadcasts', *treno merci* 'goods train', and, with elements producing juxtaposed pairs used adjectivally, *formato cartolina* 'postcard format', *tipo cameriere* 'waiter style', *uso spiaggia* 'beach style'; and, with coordinated terms, *testa coda* 'right about turn', *missile terra aria* 'land-air missile'.

(g) In the field of syntax we find an accentuation of the tendency, developed since the eighteenth century, to abandon complex, subordinating, Latin-style sentences, in favour of shorter, coordinating, French-style ones. In particular we may note:

(i) a remarkable increase in the use of nominal style (fairly common in the nineteenth century as well); nominal sentences are particularly frequent in newspaper headlines (*sulle misure anti-crisi confronto tra i partiti* 'anti-crisis measures inter-party debate') and in descriptions (*macchine velocissime sulla strada* 'cars speeding along the road'); nominal forms of the verb are commonly employed (*sfrecciare di macchine sulla strada* 'cars shooting along the road');

(ii) pronominal enclisis (except for imperatives and infinite forms of the verbs) has become obsolete and survives only in crystallized forms like *affittasi* 'to let', *vendesi* 'for sale', or *come dovevasi dimostrare* 'QED';

(iii) a much more limited use of the past historic particularly in informal spoken language;

(iv) a large use of the narrative imperfect, originating apparently in war bulletins during the first world war, and now widely used in newspaper reporting, often without any intention of raising the stylistic level of the narrative: *il ladruncolo, vistosi scoperto, si allontanava precipitosamente* 'the petty thief, on seeing he was discovered, rushed away';

(v) a more and more limited use of the subjunctive, replaced in subordinate clauses by the indicative, in conformity with informal spoken style, as in *credo che parte* 'I think he is leaving', *spero che sta bene* 'I hope he is well'. This is avoided in formal literary Italian;

(vi) the use of *a* instead of *in* for 'at' with place names, originally limited to central Italian, has been generalized: *a Roma* is now the norm, rather than *in Roma*;

(vii) since the beginning of the century it has been quite common to find elliptic expressions of different kinds like *votate socialista* 'vote Socialist', frequently used in advertising: *brindate Gancia* 'toast with Gancia', *camminate Pirelli* 'travel Pirelli', *comprate Marzotto* 'buy Marzotto'; and, on the model of *parlare forte* (with an adjectival form for the adverb) 'to speak loudly', *fissa morbido* 'sets softly', *lava pulito* 'washes clean', *sorride giovane* 'has a youthful smile'; and, in affected speech, *fa Capri* 'looks Capri', *fa fino* 'looks, sounds refined', *fa moderno* 'looks modern', *fa notizia* 'makes news'.

(h) In the field of lexis it would of course be quite easy, but not very revealing, to provide long lists of words introduced, or used with a new meaning, during the last hundred years: neologisms and foreign words, often ephemeral, adopted either for their snob value, or to talk about new things, usually attract most attention from purists who complain that they are unnecessary and defile the Italian language. De Mauro however worked out that in the mid-twentieth century 94.8 per cent of Italian lexis was made up of traditional words; the remaining 5.2 per cent consisted of non-adapted Latinisms and Graecisms (2.2 per cent) and of foreign words, adapted (1.6 per cent) or non-adapted (1.4 per cent). As for the frequency of use in actual texts of this 5.2 per cent of non-Italian words, it is merely 0.48 per cent. If one considers only the most frequently used words in twentieth-century Italian, it turns out that 90 per cent of them go back to the thirteenth and fourteenth centuries, and 7 per cent to the Renaissance, leaving only 3 per cent for words adopted subsequently. The vocabulary of Italian hardly seems to be undergoing revolutionary changes.

More interesting than neologisms as such are those groups of words which seem to characterize certain periods or cultural fashions. For instance:

(i) from the first world war we find the popularization of terms like *asso* 'ace', *bombarda* 'mortar', *il fronte* 'front' (previously feminine), *lanciafiamme* 'flamethrower', *di punta* 'spearhead', *settore* 'sector', *silurare* 'to torpedo', *cecchino* '(Austrian) sharpshooter';

(ii) during the Fascist period considerable popularity was enjoyed by words like *dinamico* 'dynamic', *ferreo* 'of iron', *folgorante* 'flashing', *granitico* 'granite-like', *inconfondibile* 'unmistakable', *indefettibile* 'unfailing', *inequivocabile* 'unequivocal', *inesorabile* 'inexorable', *integrale* 'integral', *invitto* 'unvanquished', *oceanico* 'oceanic', *scultoreo* 'sculpturesque', *totalitario* 'totalitarian', *travolgente* 'overwhelming', as well as by Latinisms taken off the shelf like *duce* for the Fascist leader;

(iii) from the second world war: *asse* 'axis', *belligeranza* 'belligerence', *guerra lampo* 'blitzkrieg', *picchiata* 'nose-dive', *repubblichini* 'Fascists of the Republic of Salò';

(iv) from political terminology of the post-war period there is a rich collection of terms referring to political parties, like *azionista* from the *Partito d'azione*, or *qualunquista* from the *Partito dell'uomo qualunque* – later used also to mean 'politically philistine'; and from factions of the Christian Democrat party, *dorotei* (from the convent of the *Dorotee* nuns in Rome, where a group of Christian Democrats met in 1959), *morotei* (followers of A. Moro), *moro-dorotei* (from the two preceding groups); *gregoriani* (who on the night of St Gregory, 25 June 1963, criticized the programme of the four-party coalition), etc.

Among frequently used allusive formulas we find *compromesso storico* and *repubblica conciliare*, referring to a possible alliance between Communists and Christian Democrats, and many expressions like *convergenze* 'convergences', *convergenze parallele* 'parallel convergences' (used by A. Moro; and on its model *divergenze parallele* 'parallel divergences', *divergenze convergenti* 'convergent divergences'), *costanti* 'constants', *direttrici* 'directrices', a geometrical term, used in the sense of policies, *equilibri più avanzati* 'more advanced balance of power' (i.e., a movement towards the left), *verifica* 'test'. Over the last ten years we find a very frequent use of terms like *alienazione* 'alienation', *consumismo* 'consumer society', *contestazione* 'protest', *demistificare* 'demystify', *dissacrare* 'desecrate', *emarginare* 'to put aside', *eversivo* 'subversive', *mercificazione* 'commercialization', *mistificante* 'obfuscating', *repressivo* 'repressive';

(v) science and technology are the source of many expressions used metaphorically in everyday language, like *ad alta tensione* 'highly charged', *capillare* 'far reaching, widespread', *al rallentatore* 'in slow motion', *emorragia* 'draining', *in quarta* 'at the double', *in orbita* 'in orbit', *sfasato* 'confused', *sintonizzato* 'in tune with', *sincronizzare* 'to synchronize', *su di giri* 'bubbling over', *tonificare* 'to invigorate';

(vi) there are many terms which can be called popular, often originating in the underworld, or in military or student slang, and sometimes of dialectal origin; they are now supraregional. Some also have straight, non-slang meanings, but we give here the slang ones: *abbuffarsi* 'to gorge oneself', *ammappete, ammazzelo* 'blimey', *balle* 'nonsense' or 'lies', *ballista* 'someone who talks nonsense' or 'tells lies', *balordo* recently used by newspapers for 'thug' rather than 'crank' or 'fool', *batosta* 'blow', *battersela* 'to beat it', *bullo* 'young tough', *burino* 'boor', *cafone* 'lout', *cagnara* 'uproar', *camorra* 'racket', *cantare* 'to squeal', *colpo* 'job', *cosca* 'group of mafiosi', *dentro* 'in prison', *dritto* 'crafty', *far fuori* 'to polish off', *fasullo* 'phoney', *fesso* 'idiot', *fesseria* 'idiotic action', *fifa* 'funk', *fregare* 'to swindle', *fuori* 'out of prison', *fusto* 'handsome fellow', *gagà* 'dapper', *grana* 'trouble' or 'dough', *grinta* 'toughness', *guappo* 'young turkey-cock', *imbranato* 'raw', *inghippo* 'hitch', *intrallazzo* 'swindle' or 'racket', *lavativo* 'dead loss', *malloppo* 'loot', *mollare* 'to let fly', *omertà* 'the mafia's law of silence' (from *umiltà*), *pacchia* 'godsend', *pappagallo* 'a man who tries to pick up girls in the street', *pestaggio* 'beating up', *pignolo* 'finicky', *pivello* 'green', *racchio* 'ugly', *regolare i conti* 'to get even', *sbafare* 'to scrounge', *sberla* 'whack', *sboba* 'dishwater', *sbolognare* 'to palm off', *scassare* 'to smash', *schiappa, schiappino* 'a wash-out', *scocciare* 'to bore', *scorfano* 'ugly individual', *scucire* 'to cough up', *sfasciare* 'to smash', *sfottere* 'to make fun of', *sganassone* 'whack', *sganciare* 'to fork out', *sgraffignare* 'to nick', *soffiata* 'tip off', *spaghetto* 'jitters', *stangata* 'blow', *strafottente* 'arrogant', *tagliare la corda* 'to beat it'.

Notes

[1]We use the descriptions by CAMILLI, A., *Pronuncia e grafia dell'italiano, terza edizione riveduta a cura di P. Fiorelli*, Florence, 1965; FIORÈLLI, P., *Córso di pronùnzia italiana*, Padova, 1965; TAGLIAVINI, C., *La corretta pronuncia italiana*, Bologna, 1965, both for Florentine and for many of the non-Tuscan pronunciations which they quote as faulty.

[2]We are using the terms 'double' and 'single' conventionally, without of course implying that it is a question of two phonetic units vs. one. In our transcription we shall represent double consonants by repeating the symbols of the single consonants, except for [ts] [dz] [tʃ] [dʒ] in which, in accor-

dance with accepted practice, only the first element of the symbol is repeated: [tts] [ddz] [ttʃ] [ddʒ]; this is purely a notational convention and does not imply an interpretation of these sounds as clusters or single units.

[3]There is also a less common pronunciation with a single intervocalic [ts], accepted by purists when it derives from Latin TI and is therefore 'etymologically justifiable', as in *nazione* 'nation', *vizio* 'vice', *Venezia* 'Venice', but not when it derives from PTI, CTI as in *concezione* 'conception', *lezione* 'lesson' (see below for central and southern usage).

[4]But in the case of *gli* it is also possible to have a single [ʎ] (admitted by purists as 'correct'), after the final vowel of a preceding word, unless of course the rules of syntactic doubling operate: one can have [lóro ʎi díkono] *loro gli dicono* 'they tell him', but one must have [tu ʎʎi dítʃi] *tu gli dici* 'you tell him' because *tu* causes syntactic doubling.

[5]Cf. CLIVIO, G. L., 'The Pronunciation of Italian in Piedmont', in *Actes du Xe Congrès international des linguistes* (1967), Bucharest, 1970, vol. IV, pp. 275–280.

[6]Writers sometimes play with these features; for instance: ' "*Che succïede qui?*" *domanda allarmato un carabiniere d'un'altra parte d'Italia*' "What's going on here?" asks an alarmed carabiniere from another part of Italy' (BRERA, G., *Il corpo della ragassa*, Milan, 1969, p. 72); '*Lui può sempre dire: "Io non c'entro, io avevo i miei stupefaci-enti!" si accalorava un barbiere con forte accento napoletano.*' 'He can always say: "I am not involved, I had my drugs," a barber insisted with a strong Neapolitan accent.' (CATTANEO, G., *Il gran lombardo*, Milan, 1973, p. 89); ' "*Interratemi,*" *ripeteva*, "*interratemi, cosí stanotte dormo tranquillo in cíelo!*" *E la nonna sua moglie all'udirlo esclamava con voce acuta: "Gíesú! Gíesú!*" ' ' "Bury me," he repeated, "bury me, so that tonight I may sleep peacefully in heaven!" And the grandmother, his wife, on hearing him exclaimed with a shrill voice: "Jesus! Jesus!" ' (this is an exchange between two Neapolitan characters in MORANTE, E., *La storia*, Turin, 1974, pp. 277–278).

[7]Qualifications like 'frequent', 'common', etc., or 'rare', 'unusual', etc., do not here refer to statistical computation but to what is felt to be normal or expected in a given context.

[8]See RÜEGG, R., *Zur Wortgeographie der italienischen Umgangssprache*, Cologne, 1956, (*Kölner romanistische Arbeiten*, Neue Folge, Heft 7).

[9]We transcribe according to the system described in chapter V. 1; in Florentine one finds [dittʃí] for *DC*, [diddittí] for *DDT*, etc.

Part Two
The Grammar of Italian

V An Outline

1 Phonology

(a) On the basis of the points made in the previous chapters, foreign students of Italian may find it practical to adopt the following **phonological system**:

i			u	p	t		ts	tʃ	k
	e		o	b	d		dz	dʒ	g
		a		f		s		ʃ	
				v					
				m		n		ɲ	
						l		ʎ	
						r			

(i) No distinction is made between open and closed mid vowels. Vowel sounds intermediate between cardinal [e] and [ɛ] and between cardinal [o] and [ɔ] are suggested as the best choice. We transcribe them here as [e] and [o]. The situation in Italy is, as we have seen, so varied, both for the kind of mid vowels used and the individual words in which they are used, as to make it pointless for a foreign learner not living in Italy to adopt in its entirety the usage of one or another local variety of Italian.

(ii) When unstressed /i/ and /u/ are adjacent to a vowel they are pronounced [j] and [w]. This happens, at normal conversational speed, with many speakers who, at a slower rate of delivery, and in a careful style, would distinguish [i] as in *spiare* [spiàre] 'to spy', *spianti* [spiànti] 'spying', from [j] as in *spiantare* [spjantàre] 'to uproot', *spianti* [spjànti] 'you uproot', and [u] as in *acuità* [akuità] 'sharpness', *arcuata* [arkuàta] 'arched' from [w] as in *equità* [ekwuità] 'equity', *Arquata* [arkwàta] (a place-name).

(iii) For double consonants one can adopt a pronunciation which is unambiguously represented by traditional spelling. All consonants can be single or double, apart from [ɲ], [ʎ], and [ʃ], for which an invariably long or an invariably short pronunciation is acceptable. There is no syntactic doubling, apart from the fossilized forms in which doubling is represented in spelling. So we have *cade* [kȧde] 'he falls' vs. *cadde* [kȧdde] 'he fell', *vizi* [vɪtsi] 'vices' vs. *vizzi* [vɪttsi] 'withered', *a picco* [a pɪkko] 'vertically' vs. *appicco* [appɪkko] 'I hang'.

(iv) The alveolar sibilant is voiceless ([s]) (A) initially before a vowel, as in *sale* [sȧle] 'salt', (B) before voiceless consonants, as in *spala* [spȧla] 'he shovels', *asta* [ȧsta] 'auction', (C) after consonants, as in *orso* [ȯrso] 'bear', (D) when it is double, as in *passo* [pȧsso] 'step'. It is voiced ([z]) in all other cases, i.e., (E) before voiced consonants, as in *sbattere* [zbȧttere] 'to slam', *asma* [ȧzma] 'asthma', (F) intervocalically, as in *casa* [kȧza] 'house', *naso* [nȧzo] 'nose'. This last condition can be waived when the intervocalic sibilant is morpheme initial, as in *trasognato* 'dreamy', *presentire* 'to have a premonition', *risanare* 'to heal', etc., which are usually pronounced with a voiceless [s].

(v) The alveolar affricate is voiced ([dz]) initially, as in *zero* [dzėro] 'zero', *zio* [dzɪo] 'uncle'. Medially it may be voiced as in *mezzo* [mėddzo] 'half', *azzurro* [addzȯrro] 'blue', *orzo* [ȯrdzo] 'barley', *bronzo* [brȯndzo] 'bronze', or voiceless as in *pazzo* [pȧttso] 'mad', *ozio* [ȯtsjo] 'idleness', *anzi* [ȧntsi] 'on the contrary', *alza* [ȧltsa] 'he raises'.

These proposals incorporate the aspects of Florentine phonology which have become national, and disregard those which have remained parochial. If the reader prefers to adopt Florentine phonology in its integrity, he can ignore the present section and refer to chapter IV. 1 (a)(i), keeping in mind, though, that points (A), (B), (D), (E), and (F) are usually not recommended even by purists.

We are trying to provide foreign students with a phonological system which has the following advantages over those proposed by puristic grammars: firstly, it is more faithfully represented by conventional spelling; secondly, it is nearer to an overall national system as it ignores phonemic oppositions which are treated differently in different varieties of Italian; thirdly, where a choice has to be made between conflicting varieties, it leans towards a northern standard,[1] which enjoys high prestige, is gaining ground in the country as a whole, and sounds less parochial than other varieties. This we believe to be a fact concerning actual linguistic behaviour and linguistic attitudes in Italy, notwithstanding the purely theoretical homage still paid to Tuscan pronunciation.

Concerning the first point, which has its importance for foreign students, one could go even further. In our model the only phonemic opposition not represented in spelling is [ts] vs. [dz]. But there is a series of words, some fairly common (such as *aguzzino* 'tormentor', *bizze* 'tantrums', *brezza* 'breeze', *frizzante* 'sparkling', *frizzo* 'witticism', *ghiribizzo* 'whim', *intirizzito* 'numb', *mozzo* 'hub', *parabrezza* 'windscreen', *pettegolezzo* 'gossip', *razzo* 'rocket', *ribrezzo* 'disgust', *schizofrenico* 'schizophrenic', *sgabuzzino* 'closet'), some less common (such as *amazzoni* 'Amazons', *lapislazzuli* 'lapislazuli', *lezzo* 'stench', *olezzo* 'fragrance', *rezzo* 'shade') which in northern Italy generally have a voiceless affricate, and in Tuscan a voiced one. In everyday words such as *pranzo* a pronunciation with voiceless [ts] is becoming more and more widely used in the north. By extrapolating this tendency it might not be unreasonable for the foreign learner to adopt as a rule a voiceless pronunciation for the alveolar affricate in internal position. If one is not prepared to accept a voiceless pronunciation (which in fact is occasionally heard in northern Italy) in words such as *mezzo* 'half', or *manzo* 'beef', one could always learn them as individual exceptions to the rule.

This is not the place to provide practical suggestions for the pronunciation of Italian, but some hints for speakers of English would include: (1) [p t k] are usually not aspirated, (2) [t d] are dental and not alveolar, (3) [r] is a vibrant (usually apical, but for some speakers uvular) and not a fricative; attention must be paid to its careful articulation in a post-vocalic and pre-consonantal position, (4) the alveolar sibilant is voiced before voiced consonants, as in *smetto* 'I stop', *sloggio* 'I move out', whereas in English it is voiceless, as in 'smoke, slot', (5) unlike English, Italian does not diphthongize its long vowels (stressed in a free syllable), and does not weaken its unstressed vowels to [ə], (6) double (long) consonants must be clearly distinguished from single (short) ones. They are pronounced with greater tension and energy, and are necessarily preceded by a short vowel: making this vowel clearly short contributes greatly to the following consonant being perceived as long.

(b) Stress

(i) The position of stress in Italian is important: a stress on the wrong syllable may make the word unintelligible. The position of the stress may be responsible for the difference between one word and another, as can be seen from minimal pairs such as [fíni] *fini* 'ends' vs. [finí] *finì* 'he finished', [ámbito] 'context' vs. [ambíto] 'desired' *ambito*, [bátʃino] 'let them kiss' vs. [batʃíno] 'basin' *bacino*, [kápita] 'it happens' vs. [kapíta] 'understood' (feminine singular) *capita*, [kómpito] 'task' vs. [kompíto] 'courteous' *compito* vs. [kompitó] 'he spelled out' *compitò*, [frústino] 'let them whip' vs. [frustíno] 'whip' *frustino*, [íntimo] 'intimate' vs. [intímo] 'I order' *intimo* vs. [intimó] 'he ordered' *intimò*, [púntino] 'let them point' vs. [puntíno] 'dot' *puntino*, [rúbino] 'let them steal' vs. [rubíno] 'ruby' *rubino*, [súbito] 'at once' vs. [subíto] 'undergone' *subito*, [stúdjati] 'study yourself' vs. [studjáti] 'studied' *studiati*.

Italian is known as a free stress language, i.e., there is no way of predicting on which syllable of a word the stress will fall. One can however list elements which require or reject stress; for instance, these are some of the suffixes which require stress: *-accio* (*fattaccio* 'criminal deed'), *-ano* (*romano* 'Roman'), *-ello* (*studentello* 'little student'), *-esco* (*romanesco* 'Romanesque', used for the dialect), *-etto* (*libretto* 'little book'), *-ino* (*gattino* 'kitten'), *-one* (*cagnone* 'large dog'), *-oso* (*famoso* 'famous'), *-uccio* (*caruccio* 'pretty'), and these are some which reject stress: *-bile* (*commestibile* 'edible', *potabile* 'drinkable'), *-fero* (*sonnifero* 'sleeping pill'), *-filo* (*cinofilo* 'dog lover'), *-fobo* (*idrofobo* 'rabid'), *-fono* (*megafono* 'loudspeaker'), *-grafo* (*telegrafo* 'telegraph').

(ii) In a polysyllabic word the stressed syllable has greater prominence than the unstressed ones; the latter can have different degrees of prominence. Reliable experimental analyses are not available, but standard textbooks suggest that there is a rhythmic rule as follows:

A secondary degree of prominence is automatically introduced before the main stress at intervals of one from the stressed syllable, and after the main stress, on the last syllable unless it immediately follows the stressed syllable. This may not be clearly perceivable in normal pronunciation, but seems to correspond to the notion of 'stressability': the syllables in question may acquire considerable prominence in an emphatic pronunciation.

A secondary degree of prominence whose presence and location is not automatically determined by a rhythmic rule may be found in compound words. The main stress of the compound is always on the last component word. The main stress of the first component(s) becomes the secondary stress of the compound. In *radiosomaggismo* (a term which refers to the celebration of the *radioso maggio* 'glorious May' in which Italy entered the first world war) the secondary stress is on the second syllable: [radjọzomaddʒízmo]; the word would be unintelligible if it were pronounced with a secondary stress on a different syllable, say [rạdjozomaddʒízmo].

Minimal pairs can be found or constructed for the presence vs. absence of a secondary stress: [ạtomĭstiko] 'not in the manner of Aquinas' vs. [atomĭstiko] 'atomistic'; and for the different positions of a secondary stress: [ạwtoreattóre] 'ram-jet engine' vs. [awtọreattóre] 'actor-author'; and, if one accepts rather contrived examples, [affạ∫inawómini] 'one who fascinates men' vs. [affa∫ịnawómini] 'one who collects men in bundles'; [ạntikotestamentárjo] 'against joint wills' vs. [antịkotestamentárjo] 'of the Old Testament'.

With adverbs in *-mente* the secondary degree of prominence may be introduced automatically, according to the rhythmic rule mentioned above, as in [fịnalménte] 'at last', or on the syllable which was originally stressed, as in [ạvidaménte] 'avidly'.

In Italian a word is said to be, according to stress position: *tronca* (oxytonic: stressed on the last syllable): *telefonò* 'he telephoned'; *piana* (paroxytonic: stressed on the penultimate syllable): *telefonare* 'to telephone'; *sdrucciola* (proparoxytonic: stressed on the antepenultimate syllable): *telefonarmelo* 'to tell it to me over the phone'; *bisdrucciola* (stressed on the last syllable but three): *telefonami* 'ring me'; *trisdrucciola* (stressed on the last syllable but four): *telefonamelo* 'tell it to me over the phone'; *quadrisdrucciola* (stressed on the last syllable but five): *telefonamicelo* 'tell it to me there over the phone'. The limit to the number of post-tonic syllables would not seem to be set by phonological rules.

An unstressed element is called 'clitic': it is proclitic if it goes with the following stressed word (*lo guardi* 'you look at it') and enclitic if it goes with the preceding one (*guardalo* 'look at it').

Many words are heard with alternative stresses: we shall list some, giving first the accentuation recommended by purists, but specifying when the second one is more common: *adula* 'he adulates' [adúla] vs. [ádula], *alacre* 'active' [álakre] vs. [alákre], *bolscevico* 'Bolshevik' [bol∫evíko] vs. [bol∫éviko], *correo* 'accomplice' [kórreo] vs. [korréo], *cuculo* 'cuckoo' [kukúlo] vs. [kúkulo], *devia* 'he deviates' [devía] vs. [dévja], *edile* 'architectural' [edíle] vs. [édile], *educo* 'I educate' [edúko] vs. (more common) [éduko], *eutanasia* 'euthanasia' [ewtanazía] vs. [ewtanázja], *elzeviro* 'short literary article' [eldzevíro] vs. [eldzéviro], *evapora* 'it evaporates' [evapóra] vs. (more common) [evápora], *infido* 'unreliable' [infído] vs. [ínfido], *leccornia* 'delicacy' [lekkornía] vs. [lekkórnja], *lubrico* 'lascivious' [lúbriko] vs. (more common) [lubríko], *magiaro* 'Magyar' [mádʒaro] vs. (more common) [madʒáro], *microbi* 'microbes' [mikróbi] vs. (more common) [míkrobi],[2] *missile* 'missile' [míssile] vs. [missíle], *mollica* 'crumb' [mollíka] vs. [móllika], *pedule* 'rock climbing boots' [pedúle] vs. [pédule], *rubrica* 'index book' [rubríka] vs. [rúbrika], *salubre* 'salubrious' [salúbre] vs. (more common) [sálubre], *scandinavo* 'Scandinavian' [skandinávo] vs. (more common) [skandínavo], *utensile* 'tool' [utensíle] vs. (more common) [uténsile], *valuto, sopravvaluto* 'I estimate, I overestimate' [valúto] [soprav-valúto] vs. (more common) [váluto] [sopravváluto], *zaffiro* 'sapphire' [dzaffíro] vs. [dzáffiro].

With many classical names there is a learned pronunciation (which pre-serves the position of the stress in Latin, even in the case of Greek names) and a more common, popular pronunciation; for example, giving the learned pronunciation first, *Aristide* 'Aristides' [arístide] vs. [arìstide], *Euridice* 'Eurydice' [ewrídit∫e] vs. [ewridìt∫e] (stress as in Greek), *Orfeo* 'Orpheus' [órfeo] vs. [orféo] (stress as in Greek). In some cases words with one element in common are stressed differently: *piroscafo* 'ship' [piróskafo] (which conforms to Latin accentuation) vs. *motoscafo* 'motorboat' [motoskáfo] (which does not).

(c) Fall of final vowels

Traditionally a distinction is made between truncation (in front of either a vowel or a consonant) and elision (in front of a vowel only). Truncation: the final vowel of a polysyllable may fall if the resulting form ends in [l] [r] [n] [m]: *sottil argomento* 'subtle argument', *sottil ragionamento* 'subtle reasoning', *andar piano* 'to go slowly', *andar avanti* 'to go forward', *son troppi* 'they are too many', *son andati* 'they have gone', *siam pochi* 'we are few', *siam arrivati* 'we have arrived'. Elision: in front of a vowel a final vowel may fall, whatever consonant thus becomes final: *dev'essere* 'it must be', *quest'opera* 'this work', *quand'era* 'when he was', etc. The foreign learner does not need to use elision or truncation, apart from the cases, specified in the grammar below, in which they are compulsory (*l'amico* 'the friend', *un amico* 'a friend', etc.), and in fixed expressions like *amor proprio* 'self esteem', *d'altra parte* 'on the other hand' (but *l'ho saputo da altra fonte* 'I learnt it from another source'), *mal fatto* 'badly done', *ben fatto* 'well done', etc.

2 Spelling

We can now draw up two lists representing Italian spelling conven-tions.

From sounds to letters		From letters to sounds	
[i]	*i*	*a*	[a]
[e]	*e*	*b*	[b]
[a]	*a*	*c* (+ *a, o, u,* consonant)	[k]

From sounds to letters

[o]	o
[u]	u
[p]	p
[b]	b
[t]	t
[d]	d
[k]	c (+a, o, u, consonant)
	ch (+i, e)
[g]	g (+a, o, u, consonant)
	gh (+i, e)
[f]	f
[v]	v
[s]	s
[ʃ]	sc (+i, e)
	sci (+ vowel)
[ts]	z
[dz]	z
[tʃ]	c (+i, e)
	ci (+ vowel)
[dʒ]	g (+i, e)
	gi (+ vowel)
[m]	m
[n]	n
[ɲ]	gn
	gni (+ vowel)
[l]	l
[ʎ]	gl (+i)
	gli (+ vowel)
[r]	r

From letters to sounds

c (+i, e)	[tʃ]
ch	[k]
ci (+ vowel)	[tʃ]
d	[d]
e	[e]
f	[f]
g (+ a, o, u, consonant)	[g]
g (+ i, e)	[dʒ]
gh	[g]
gi (+ vowel)	[dʒ]
gl (+i)	[ʎ]
gli (+ vowel)	[ʎ]
gn	[ɲ]
gni (+ vowel)	[ɲ]
h	—
i	[i]
l	[l]
m	[m]
n	[n]
o	[o]
p	[p]
q	[k]
r	[r]
s	[s]
sc (+i, e)	[ʃ]
sci (+ vowel)	[ʃ]
t	[t]
u	[u]
v	[v]
z	[ts]
	[dz]

The names of the letters of the alphabet in Italian are: *a* [a], *b* [bi], *c* [tʃi], *d* [di], *e* [e], *f* [effe], *g* [dʒi], *h* [akka], *i* [i], *j* [i lungo], *k* [kappa], *l* [elle], *m* [emme], *n* [enne], *o* [o], *p* [pi], *q* [ku], *r* [erre], *s* [esse], *t* [ti], *u* [u], *v* [vi], *w* [vi doppjo], *x* [iks], *y* [ipsilon] or [i greko], *z* [dzeta]. These names can be considered masculine or feminine, so one also has [i] *lunga*, [vi] *doppia*, [i] *greca*. There are other, more local ways of naming them with a supporting [e] in [be], [tʃe], etc., or with [u] in [vu]. Conventional 'spelling' over the phone, to indicate how to write a word, is normally done by giving place names or other words which begin with the letter in question. For instance, *Livorno, Empoli, Pisa, Savona, Como, Hotel, i greco* spells *Lepschy*.

The letter *h* is only used (i) to indicate the velar pronunciation of *c* and *g*,

(ii) as an etymological spelling, with no phonetic counterpart, in the forms *ho, hai, ha, hanno* 'I have, you have, he has, they have', of the verb *avere* 'to have', thus distinguishing them in spelling from *o* 'or', *ai* 'to the', *a* 'to', *anno* 'year', (iii) in exclamations, either without phonetic value, as in *ahi, eh*, or representing a velar fricative as in *bah, poh* (in one of their possible pronunciations). In Italian the conventional representation of laughter, equivalent to the English 'ha ha', is *ah! ah!* pronounced [ha ha].

In the first two lists we have not given *k, w, x, y*, which are usually pronounced [k], [v], [ks] or [gz], [i]. We have also ignored assimilation: for instance *n* in *in piedi* 'standing' may represent [m].

As appears from the lists, *c* and *g* in front of *a, o, u* represent the velars [k] and [g], and in front of *i, e*, they represent the palatals [tʃ] and [dʒ]. To represent the velars in front of *i, e*, one adds *h* after *c* and *g*, and to represent the palatals in front of *a, o, u*, one adds *i* after *c* and *g*. Similarly *sc* represents [sk] in *sca, sco, scu, schi, sche*, and [ʃ] in *sci, sce, scia, scio, sciu*;[3] *gl* in front of *i* represents [ʎ], as in *gli*, or [gl] as in *glicerina* 'glycerine', *glicine* 'wistaria'; in front of other vowels *gl* represents [gl]; *gli* in front of a vowel represents [ʎ], as in *moglie* 'wife', *cogliere* 'to pick'; *gn* represents [ɲ] as in *gnocco* 'a kind of noodle', *gnomo* 'gnome', but words such as *gnoseologia* 'gnoseology' are sometimes pronounced with [gn] (and of course *wagneriano* is [vagnerjàno]); *gni* represents [ɲ] in the subjunctives like *sogniate* 'may you dream' (cf. the homophonous indicative *sognate* 'you dream').

The letter *i* may be used before *e*, where the pronunciation of *c, g* and *sc* would in any case be palatal; according to spelling tradition we have *cielo* 'sky', but *celeste* 'blue'; *cieco* 'blind', but *cecità* 'blindness'; *sufficiente* 'sufficient', *deficiente* 'deficient', *efficiente* 'efficient', but *beneficenza* 'charity'; *società* 'society', *specie* 'species', *superficie* 'surface', but *innocente* 'innocent', *facendo* 'doing', *pasticceria* 'patisserie'; and *igiene* 'hygiene', *effigie* 'effigy', but *leggero* 'light' (sometimes also *leggiero*); *scienza* 'science', *scientifico* 'scientific', *scienziato* 'scientist', *coscienza* 'conscience', *cosciente* 'conscious', but *convalescenza* 'convalescence', *convalescente* 'convalescent'.[4]

There are other cases in which one has to know the accepted tradition, as the spelling cannot be deduced from the pronunciation: for instance with *q* vs. *c*: *quando* 'when', *quota* 'quota', but *cuore* 'heart', *cuoco* 'cook'; *squadra* 'team', but *scuola* 'school'; *acquisto* 'acquisition', *soqquadro* 'confusion', *taccuino* 'notebook'.

In some cases either a single or a double consonant may be found: *bagatella* and *bagattella* 'trifle', *caffelatte* and *caffellatte* 'white coffee', *contradittorio* and *contraddittorio* (also *contradditorio*) 'contradictory', *cosidetto* and *cosiddetto* 'so-called', *retorico* and *rettorico* 'rhetorical', *scopola* and *scoppola* 'a smack on the head', *sopraluogo* and *sopralluogo* 'on the spot investigation', *sopratutto* and *soprattutto* 'above all', *sovraprezzo* and *sovrapprezzo* 'surcharge'.

Of the two forms *familiare* and *famigliare* the former used to be recommended as correct, the second is now acceptable; some people distinguish *familiare* 'familiar' from *famigliare* 'of the family'.

(b) The apostrophe

One is traditionally taught that the apostrophe is used in cases of elision but not of truncation (see above), i.e., when the shortened form could not exist in front of a consonant: *un artista* 'an artist' (male), as *un cane* 'a dog', but *un'artista* 'an artist' (female), because one cannot have *un cagna* for *una cagna* 'a bitch'; so also *pover'uomo* 'poor man', but *tal amico* 'such a friend', *fin allora* 'until then', *qual è* 'which is', etc. The apostrophe is commonly used also in *un po'* 'a bit', *a mo' di* 'by way of', and may be used in the imperatives *da'* 'give', *di'* 'say', *fa'* 'do', *sta'* 'stay', *va'* 'go'. Note that in these last cases there is a space between the apostrophe and the following word, whereas in the ones mentioned above the elided word and the following one are not separated: *l'amico* 'the friend', *un'onda* 'a wave'.

(c) Accent marks are generally used (i) in all polysyllables stressed

on the last syllable: *però* 'however', *perchè* 'because', *così* 'so', *andò* 'he went', *finì* 'he ended',

but not if the last syllable ends in a falling diphthong: *andai* 'I went', *eroi* 'heroes' (in metre these words may count as trisyllabic, in which case the last syllable is unstressed);

(ii) in some monosyllables like *può* 'he can', *più* 'more', *ciò* 'that', *giù* 'down', *già* 'already' which, without an accent mark could be read as paroxytonic bisyllables (*gia* [dʒla] 'he went' is the imperfect of the literary *gire* 'to go'); (iii) in some monosyllables where the spelling without an accent mark represents another word: *sì* 'yes' vs. *si* 'oneself', *sè* 'oneself' vs. *se* 'if', *è* 'he is' vs. *e* 'and', *dà* 'he gives' vs. *da* 'from', *dì* 'day' vs. *di* 'of', *là* and *lì* 'there' vs. *la* and *li* article and pronoun.

Note that *qui* and *qua* are written without accent marks: there are no homophones with which they could be confused, and the *q* indicates that the following *u* cannot be stressed ([kùi] 'to whom' is spelled *cui*). One can thus distinguish *dà* 'he gives', *da* 'give' imperative, *da* 'from'. It used to be quite common to distinguish *sù* adverb 'up' from *su* preposition 'on', as in *vado sù* 'I am going up', but *su di me* 'on me'; *dò* 'I give' from *do* the musical note, *dànno* 'they give' from *danno* 'damage', and *sè* from *se stesso, se medesimo* 'himself' (because in the latter expressions *se* cannot mean 'if'). Nowadays it is more common to write *su, do, danno* always without an accent mark, and *sè* always with an accent mark when it is a pronoun (*se* 'if' always without). It is also old-fashioned to use the circumflex to indicate a so-called contraction, as in *côrre* literary for *cogliere* 'to pick' vs. *corre* 'he runs', *cerchî* 'circles' vs. *cerchi* 'you search' (the usual form is *cerchi* for both) (cf. chapter V. 5 (a)).

A convention which has become more and more widely accepted by publishers (also by newspapers, but not in personal manuscripts and typescripts, where a grave throughout is preferred) makes use of the grave for [ɛ] and [ɔ] and of the acute for [e] (with reference to Florentine pronunciation): *è* 'he is', *cioè* 'that is', *caffè* 'coffee', (with [ɛ]), *perché* 'because', *né* 'neither', *sé* 'oneself' (with [e]); stressed final *-o* always represents [ɔ], hence it is written with a grave: *ciò* 'that', *può* 'he can', *portò* 'he carried'. As there is no distinction to be made between open and closed [a], [i], [u] the grave is usually employed on the letters representing these vowels (but some people use the grave on *a* because it represents an open vowel, and the acute on *i* and *u* because they represent closed vowels: *là* but *lí, piú*).

The use of grave and acute accents to distinguish between Florentine [ɛ] [ɔ] and [e] [o] is sometimes extended to non-final syllables to distinguish words which would otherwise have the same spelling: *scòrsi* 'I glimpsed' vs. *scórsi* 'past', *corrèsse* 'he corrected' vs. *corrésse* '(if) he ran'.

Occasionally accent marks are used to distinguish between homographs representing words with the stress on different syllables: *prìncipi* 'princes' vs. *principi* (or *principî*) 'principles', *àrbitri* 'referees' vs. *arbitri* (or *arbitrî*) 'arbitrary acts' (cf. chapter V. 5(a)).

Many proposals have been made, along the lines of the three paragraphs above, to introduce a consistent system of accent marks in Italian indicating unambiguously (i) where the stress falls, (ii) when the stressed vowel is *e* or *o*, whether it is open (with a grave) or closed (with an acute). The simplest and most explicit system would be to put an accent mark on the stressed vowel of every word. As most Italian words are paroxytonic, a more economic system would be not to put an accent mark on these, unless the stressed vowel is *e* or *o* (in which case one needs the accent mark to indicate whether they are closed or open). So one would write for instance: *tàvolo* 'table', *dècade* 'decade', *dèmoni* 'demons' (plural of *dèmone*), *móndano* 'they clean', *decade* 'it declines', *demòni* 'demons' (plural of *demònio*), *parte* 'part', *pòrta* 'door'.

Some authors see these systems as purely didactic artifices to be used in texts for teaching, others present them as projects of spelling reforms (with the ultimate aim of reforming pronunciation as well, making it conform to the Florentine standard more systematically). These proposals, however, particularly if they are presented as spelling reforms, seem not only unwieldy and impractical, but also basically ill-conceived. The elimination of a few ambiguities is pointless, because there are countless more (this is how language works), and unnecessary, because the context almost always disambiguates the word. As for the distinction between open and closed *e* and *o*, given the Italian situation, it is better to leave the choice to the reader. As a consequence of the linguistic history of Italy, people can now write *piede* and *quattordici* which are national forms; if one is made to indicate that *piède* must be with an [ɛ] and *quattórdici* with an [o], one is at the same time being made to use a form which is characterized as regional. The introduction of these accent marks would probably not make Italian speech more national, but Italian spelling less so. The adoption of these projects would not bring Italian spelling any nearer to a phonological representation, but rather take it further away: Italians who pronounce *è* [ɛ] and *perchè* [perkέ], would learn a spelling vagary ([ɛ] spelled with a grave accent in *è* and with an acute accent in *perché*) rather than change their speech.

For the foreign learner the best solution is to put a grave accent on vowels which traditionally require an accent mark (which is, as noted above, what most Italians do).

(d) **Punctuation**

A contrastive discussion of the use of comma, colon, semicolon and full stop in English and Italian would be out of place here, but it is worth noting that (i) Italian does not normally use a question mark in indirect questions: the English 'I wonder if . . .?' corresponds to '*mi chiedo se . . .*'; (ii) a dash sometimes used without a preceding and following space as a breaking mark in English is easily interpreted by Italians as a hyphen joining the two elements it separates, because of the lack of spaces. Compared with English the dash is less often used in Italian, where it mostly introduces exchanges in a dialogue, as an alternative to inverted commas, or delimits a parenthetic expression, instead of brackets. An English student writing in Italian tends to use it inappropriately for colon, semicolon or full stop.

(e) **The division of words** at the end of the line conforms in Italian to syllabic boundaries (as codified by orthographic conventions). Vowels may be separated from each other if they do not form a diphthong: *a-cu-i-to* 'sharpened', *ma-ia-le* 'pig', *si-a* 'let it be', *mai* 'never', *più* 'more'; single consonants go with the following syllable: *ma-ri-to* 'husband', *ta-vo-li-no* 'little table'; also *mo-glie* 'wife', *e-sce* 'he goes out', *o-gnu-no* 'each one'; double consonants and con-

sonant clusters are divided between the syllables, but if there is a group of stop + *l, r* it goes with the following syllable; if the consonant cluster begins with *s*, the *s* goes with the following syllable: *fat-to* 'done', *ac-qua* 'water', *cor-sa* 'run', *al-to* 'high', *a-pren-do* 'opening', *ap-pren-do* 'I learn', *o-ste* 'publican', *ma-e-stro* 'teacher'.

As can be seen from these examples, a practical rule could be: put as many consonants as possible with the following syllable, as long as you get a cluster which can occur at the beginning of a word. The rule leads to different treatment of comparable clusters: *cap-zio-so* 'captious', *ab-nor-me* 'abnormal', but *di-spe-pti-co* 'dyspeptic' (with *-pti-* as in *pterodattilo* 'pterodactyl'), *di-spe-psi-a* 'dyspepsia' (with *-psi-* as in *psicologia* 'psychology'), *ri-tmo* 'rhythm' (with *-tmo* as in *tmesi* 'tmesis'). There are also exceptions: *a-vrò* 'I shall have', *do-vrei* 'I should' although no Italian word begins with *vr-*.

It is considered undesirable to end the line with an apostrophe (with or without a hyphen): *l'-amico* 'the friend', *un'-amica* 'a friend' are avoided, and *l'a-mico, un'a-mica* or *u-n'amica* are preferred. Also to be avoided is the habit which many printers have in these cases of using the full form of the article at the end of the line: *lo / anno* 'the year', *una / ora* 'an hour'.

(f) Capitals

In modern Italian there is a strong tendency not to use capitals, except where their use is compulsory as in proper names. In many cases in which a capital is found in English, it is not used in Italian, e.g., in the names of the months and of the days of the week. With names deriving from states, nations, towns, etc., capitals are often used for the substantives (*gli Italiani* 'the Italians'), but not for the adjectives (*il popolo italiano* 'the Italian people'), nor to refer to the language (*studiare l'italiano* 'to study Italian'), or individuals (*c'erano due italiani* 'there were two Italians').

(g) Note that in quoting **titles** of books and newspapers one need not retain a capital or italics for an initial article belonging to the title. Manzoni's novel is *I promessi sposi*; a critic may write: *leggendo 'I promessi sposi'* (or '*I Promessi Sposi*', or *i 'Promessi Sposi'*) *per l'intreccio* 'reading the *Promessi Sposi* for the plot', but, with a preposition, preferably: *l'oratoria dei 'Promessi Sposi'* 'the oratory of the *Promessi Sposi*'. If the article is retained as part of the title a preposition in front of it may have the form it takes when fused with the article: *i racconti de* (or *di*) '*Il Mondo*' 'the stories of *Il Mondo*', *lo stile di Moravia ne* (or *in*) '*La Noia*' (or '*La noia*') 'Moravia's style in *La Noia*'. (But when speaking one will generally use *del Mondo* for *de 'Il Mondo*', *nella Noia* for *ne 'La Noia*').

3 The article

(a) The different forms of the article are set out in the following table:

	Masculine	Feminine
Indefinite (singular)	*un uno*	*una un'*
Definite (singular)	*il lo l'*	*la l'*
Definite (plural)	*i gli gl'*	*le l'*

The form of the article depends on the initial sound of the following word (which need not be the noun that goes with the article).

(b) **Masculine**   *uno, lo, gli* are used before *s*+consonant, *z, ps,* and normally before *pn, gn, x,* and unstressed *i*+vowel; otherwise *un, il, i* (but *l'* is used before a vowel and *gl'* may be used before *i*).

Examples: *un ragazzo* 'a boy', *uno strano ragazzo* 'a strange boy', *il ragazzo* 'the boy', *lo strano ragazzo* 'the strange boy', *i ragazzi* 'the boys', *gli strani ragazzi* 'the strange boys'; *uno studio* 'a study', *un piccolo studio* 'a small study', *lo studio, il piccolo studio, gli studi, i piccoli studi; un inglese* 'an Englishman', *l'inglese, gli inglesi* or *gl'inglesi; uno pseudonimo* 'a pseudonym', *lo pseudonimo, gli pseudonimi; uno* or *un pneumatico* 'a tyre', *lo* or *il pneumatico, gli* or *i pneumatici; uno* or *un gnocco* 'a kind of noodle, or a bump', *lo* or *il gnocco, gli* or *i gnocchi; uno* or *un xilofono* 'a xylophone', *lo* or *il xilofono, gli* or *i xilofoni; uno* or *un iugoslavo* 'a Jugoslav', *lo* or *l'iugoslavo, gli iugoslavi.* Words beginning with *i*+vowel may take *l'* (as *l'ieri* 'the yesterday') as well as *lo* (as *lo iato* 'the hiatus'); the plural in both cases is *gli (gli ieri, gli iati).*

Articles with foreign words beginning with (i) [w]: *un whisky, il* or *l'whisky, i* or *gli whisky; un weekend, il* or *l'weekend, i* or *gli weekend*; (ii) [j]: *un* or *uno yacht, lo* or *l'yacht, gli yacht*; (iii) [h]: *uno Hennessy, lo Hegel, gli Humboldt.* The [h] is here treated like an Italian spirant such as [ʃ]; one also finds a more affected *il Hegel* with an [h], and a more popular *l'Hegel* without an [h]; when there is no [h] the normal prevocalic form of the article is used: *un hotel, l'hotel, gli hotel.* It has been suggested that with French names one should adopt French usage, i.e., *l'Havet* but *lo Hugo*.

Note some exceptions which mostly preserve old Italian forms: *per lo più* 'for the most part', *per lo meno* 'at least', *gli dei* 'the gods', *un zinzin* 'a pinch' (of something), *passata la festa gabbato lo santo* 'once on shore we pray no more'. In an old-fashioned or bureaucratic style one may find the date written like this: *li 18 agosto 1974*, where *li* is an old form of the plural article. As this form is unknown in modern Italian it is sometimes found with an accent as if it were the locative pronoun *lì*, and also used with the first of the month instead of *il*.

(c) **Feminine**   in the singular *una*, *la* are used before a consonant and also before [w] and [j], *un'*, *l'* are used before a vowel; in the plural *le* is used; it is preferred to *l'* even in front of *e-*: *le erbe* 'the herbs'.

Examples: *una ragazza* 'a girl', *la ragazza, le ragazze; una iugoslava* 'a Jugoslav woman', *la iugoslava, le iugoslave; un'idea* 'an idea', *una vecchia idea* 'an old idea', *l'idea, la vecchia idea, le idee, le vecchie idee*. In front of surnames of women even beginning with a vowel, *la* is always used: *la Ingrao, la Antinucci; l'* would refer to a man; but cf., with Christian names, where no confusion is possible, *l'Ida, l'Anna*.

For the use of the article see chapter VI. 2.

4 Prepositions with the article

(a) Many prepositions combine with the definite article to form a single word. They all belong to the traditional list of prepositions proper; this list consists of the following weak forms used as prepositions only (apart from *su* which can also be used adverbially and is thus comparable to *contro* 'against', *dentro* 'inside', *fuori* 'outside', *sopra* 'over', *sotto* 'under', etc.). Some of the most common meanings are provided:

a 'to, at, in': *vado a scuola* 'I go to school', *sono a casa* 'I am at home', *vivono a Venezia* 'they live in Venice'.

con 'with': *vieni con me* 'come with me'.

da 'from, by, to, at, with': *vengo da Roma* 'I come from Rome', *è scritta da Ugo* 'it is written by Ugo', *vado dal macellaio* 'I'm going to the butcher's', *sta da noi* 'he's staying with us' (cf. French *chez* for the last two examples).

di 'of, by, from': *questo è fatto di legno* 'this is made of wood', *questo libro è di Ugo* 'this book is Ugo's', *una poesia di Dante* 'a poem by Dante', *è di Milano* 'he comes from Milan', i.e., he is a native of Milan.

fra, tra 'between, among, in (of future time)': *leggere fra le righe* 'to read between the lines', *fra amici* 'among friends'; *fra* and *tra* have the same meaning, but one or the other may be preferred to avoid alliteration: *tra fratelli* 'between brothers' rather than *fra fratelli; fra tre giorni* 'in three days' time' rather than *tra tre giorni*.

in 'in, to, into': *siamo in campagna* 'we are in the country', *andiamo in Italia* 'we are going to Italy', *l'ho buttato in acqua* 'I threw him into the water'.

per 'for, through': *questo è per te* 'this is for you', *camminando per le strade di Milano* 'walking through the streets of Milan'.

su 'on': *mettilo su una sedia* 'put it on a chair'.

(b) In modern Italian when there is an article the combined form is compulsory with these prepositions, except with *fra* and *tra* which never combine, *per* for which the combined forms (*pel, pei,* etc.) are practically obsolete, and *con* for which they are optional:

	il	*lo*	*l'*	*i*	*gli*	*la*	*le*
a	*al*	*allo*	*all'*	*ai*	*agli*	*alla*	*alle*
con	*col*	*collo*	*coll'*	*coi*	*cogli*	*colla*	*colle*
da	*dal*	*dallo*	*dall'*	*dai*	*dagli*	*dalla*	*dalle*
di	*del*	*dello*	*dell'*	*dei*	*degli*	*della*	*delle*
in	*nel*	*nello*	*nell'*	*nei*	*negli*	*nella*	*nelle*
su	*sul*	*sullo*	*sull'*	*sui*	*sugli*	*sulla*	*sulle*

Examples: *all'ultimo momento* 'at the last moment', *negli esami* 'in the exams', *sulla tavola* 'on the table', *col pretesto* 'with the pretext'.

(c) *di* + definite article is used in the so-called 'partitive' construction: *ho comprato dei fiori* 'I have bought some flowers', *vuoi del pane?* 'do you want any bread?'; but in negative sentences: *non ho matite* 'I have no pencils' (for the particular meaning of *di* + article in negative sentences see chapter VI. 2(b) (ii)). Note that the partitive cannot be preceded by *di*; whereas one can contrast *vedo quadri* 'I see pictures' and *vedo dei quadri* 'I see some pictures', one cannot contrast *parlo di quadri* 'I am talking of pictures' and *parlo di + dei quadri* 'I am talking of some pictures'. Instead of *di*+partitive, *un po' di, alcuni, certi*, etc., would be used.

5 Nouns and adjectives

(a) Noun endings in Italian may be grouped into three main categories. These three categories also apply to adjectives.

	(i)	(ii)	(iii)
Singular	*-o*	*-a*	*-e*
Plural	*-i*	*-e*	*-i*
	masculine	feminine	masculine and feminine

Exceptions: *la mano, le mani* 'hand, -s', *l'eco* (feminine), *gli echi* 'echo, -es', *il dio, gli dei* 'god, -s' (with an irregular use of the article, cf. chapter IV. 1(a)(i)(C)), *l'uomo, gli uomini* 'man, men', *il bue, i buoi* 'ox, -en', *il carcere, le carceri* 'prison, -s'.

Adjectives always agree in number and gender with the noun they qualify: *il padre severo, i padri severi* 'the strict father, -s', *la madre indaffarata, le madri indaffarate* 'the busy mother, -s', *il ragazzo grande, i ragazzi grandi* 'the big boy, -s', *la ragazza forte, le ragazze forti* 'the strong girl, -s'.

Plurals of nouns and adjectives in -co and -go

Words of so-called popular tradition (mostly paroxytones) tend to preserve the velar: *ago, aghi* 'needle, -s', *fuoco, fuochi* 'fire, -s', *impiego, impieghi* 'employment, -s', *sacco, sacchi* 'sack, -s'; *lungo, lunghi* 'long', *poco, pochi* 'little, few'. But: *amico, amici* 'friend, -s', *nemico, nemici* 'enemy, -ies', *greco, greci* 'Greek, -s', *porco, porci* 'pig, -s'. Words belonging to the so-called learned tradition (mostly proparoxytones) tend to change the velar to a palatal: *asparago, asparagi* 'asparagus', *biologo, biologi* 'biologist, -s', *filologo, filologi* 'philologist, -s', *teologo, teologi* 'theologian, -s'; *pacifico, pacifici* 'peaceful'. But: *catalogo, cataloghi* 'catalogue, -s', *dialogo, dialoghi* 'dialogue, -s'; *analogo, analoghi* 'analogous', *carico, carichi* 'loaded'.

Feminine nouns and adjectives in -ca and -ga

These always have their plural in *-che* and *-ghe: amica, amiche* 'friend, -s', *droga, droghe* 'drug, -s'; *larga, larghe* 'large', *poca, poche*; 'little, few').

Note *il, la belga, i belgi, le belghe* 'Belgian, -s'.

Plurals of nouns and adjectives in -io

When the *i* is stressed the plural is in *-ii: pendio, pendii* 'slope, -s', *zio, zii* 'uncle, -s'; *pio, pii* 'pious'; when the *i* is unstressed the plural is usually in *-i: studio, studi* 'study, -ies'; *vario, vari* 'varied', although *-ii, -î* (or, obsolete, *-j*) may also be found, particularly to avoid ambiguity (in spelling, as the pronunciation is normally with a final single [i]): *principio, principi, principii, principî* (or *principj*) 'principle, -s' vs. *principe, principi* 'prince, -s' (cf. chapter V. 2(c)).

Feminine nouns and adjectives in -cia and -gia

When the *i* is stressed it is retained in the plural: *farmacia, farmacie* 'chemist's shop, -s'; when the *i* is unstressed (and so is only there to indicate that the preceding consonant is a palatal) the following spelling convention is the most widely used: the plural is without an *i* if *-cia* and *-gia* are preceded by a consonant: *provincia, province* 'province, -s', *spiaggia, spiagge* 'beach, -es'; *lercia, lerce* 'filthy', *greggia, gregge* 'raw', and with an *i* if they are preceded by a vowel: *camicia, camicie* 'shirt, -s', *valigia, valigie* 'suitcase, -s'; *fradicia, fradicie* 'soaking wet', *grigia, grigie* 'grey'.

The adjectives *bello* 'beautiful' and *quello* 'that' have endings like those of the definite article when they precede the noun: *un bel libro* 'a fine book', *begli esempi* 'good examples', *quel libro* 'that book', *quei libri* 'those books', but *quell'oggetto è bello* 'that object is beautiful', *quegli oggetti sono belli*.

Buono 'good', *grande* 'big', *Santo* 'Saint' in the singular have endings similar to those of the indefinite article if they precede the noun; *buon, gran, San* in the masculine before a consonant: *un buon pasto* 'a good meal', *un gran libro* 'a great book', *San Pietro* 'Saint Peter'. *Buon* (feminine *buon'*), *grand'* (and frequently *grande*), *Sant'* are used before a vowel: *buon esempio* 'good example', *buon'idea* 'good idea', *grand'uomo* 'great man', *grande amore* 'great love', *Sant'Antonio* 'Saint Anthony'; whilst the full forms *buono, grande, Santo* are used before s + consonant: *un buono studio* 'a good study', *un grande schiaffo* 'a great smack', *Santo Stefano* 'Saint Stephen'.

In front of the other initial sounds which require *uno* rather than *un* both *buon, gran, San,* and *buono, grande, Santo* are used: *un buon sciroppo* 'a good syrup', *un gran gnocco* 'a big bump', *un buono psicologo* 'a good psychologist', *un grande scendiletto* 'a large bedside mat', but only the form *San* is used before *z: San Zenone* 'Saint Zeno', *San Zaccaria* 'Saint Zachariah', etc. Note the expressions *gran cose* 'great things', *gran belle notizie* 'splendid news', *gran brutti fatti* 'terrible things'.

(b) Besides the endings listed in the above three categories (i)–(iii), nouns may have the following endings:

	(iv)	(v)	(vi)
Singular	*-a* (masculine)	*-o* (masculine)	*-o* (masculine)
Plural	*-i* (masculine)	*-a* (feminine)	*-i* (masculine)
			-a (feminine)

Examples (iv): *il dentista, i dentisti* 'dentist, -s', *il pianista, i pianisti* 'pianist, -s' (the feminine *la dentista, le dentiste, la pianista, le pianiste* follow category (ii)), *il poeta, i poeti* 'poet, -s', *il problema, i problemi* 'problem, -s', *il programma, i programmi* 'programme, -s', *il telegramma, i telegrammi* 'telegram, -s', *il tema, i temi* 'theme, -s'; (v) *il paio, le paia* 'pair, -s', *il riso, le risa* 'laughter', *l'uovo, le uova* 'egg, -s'; note the agreement in *una delle più grosse uova* or *un uovo dei più grossi* 'one of the biggest eggs'; (vi) the different plurals in this category usually have different meanings: *il braccio* 'arm', *le braccia* 'arms' (of the body), *i bracci* 'arms' (of an object), *il dito* 'finger', *le dita* 'fingers', but *i diti* when considered individually, as in *i diti mignoli* 'little fingers', *il fondamento* 'foundation', *le fondamenta* 'foundations' (of a house), *i fondamenti* 'foundations' (metaphorical), *il membro* 'member', *le membra* 'limbs', *i membri* 'members' (of a society), *il muro* 'wall', *le mura* 'city walls', *i muri* 'walls' (of a house). Sometimes however the plurals may have the same meanings: *il ginocchio* 'knee', *le ginocchia* or *i ginocchi, il lenzuolo* 'sheet', *le lenzuola* or *i lenzuoli, l'orecchio* 'ear', *le orecchie* or *gli orecchi.* Note *il frutto, i frutti* 'fruit, -s', but *la frutta* collective.

(c) Invariable nouns and adjectives belong to the following groups: (vii) Nouns ending with a stressed vowel: *il caffè, i caffè* 'coffee, -s', *la città, le città* 'town, -s', *la virtù, le virtù* 'virtue, -s'; here one can add monosyllabic nouns: *la gru, le gru* 'crane, -s', *il re, i re* 'king, -s'. (viii) Feminine nouns ending in *-ie: la serie, le serie* 'series', *la specie, le specie* 'species', *la superficie, le superficie* (but also *le superfici*) 'surface, -s'. (ix) Nouns and adjectives ending in *-i: la crisi, le crisi* 'crisis, -es', *un numero dispari, dei numeri dispari* 'odd number, -s', *un numero pari, dei numeri pari* 'even number, -s'. (x) Nouns and adjectives of foreign origin: *il bar, i bar, il film, i film, lo sport, gli sport, il tram, i tram; una gonna beige, delle gonne beige* 'beige skirt, -s', *la sciarpa blu, le sciarpe blu* 'blue scarf, -ves', *la borsa marron, le borse marron* 'brown bag, -s'.

Note that there is no obvious rule for making a foreign noun masculine or feminine in Italian. With French and German nouns it is advisable to keep the original gender (treating the German neuter as a masculine); but sometimes the gender of an Italian word, etymologically or semantically related, prevails: *una Fräulein* 'a (German) Miss' or 'a (German) nanny'; as well as *le 'Fleurs du mal' di Baudelaire* one also meets *i 'Fleurs du mal'*, on the model of Italian *fiori*. With English words, after a period of uncertainty, the masculine has become standard for instance in *il film, il radar*, and the feminine in *la coca-cola, la jeep*; with words like *pub* and *suspense* both genders are found.

(xi) Adjectives which were originally nouns: *il guanto marrone, i guanti marrone* 'brown glove, -s' (*marrone* can be used as well as *marron* quoted in (x) above; there is also a plural *marroni*), *un fazzoletto rosa, dei fazzoletti rosa* 'pink handkerchief, -ves', *la cravatta viola, le cravatte viola* 'mauve tie, -s'.

(d) As a last point observe that Italian normally uses the singular (whereas English uses the plural) when there is a plurality of things of which each individual has one: *avevano il naso rosso* 'their noses were red', *portavano tutti il cappotto* 'they all had their coats on'.

6 Comparatives and superlatives

Più 'more' and *meno* 'less' are used to form comparatives; *il più* and *il meno* are used to form the relative superlative (indicating the highest degree); the absolute superlative (indicating a very high degree) is formed by adding the suffix *-issimo* to the stem of the adjective.

	Comparative	Relative superlative	Absolute superlative
bello	*più bello* *meno bello*	*il più bello* *il meno bello*	*bellissimo*

brutto	*più brutto*	*il più brutto*	*bruttissimo*
	meno brutto	*il meno brutto*	

Examples: *questo è più bello* 'this is nicer', *quello è il più brutto* 'that is the ugliest', *lei è gentilissima* 'she is very kind', *questo è meno difficile* 'this is less difficult', *questo è il meno costoso* 'this is the least expensive'. The distinction between comparative, with no article, and superlative, with the definite article, is neutralized when they are attributes of a noun with a definite article: *questa scatola è più grande* 'this box is bigger', *questa scatola è la più grande* 'this box is the biggest', *ecco la scatola più grande* 'here is the bigger box' and 'here is the biggest box'.

(a) *più* and *meno* can also be used adjectively, as in *mi piace con più zucchero* 'I like it with more sugar', *vorrei avere meno difficoltà* 'I wish I had fewer difficulties', or adverbially, as in *non ne voglio più* 'I don't want any more (than I've had)' literally 'any of it any longer' (*non ne voglio di più* means 'I don't want more (than I've got)'), *non mi piace più* 'I don't like it any more' (*non mi piace di più* means 'I do not like it more');

(b) in the form *questi sono i più piccoli possibile* 'these are the very smallest' *possibile* is invariable;

(c) Italian uses *tutti* where English uses 'any' in sentences like *è più vecchio di tutti i miei amici* 'he is older than any of my friends';

(d) the suffix -*issimo* may also be added to nouns, but apart from expressions which have become almost technical, like *il campionissimo* 'the super champion', *canzonissima* (the name of a television song contest), other forms like *augurissimi* 'very best wishes', *salutissimi* 'best greetings' are rather affected. With nouns intensification can also be obtained by doubling: *caffè caffè* 'real coffee' (and not a substitute);

(e) intensification of an adjective can be obtained (as well as by combining it with an adverb) by doubling it: *una stanza molto piccola* or *piccola piccola* 'a very small room'. Another adjective can also be added, producing pairs in a fixed order like *bagnato fradicio* 'soaking wet', *pieno zeppo* 'chock full', *sporco lurido* 'filthy dirty', *stanco morto* 'dead tired', *vecchio decrepito* 'old and decrepit'.

Certain adjectives, alongside forms which follow the above pattern, have forms which derive from Latin comparatives and superlatives:

	Comparative	Relative superlative	Absolute superlative
buono	*migliore*	*il migliore*	*ottimo*
cattivo	*peggiore*	*il peggiore*	*pessimo*
grande	*maggiore*	*il maggiore*	*massimo*
piccolo	*minore*	*il minore*	*minimo*

The two forms may be interchangeable: *abbiamo fatto un ottimo* or *buonis-simo pranzo* 'we had an excellent meal', *questo vino ha un gusto pessimo* or *cattivissimo* 'this wine has a horrible taste'; but expressions like *il minimo disturbo* 'the least trouble', *la massima ammirazione* 'the greatest admiration' correspond to *il più piccolo disturbo*, not to *il piccolissimo disturbo*, and to *la più grande ammirazione*, not to *la grandissima ammirazione*.

In comparative sentences *di* 'than' is normally used: *è più intelligente di te* 'he is more intelligent than you', *meno di due ore* 'less than two hours', *oggi c'è più vento di ieri* 'today is windier than yesterday'; but *che* is sometimes found in its place: *oggi c'è più vento che ieri. Che* is used when two terms are compared directly (and not by means of another term as in *Ugo è più intelligente di te*): *fa meno caldo al mare che in città* 'it is less hot by the sea than in town', *ho più stampe che quadri* 'I have more prints than paintings' (but *apprezza più le stampe dei* or *che i quadri* 'he appreciates prints more than paintings'), *Ugo è più furbo che intelligente* 'Ugo is more crafty than intelligent', *si comporta vilmente più che prudentemente* 'he is behaving in a cowardly rather than in a cautious manner'.

Comparative clauses can be constructed in a variety of ways: *è arrivato più presto che non mi aspettassi*, or *è arrivato più presto di quanto (non) mi aspettavo* (or *aspettassi*), or *è arrivato più presto di quello che mi aspettavo* (or *aspettassi*) 'he arrived earlier than I expected'; *mi diede meno carta che non ne avessi chiesta*, or *mi diede meno carta di quanta (non) ne avevo* (or *avessi*) *chiesta*, or *mi diede meno carta di quella che avevo* (or *avessi*) *chiesta* 'he gave me less paper than I had asked for'; *è più piccolo che non immaginassi*, or *è più piccolo di quanto (non) immaginavo* (or *immaginassi*), or *è più piccolo di quello che immaginavo* (or *immaginassi*), or *è più piccolo di come lo immaginavo* (or *immaginassi*) 'he is smaller than I imagined' (Note the use of pleonastic *non*; cf. chapter VI note 9).

Correlative terms introducing comparisons are *così . . . come, tanto . . . quanto, altrettanto . . . quanto*; *che* may replace the adverbial *quanto* (purists object to this use of *che*, as also to *sia . . . che* replacing *sia . . . sia* 'both . . . and', 'whether . . . or'; the forms with *che* are more colloquial): *riesce tanto nella pittura quanto* (or *che*) *nella scultura* 'he is as good at painting as he is at sculpture', *non ho tanti libri quanti mio fratello* (*quanti* is used adjectivally and cannot be replaced by *che*) 'I haven't as many books as my brother', *è uno scrittore altrettanto noto all'estero quanto* (or *che*) *in Italia* 'he is a writer who is as well known abroad as in Italy'. *C'erano tanto uomini quanto donne* means 'there were both men and women', whereas *c'erano tanti uomini quante donne* means 'there were as many men as women'; in sentences like the latter the agreement is with the noun that follows: *quante* (not *quanti*) *donne*.

7 Adverbs

Adverbs are usually formed by adding *-mente* to the feminine singular of the adjective: *lentamente* 'slowly', *rapidamente* 'quickly', *certamente* 'certainly'; if the adjective ends in *-le* or *-re*, the *-e* is dropped before *-mente*: *facilmente* 'easily', *gentilmente* 'kindly', *particolarmente* 'particularly' (but also *benevolmente, leggermente, violentemente*, corresponding to *benevolo* 'benevolent', *leggero* 'light', *violento* 'violent').

Sometimes an adverb consists of the form of the masculine adjective: *parla piano* 'speak quietly', *abitiamo vicino* 'we live nearby', or of *di* followed by a masculine adjective: *di nuovo* 'again', *di recente* 'recently'. Many adverbs of time and place are unconnected with adjectives: *adesso* 'now', *oggi* 'today', *qua* 'here', *lì* 'there', etc.

Adverbs have comparative and superlative forms parallel to the adjectival ones: *glielo ha detto gentilmente* 'he told him in a kind way', *glielo ha detto più gentilmente* 'he told him in a kinder way', *glielo ha detto gentilissimamente* or *molto gentilmente* 'he told him in a very kind way'; note the equivalence of the relative superlative followed by *possibile* and of the comparative followed by *che* and the required form of the verb *potere*: *glielo ha detto il più gentilmente possibile* or *glielo ha detto più gentilmente che poteva* 'he told him in as kind a way as possible'.

Bene 'well' and *male* 'badly' also have forms which derive from the Latin comparatives and superlatives: *bene, meglio, il meglio possibile, ottimamente; male, peggio, il peggio possibile, pessimamente: l'ha aggiustato il meglio possibile* or *l'ha aggiustato meglio che poteva* 'he mended it as well as possible' or 'as well as he could', *l'ha aggiustato ottimamente* or *benissimo* or *molto bene* 'he mended it very well'. Italian frequently uses adjectives where English uses adverbs: *parlava tranquilla* 'she was speaking calmly', *camminavano svelti* 'they were walking quickly'.

8 Personal pronouns

			Stressed (or Disjunctive)			Unstressed (or Conjunctive)	
			Subject	Direct object	Indirect object (only after preposition)	Direct object	Indirect object
Singular	1		io	me	me	mi	mi
	2		tu	te	te	ti	ti
	3	{	egli	lui	lui	lo	gli
Masculine		{	esso		esso		ne
		{	lui				
		{	ella	lei	lei	la	le
Feminine		{	essa		essa		ne
		{	lei				
Reflexive				sè	sè	si	si
Plural	1		noi	noi	noi	ci	ci
	2		voi	voi	voi	vi	vi
	3	{	essi	loro	loro	li	loro
Masculine		{	loro		essi		gli
							ne
Feminine		{	esse	loro	loro	le	loro
		{	loro		esse		ne
Reflexive				sè	sè	si	si

(a) **Subject pronouns** are omitted in Italian unless they are needed for emphasis, contrast or clarity: *ho aperto la porta* 'I opened the door', but *mi ha autorizzato lei* 'it is she who gave me permission', *io vado, e tu?* 'I am going, what about you?', *mi chiese cosa tu volessi* 'he asked me what you wanted' (without *tu* the meaning might be 'what I wanted'). The pronoun is often used in a coordinated clause if the subject has not been mentioned in a preceding one: *quando cominciò a piovere chiuse la finestra* (subordinate without pronoun) 'when it began to rain he shut the window', but *cominciò a piovere e lui chiuse la finestra* (coordinate with pronoun) 'it began to rain and he shut the window', *hanno suonato il campanello e lui si è alzato in piedi* 'they rang the bell and he got up', *hanno scritto varie volte ma lui non ha risposto* 'they wrote several times but he did not answer'.

Note the difference between Italian and English usages in cases like *Chi è? – Io* 'Who is it? – Me'; *anch'io* 'me too'; *io far così?* 'what, me do that?'.

(i) When pronouns (or pronouns and proper names) are coordinated, their order is free in Italian, unlike English; after *e* 'and', however, the form *te* is more common than *tu: tu e io* or *io e te* 'you and I'; *tu e lui* or *lui e te* 'you and he'; *tu e Ugo* or *Ugo e te* 'you and Ugo'; *io, tu e lui* or *io, lui e te*, etc. 'he, you and I'.

(ii) The most commonly used third person pronouns are *lui, lei, loro; egli, essi* are used in the literary (or formal spoken) language, referring to people, so are *essa* and *esse*, which can however also refer to things and animals. *Esso* usually refers to a thing or an animal, but it is not used in colloquial Italian. *Ella* is more formal than *essa* and only refers to a person.

(iii) In forms of address *lei* (which may be written with a capital initial: *Lei*) is the polite pronoun in the singular; its plural counterpart *loro* (or *Loro*) is more formal and tends to be substituted by *voi*. *Ella* can be used as a more formal alternative to *lei*. Even though *lei* was originally a feminine pronoun, if the person addressed is a man an accompanying adjective or past participle is normally masculine: *lei è sicuro di venire?* 'are you sure you are coming?'.

Another polite form of singular address is *voi*. The relative formality of *lei* and *voi* varies in different parts of Italy, but *voi* is in any case disappearing as a singular form of address and foreigners should use *lei* for acquaintances and *tu* for friends and colleagues; the use of *tu* roughly corresponds to being on Christian name terms in English.

(b) **Stressed direct object pronouns** are used for emphasis or contrast: *invito te, non lui* 'I am inviting you, not him', and after *come* 'as, like', *tranne* 'except': *come me, tranne te*, and in exclamations: *povero me!* 'poor me!'. *Esso* cannot be used as a direct object; either an unstressed pronoun or an expression which is not a personal pronoun has to be used. While with a human referent one has (i) *ha visto Ugo?* 'did he see Ugo?', (ii) *l'ha visto* 'he saw him', (iii) *ha visto non solo lui ma anche Ada* 'he saw not only him but also Ada', with a non-human referent one has (i) *ha perso il portafoglio?* 'did he lose his wallet?', (ii) *l'ha perso* 'he lost it', but (iii) *ha perso non solo quello* (and not *esso*) *ma anche le chiavi* 'he lost not only that but also his keys'. With the object *lei* in forms of address the agreement is usually *ad sensum: considerano lei avaro e me generoso* 'they consider you stingy and me generous' (with *lei* referring to a man).

(c) **Indirect object stressed pronouns** are used if a preposition is followed by a pronoun: *esco con lui* 'I am going out with him', *parlo di te* 'I am talking about you'. *Ha telefonato a te* 'he rang *you*' has an emphatic form of the pronoun vs. the unmarked *ti ha telefonato*, but *parla di te* has no counterpart with an unstressed pronoun and therefore is felt to be unmarked and not emphatic. *Ella* is avoided as indirect object, *per lei, a lei*, etc., being preferred to *per ella, ad ella*, etc.

A systematic use is made of the difference between the third person *lui* and the third person reflexive *sè: lo fa per lui* 'he does it for him' vs. *lo fa per sè* 'he does it for himself'; *sè* and *sè stesso* are always objects and cannot be used for the subject: what corresponds to 'he said it himself' is *l'ha detto lui* or *lui stesso*, and not *sè* or *sè stesso*. English and Italian differ in sentences like *guarda dietro a sè* (with *sè* referring to the subject of *guarda*) and *guarda dietro a lui* (with *lui* being different from the subject of *guarda*) which both correspond to 'he looks behind him'.

(d) **Unstressed pronouns** precede the verb (except for the cases discussed below): *ti vedo* 'I see you', *lo compro* 'I buy it', *ti sta scrivendo* 'he is writing to you', *gli parlo* 'I am speaking to him'.

Lo can be a neuter pronoun referring to a whole sentence: *E' arrivato. – Non lo sapevo* 'He has arrived. – I did not know'. It can also be used in constructions like: *Ada è magra? – Sì, lo è* 'Is Ada thin? – Yes she is'; *li credevo intelligenti ma non lo sono* 'I thought they were intelligent but they are not'; *la* can be used neutrally in expressions like *la sa lunga* 'he knows the lot', *se la vede brutta* 'he is in a fix', *ce la fa* 'he can manage', *se la sente* 'he feels up to it', *me la paghi* 'you'll pay me for it', etc.

The choice of the unstressed pronoun may depend on the verb: cf. *pensa a Ugo* 'she is thinking of Ugo', *pensa a lui, lo pensa; pensa al gatto* 'she is thinking of the cat', *pensa a lui* or *ad esso; si è abituata a Ugo* 'she got used to Ugo', *si è abituata a lui*, but no unstressed pronoun comes naturally in the above two examples; *si è abituata al pericolo* 'she got used to the danger', *si è abituata ad esso, ci si è abituata*. We find the expected use of the pronoun in *dà un calcio a Ugo* 'she kicks Ugo', *dà un calcio a lui, gli dà un calcio*; but for *dà un calcio al leggio* 'she kicks the lectern' there is no readily acceptable use of the pronouns, either stressed (*a lui, ad esso*) or unstressed (*gli, ci*).

With *loro* there are three different usages. In the literary language it could precede the verb: *Caron dimonio, con occhi di bragia/loro accennando tutte le raccoglie* 'the demon Charon, with eyes of burning coal, beckons to them and gathers them all in' (Dante, *Inferno* III, 109–110, J. D. Sinclair's translation); in modern Italian it needs to be preceded by at least one verbal element: *dopo aver loro detto* . . . 'after having told them', with *loro* unstressed like *ti* in *dopo averti detto; dopo aver detto loro* . . . which is more frequent but does not fit into the same category as the other unstressed pronouns, as it follows the verb, and so tends to alternate with the fully stressed indirect object pronoun of *dopo aver detto a loro* . . . In colloquial Italian *gli* frequently replaces the unstressed indirect object *loro: gli sto facendo un favore* 'I am doing them a favour' (in line with *ti sto facendo, vi sto facendo*) instead of *sto facendo loro un favore*.

Ne is used for the partitive: *ho molte pesche, ne vuoi?* 'I have a lot of peaches, do you want some?'; it is also used with numbers: *ne vuoi due?* 'do you want two?'. As well as corresponding to 'of it, of them' *ne* may be used for 'about it, about them': *è meglio parlarne* 'we had better talk about it'. In this case it replaces *di* + —; in *ne proviene* 'he comes from there' it replaces *di* or *da* + —, but it cannot be used indiscriminately for any *di* or *da* construction: *è stato ucciso dai nemici* 'he was killed by the enemy' cannot become *ne è stato ucciso; ne è stato colpito* 'he was hit by it' would be expanded into *è stato colpito da questa situazione* 'he was hit by this situation' rather than into *è stato colpito da un proiettile* 'he was hit by a bullet'; in *c'è stato un incendio e l'edificio ne è rimasto distrutto* 'there was a fire in which the building was destroyed', *ne* indicates 'as a consequence' rather than 'by'.

La and *le* are, as we have seen, the polite direct and indirect forms corresponding to *lei: la saluto e le faccio i miei auguri* 'I am sending you my greetings and best wishes'. With a *lei* form of address referring to a man, although an accompanying adjective or past participle is normally masculine (see (a)(iii) above), the unstressed object pronoun is *la: se lei è sicuro di venire, mio fratello può aspettarla alla stazione* 'if you are sure you are coming, my brother can meet you at the station'. If *la* is the object of a compound tense, then the past participle is normally feminine: *ricorda, signor Biffi, che l'ho incontrata l'anno scorso?* 'do you remember, Mr Biffi, that I met you last year?'. With an adjective the agreement *ad sensum* is more common: *la credevo occupato, dottore* 'I thought you were busy, doctor'; but also, more formally, *la credevo occupata, dottore*.

When two unstressed pronouns are used, the indirect object usually precedes, and *mi, ti, si, ci, vi* change before *lo, la, li, le* and *ne* to *me, te, se, ce, ve: me la dà* 'he gives it to me', *te ne parla* 'he talks to you about it' (for more details see chapter VI. 10). *Gli* and *le* change before the same pronouns to *glie* which combines with the pronoun which follows: *glielo do* 'I give it to him (or: to her)', *gliene parlerà* 'he will speak to him (or: to her) about it'.

Unstressed pronouns follow the verb in the cases set out below; except for *loro*, which in spelling always remains separate, they attach themselves to these forms of the verb (which retain their original stress):

(i) the infinitive: *per dirvi* 'to tell you', *senza dirvelo* 'without telling it to you', *per dir(e) loro* 'to tell them'; in the first two cases the final *-e* of the infinitive falls (and any final double consonant of the stem is simplified, as in *condurre* 'to lead': *condurlo*), in the third case truncation is optional. When the infinitive is part of the second person negative imperative, as in *non parlare* 'do not talk', the pronoun usually follows: *non farlo* 'do not do it', but it may also precede: *non lo fare*;

(ii) the gerund: *mostrandogli* 'showing to him', *dicendoglielo* 'saying it to him';

(iii) a past participle standing on its own: *cedutogli* 'having given in to him';

(iv) an imperative in the second person singular or plural, or first person plural: *vattene!* 'go away!' (note the *-tt-* which conforms to the rules of syntactic doubling), *bambini, salutateci* 'children, say good-bye to us', *mandiamolo* 'let us send it'. But if the imperative is in the *lei* and not in the *tu* form, i.e., when the third person singular or plural of the subjunctive is used, the pronoun precedes the verb: *lo guardi pure* vs. *guardalo pure* 'do look at it'. Here is a full table of the imperative (and its negative forms) with pronouns:

compralo 'buy it'; *non comprarlo* or *non lo comprare*

lo compri 'let him buy it' or 'buy it' (with the *lei* form of address); *non lo compri*

compriamolo 'let's buy it'; *non compriamolo* or *non lo compriamo*

compratelo 'buy it' (plural); *non compratelo* or *non lo comprate*

lo comprino 'let them buy it' or 'buy it' (with the *loro* form of address); *non lo comprino*.

(v) in rare cases, in non-colloquial usage, the present participle may also be followed by a (reflexive) pronoun: *la nota riferentesi a questo* 'the note referring to this'.

In constructions of verb + infinitive the direct or indirect object pronoun may go either after the infinitive which governs it, or with the first verb (before or after it, according to the above rules): *lo voglio vedere* or *voglio vederlo* 'I want to see him', *vallo a vedere* or *va a vederlo* 'go and see him'. But there are limitations depending on the syntactic function of the pronoun: a clitic cannot follow the infinitive if it represents its subject: *lo ho sentito gridare* may mean 'I heard him shout' or 'I heard it shouted', but *ho sentito gridarlo* only means 'I heard it shouted'. Cf. the contrast between *lo pregano di ascoltare* 'they ask him to listen' and *pregano di ascoltarlo* 'they ask that he be listened to'. With reflexives, when the clitic goes with the main verb this then takes the auxiliary *essere* (cf. chapter V. 15(l)): *mi sono potuto adattare* or *ho potuto adattarmi* 'I was able to adapt myself', *essendoti dovuto fermare* or *avendo dovuto fermarti* 'as you had to stop', *per essersi voluto impegnare* or *per aver voluto impegnarsi* 'because he chose to commit himself', *si è cominciata a preoccupare* or *ha cominciato a preoccuparsi* 'she started worrying'.

(A) If the infinitive follows a modal (*potere* 'can', *dovere* 'must', *volere* 'will') and some other verbs (like *sapere* 'to know how to', *solere* 'to have the habit of', *cominciare a* 'to begin to', *provare a* 'to try to', etc.) the reflexive clitic may be attached either to the infinitive or to the main verb: *Ugo deve alzarsi* or *Ugo si deve alzare* 'Ugo must get up'.

(B) If the infinitive follows *parere*, *sembrare* 'to seem to', other verbs like *aspirare a* 'to aspire to', or reflexives like *mettersi a* 'to start to', the reflexive clitic can only follow the infinitive: *Ugo pare alzarsi* (and not *si pare alzare*) 'Ugo seems to be getting up'.

(C) If the infinitive follows verbs of perception (*sentire* 'to feel', 'to hear', *vedere* 'to see', etc.) the reflexive clitic referring to the subject of the main verb can only precede it, but note that *Ugo si sente alzare* is more readily interpreted as 'Ugo feels that he is being lifted up' than as 'Ugo feels himself getting up'; the latter (suggesting perhaps that he is getting up under some mysterious compulsion rather than of his own free will) would be rendered by other expressions like *Ugo sente che si sta alzando*, or even, more clumsily, *Ugo si sente alzarsi*, but in any case not by *Ugo sente alzarsi* where the clitic would refer to the subject of the infinitive and this would need to be expressed: *Ugo sente qualcuno alzarsi* 'Ugo hears somebody get up'. If the infinitive is not reflexive, its subject need not be expressed, as in *Ugo sente camminare* 'Ugo hears (somebody) walk', or 'hears footsteps'. With *fare* 'to make' and *lasciare* 'to let', if the subject of the main verb and of the infinitive is the same, we have *Ugo si fa alzare* (but *si costringe ad alzarsi* would be more acceptable) 'Ugo makes himself get up'; otherwise the subject of the infinitive is normally expressed and the clitic must be omitted: *Ugo fa alzare* (not *alzarsi*) *Ada* 'Ugo makes Ada get up' (this can also mean 'Ugo has Ada lifted up') (cf. chapter VI. 11 (a)(iii)).

When there is a preposition between the verb and the infinitive it would seem that only *a* allows the alternative position of the pronoun: *comincio a capirlo* or *lo comincio a capire* 'I am beginning to understand it', but only *cerco di finirlo* 'I am trying to finish it', *spero di trovarlo* 'I hope to find him', *aspetto di vederlo* 'I am waiting to see him'.

If the infinitive depends on *fare* 'make', *lasciare* 'let', the pronoun goes with them and not with the infinitive: *lo faccio liberare* 'I shall have him set free', *glielo faccio mandare* 'I shall have it sent to him'. With verbs of perception like *sentire* 'feel', 'hear', *vedere* 'see', etc., we have: *gliel'ho sentita cantare* 'I heard him sing it', *gliele ho viste scrivere* 'I saw him write them', and, less acceptable, *l'ho sentito cantarla, l'ho visto scriverle* with the object of the infinitive following it and the subject preceding the main verb; one can always avoid this choice and say: *l'ho sentito che la cantava, l'ho visto che le scriveva* (cf. chapter VI. 10).

9 Possessives

		Singular		Plural		
		Masculine	Feminine	Masculine	Feminine	
Singular	1	*mio*	*mia*	*miei*	*mie*	'my, mine'
	2	*tuo*	*tua*	*tuoi*	*tue*	'your, yours'
	3	*suo*	*sua*	*suoi*	*sue*	'his, her, hers'
Plural	1	*nostro*	*nostra*	*nostri*	*nostre*	'our, ours'
	2	*vostro*	*vostra*	*vostri*	*vostre*	'your, yours'
	3	*loro*	*loro*	*loro*	*loro*	'their, theirs'

From possessive adjectives or pronouns in Italian one can gather whether (a) the possessor is first, second or third person (as in English), (b) the possessor is singular or plural (as in English), (c) the thing possessed is masculine or feminine, singular or plural (unlike English), because they agree in gender and number with the noun. English unlike Italian also conveys the gender of the possessor in the third person singular. Example: *il suo gatto* 'his (or: her) cat', *i suoi gatti* 'his (or: her) cats', *il nostro gatto* 'our cat', *i nostri gatti* 'our cats'. If one needs to avoid ambiguity one can use the heavier forms *il gatto di lui*, or *di lei*; also to avoid ambiguity *proprio* can be used instead of *suo* with reference to the subject, as 'own' can be used in English: *Ugo prese le proprie carte* 'Ugo took his (own) papers'. *Proprio* can also be used to emphasize ownership: *il mio proprio, il suo proprio,* etc.

The article is normally used before possessives (as in the above examples): *ho perso il mio accendino, posso usare il tuo?* 'I have lost my lighter, can I use yours?'. Possessives can also be used with the indefinite article, with numbers, and with demonstrative adjectives: *un mio amico* 'a friend of mine', *due tuoi ammiratori* 'two admirers of yours', *questo vostro sbaglio* 'this mistake of yours', *quel suo sorriso* 'that smile of hers'.

The article is not used with the possessive when it accompanies a singular noun, not qualified by suffixes or adjectives, denoting family relationships (*loro* however takes the article): *mia madre* 'my mother', *nostro padre* 'our father', *tuo fratello* 'your brother'; but *il tuo cugino preferito* 'your favourite cousin', *il loro zio* 'their uncle', *le mie cognate* 'my sisters-in-law', *i miei suoceri* 'my parents-in-law', *la sua cuginetta* 'his little cousin'. *Mamma* 'mother', 'mummy', *papà* and *babbo* 'father', 'daddy', *nonna* 'grandmother', *nonno* 'grandfather' are found both with and without the article: *la mia mamma* or *mia mamma, il mio nonno* or *mio nonno,* etc. The article is not used in constructions like *li consideriamo nostri amici* 'we consider them our friends', *l'hai accettata come tua collega?* 'have you accepted her as your colleague?' (see chapter VI. 2(b)(v)).

Note the difference between *questa casa è mia* 'this house is mine' (it is my property), *questa casa è la mia* 'this house is mine' (and not someone else's), and *questa è la mia casa* 'this (and not another) is my house'.

10   Interrogatives and relatives

(a) **Interrogative adjectives** *che* 'what' (invariable), *quale* (plural *quali*) 'which', *quanto (-a, -i, -e)* 'how much, how many'. Examples: *che treno prendi?* 'what train are you catching?', *che dischi avete scelti?* 'what records did you choose?', *quale sedia preferisci?* 'which chair do you prefer?', *quali fiori vuoi?* 'which flowers do you want?', *quanto cioccolato ha comprato?* 'how much chocolate has he bought?', *quante uova hai venduto?* 'how many eggs have you sold?'.

(b) **Interrogative pronouns** *chi* 'who' (invariable), *che, che cosa, cosa* 'what' (invariable) (*cosa,* frowned on by purists, is probably the most common of the three), *quale, quanto* as above. Examples: *chi è arrivato?* 'who has arrived?', *chi hai visto?* 'whom did you see?', *che* *c'è?, che cosa c'è?, cosa c'è?* 'what is the matter?', *che cosa vuoi?* 'what do you want?', *cosa ha detto?* 'what did he say?', *quale hai scelto?* 'which did you choose?', *quanto costa?* 'how much does it cost?'. The subject normally goes at the end (or at the beginning) of the clause and not between the question word and the verb: *quanto costa la sciarpa?* or *la sciarpa quanto costa?* (not *quanto la sciarpa costa?*) 'how much is the scarf?'.

If the question does not include an interrogative word, interrogation is usually conveyed in Italian not by inversion but by intonation, i.e., there is a rising tone on the last stressed word of the sentence. The rising tone remains on the same word even when interrogation is conveyed by inversion: *tua sorella vuol venire?* and *vuol venire tua sorella?* (both with rising tone on *venire*) mean 'does your sister want to come?'. With a rising tone on *sorella* both sentences would mean 'is it your sister who wants to come?'. Note that inversion does not produce *vuole tua sorella venire?*: the postposed subject normally goes at the end of the clause. Similarly: *i conigli hanno mangiato?* 'have the rabbits eaten?', or, with inversion, *hanno mangiato i conigli?*, both with a rising tone on *mangiato* (with a rising tone on *conigli* the latter sentence would mean 'have they eaten the rabbits?'); *puoi farlo?* 'can you do it?'; inversion here would result in *puoi farlo tu?* (with a rising tone on *farlo*), and not in *puoi tu farlo?*; with a rising tone on *tu*, the question corresponds to the statement *tu puoi farlo* rather than *puoi farlo* (see chapter VI. 1 for some notes on intonation and word order).

(c) **Relative pronouns** *che* 'who, whom, which'; *cui* (indirect) is normally used with a preposition: *a cui* (and more rarely *cui* by itself) 'to whom, to which', *da cui* 'from whom, from which', *di cui* 'of whom, of which'. *Che* and *cui* can be replaced by *il quale, la quale, del quale, della quale*, etc., to avoid ambiguities. Examples: *l'uomo che è entrato* 'the man who came in', *la donna che ho visto* 'the woman I saw', *il dolce che hai mangiato* 'the cake you have eaten', *la figlia di Ugo la quale arriverà domani* 'Ugo's daughter who will arrive tomorrow', *l'articolo di cui ti ho parlato* 'the article I spoke to you about', *l'amica con cui sono andata in vacanza* 'the friend I went on holiday with'.

The relative consisting of article + *quale* is more rarely employed than *che*. There would seem to be certain constraints; it is less likely to appear as direct object than as subject: *ecco la ragazza la quale sono venuto a prendere* 'here is the girl I came to collect' is less acceptable than *ecco la ragazza la quale è venuta a prendermi* 'here is the girl who came to collect me'; the relative with *quale* is more likely to introduce an appositive than a restrictive clause: it is acceptable in *ha scritto a un amico il quale l'ha aiutata* 'she wrote to a friend, and he helped her', whereas it would be less so replacing *che* in *ha scritto a un amico che l'ha aiutata* 'she wrote to a friend who helped her'.[5]

Note that relative *quale* without an article means 'such as': *piante quali crescono in montagna* 'plants such as grow in the mountains' vs. *piante le quali crescono in montagna* 'plants which grow in the mountains'.

Instead of *Ugo, la sorella del quale ho visto in montagna* 'Ugo, whose sister I saw in the mountains', one has *Ugo, la cui sorella ho visto in montagna* (not *la sorella di cui* or *la di cui sorella*); similarly *mio nonno, i cui libri ho ereditato* 'my grandfather, whose books I inherited'; here one could say *i libri del quale*, but not *i libri di cui* or *i di cui libri*.

Chi and *quanto* have the additional function of a relative: *chiedilo a chi se ne intende* 'ask someone who knows', *quanto mi dici è interessante* 'what you tell me is interesting'.

Note the following constructions with *che*:

(i) *è partito ieri, il che mi dispiace* 'he left yesterday, which I regret'; *ciò che mi dispiace* could also be used, but *che* on its own in this construction tends to be avoided.

(ii) *ricordo il giorno che sei arrivato* 'I remember the day you arrived', *è arrivato che stavamo ancora mangiando*, 'he arrived while we were still eating', *cantavano che era un piacere* 'they were singing away'; here the use of *che* instead of *in cui*, or *quando*, or *in modo tale che*, etc., is considered grammatically correct. There are many instances in which *che* (alone, or with an indirect personal pronoun, e.g., *che gli*) replaces an indirect relative pronoun (e.g., *a cui*); this has a literary tradition going back to the origins of Italian literature and is very common today in colloquial spoken Italian; as such it is also found in modern novels, particularly in dialogue: *è una povera ragazza che le hanno detto che sono tornato* in which *che le* equals *a cui* 'she is a poor girl who was told I had come back'; *quello era l'unico che gli piacevano i miei quadri*, in which *che gli* equals *a cui* 'he was the only one who liked my pictures' (both examples from Pavese). This construction is normally considered ungrammatical.

(iii) In some of the above examples *che* may be interpreted as a conjunction rather than as a relative pronoun: *è arrivato che stavamo ancora mangiando* might be paraphrased as *è arrivato tanto presto che stavamo ancora mangiando* 'he arrived so early that we were still eating'. Cases of this kind are common in which it is difficult to define the exact force of *che*: *non è arrivato, che io sappia* 'he has not arrived that I know of' or 'he has not arrived as far as I know'; in *vedevo tornare Ugo che era stanco morto* 'I saw Ugo come back dead tired' *che* may be interpreted either as a relative pronoun or as a conjunction with a consecutive value: *(in condizioni tali) che era stanco morto.* In *è lui che cercano* 'it is him they are looking for' *che* may appear to be a relative pronoun, but in *è per lui che si agitano* 'it's him they are getting worked up about' *che* appears to be a conjunction. In expressions like *lui sì che capisce* 'well, *he* understands', *lui no che non può andare* 'he certainly can't go', *che* also seems to be a conjunction. When *che* is a conjunction, it may be omitted after verbs of thinking and believing: *credo (che) sia pronto* 'I believe it's ready', *penso (che) sia stato lui* 'I think it was him', whereas the pronoun *che* is never omitted in modern Italian.

(iv) Colloquial Italian often uses *che* in exclamations: *che bello!* 'how nice!', *che bello che è!* 'how nice it is!', *che antipatico che sei!* 'how nasty you are!', *antipatico che sei!* 'nasty, you are!', *che palazzo!* 'what a building!', *che roba!* 'how awful!', *che vita!* 'what a life!'.

11 Negatives

These are the most common negative words apart from *no* 'no': *non* 'not', *niente, nulla* 'nothing', *mai* 'never', *nessuno* 'no one', 'no (adjective)', *non ... alcuno* 'not ... any', 'no (adjective)', *non ... più* 'no longer', *non ... affatto, non ... per niente* 'not at all', *non ... mica* 'not at all', *neanche, neppure, nemmeno* 'not even', *nè ... nè* 'neither ... nor'.

In a negative sentence in Italian there must always be a negative word before the verb; this may result in sentences with two negatives: *nessuno è venuto*, or *non è venuto nessuno* 'no one came' (note also *è venuto nessuno?* 'did anyone come?'), *niente lo spaventa* or *non lo spaventa niente* 'nothing frightens him', *non vedo niente* 'I do not see anything', *non è successo nulla* 'nothing has happened' (note the masculine agreement), *non ho visto nessuno* 'I did not see anyone', *non hai nessun bisogno* or *alcun bisogno di uscire* 'you have no need to go out', *non è mai venuto* 'he never came', *non è più qui* 'he is no longer here', *non è affatto vero* 'it is not true at all', *non è mica male* 'it's not at all bad' (used mainly on a colloquial level, implying that someone expected what is being denied; in this example the expectation was, modestly perhaps, that something should be bad),[6] *non ne ho neanche uno* 'I haven't got even one', *a me non piace e neanche a lui* 'I don't like it and nor does he', *non lo dico nè a te nè a lui* 'I am not telling you or him'.

Non ... punto, used similarly to *non ... affatto* (and also with *punto* inflected as an adjective) is a Tuscan regionalism: *non ne ho punto* 'I don't have any', *non ho punta sete* 'I'm not at all thirsty'.

Senza may be the antecedent of *niente, nessuno: se ne è andato senza dir niente* 'he went off without saying anything', *è restato senza niente* 'he was left without anything', *è partito senza salutare nessuno* 'he left without saying good-bye to anyone'.

Note the following colloquial usages: *non è niente vero* and *non è vero niente* 'it's not true at all', *oggi niente zucchero* 'no sugar today'.

12 Demonstratives

An earlier system (still used in Tuscan) had three terms, *questo, codesto, quello*, referring respectively to the first person, i.e., the speaker, the second person, i.e., the person addressed, and the third person; *codesto* is now disappearing, and modern Italian has a two-term system: *questo, -a, -i, -e* 'this, these', *quello, -a, -i, -e* 'that, those' (similarly *qui, costì, lì; qua, costà, là* have been reduced to *qui, lì; qua, là* 'here, there'). The adjective *quello* has the same forms as the definite article (see chapter V. 3(a)): *quegli svedesi* 'those Swedes', but *quelli svedesi* 'the Swedish ones' (where *quelli* is the pronoun and *svedesi* the adjective). *Ciò* 'that' refers to a whole concept. Examples: *questo programma è difficile* 'this programme is difficult', *quale preferisci? – Questo* 'which do you prefer? – This one', *quale vuoi? – Quello* 'which do you want? – That one', *quello che* or *ciò che mi hai detto mi ha fatto piacere* 'I was pleased by what you told me', *ciò mi sorprende* 'that surprises me'.

For the indirect object the form *ci* is used: *penso a ciò* 'I am thinking of that': *ci penso*.

Note that (a) *questo* is used rather than *quello* in sentences like *questo non è vero* 'that's not true', *questo è strano* 'that's odd', *questo è ridicolo* 'that's ridiculous', *queste sono balle* 'that's a load of rubbish', etc.; (b) *colui, colei, coloro* 'he, she, they' and *costui, costei, costoro,* with a derogatory meaning 'that individual', etc., are rarely used. Instead of *colui che, colei che, coloro che, quello che,* etc., *chi* is more commonly used as long as there is no need to distinguish the gender: *chi ha l'automobile ci arriva facilmente* 'anyone with a car can get there easily', literally 'he who has a car'; (c) in the literary language *questi* and *quegli* can be used as singulars meaning 'this person', 'that person', or 'the latter', 'the former' (normally as subjects): *considerate Manzoni e Leopardi: questi fu il maggior poeta, quegli il maggior prosatore dell'Ottocento* 'consider Manzoni and Leopardi, the latter was the greatest poet, the former the greatest prose writer of the nineteenth century'. Less

formally one uses *questo . . . quello*. The plural is in any case *questi . . . quelli*;
(d) *quel di* in a geographical context means 'the territory of': *in quel di Como*
'in the territory of Como'.

Stesso and *medesimo* 'same' are usually listed with the demonstratives: *mi
ha dato lo stesso libro* 'he gave me the same book'. *Stesso* can also be used to
reinforce: *mi ha dato il libro stesso* 'he gave me the book itself'. In the
demonstrative sense it usually precedes, and in the reinforcing sense it usually follows the noun. In the latter sense it is not always used in the same way
as the English forms with '-self'; it is used with the force of 'in person, even',
etc., but not to emphasize a term which is in contrast with others: *all'esame
gli studenti erano agitatissimi, e gli insegnanti stessi sembravano innervositi*
corresponds to 'at the exam the students were very nervous, and the
teachers themselves seemed on edge', but the equivalent of the English 'at
the exam the students were very nervous, while the teachers themselves
seemed quite calm' cannot be *mentre gli insegnanti stessi erano calmi* and
would have to be *mentre gli insegnanti invece*, or *gli insegnanti invece*, or *ma
gli insegnanti erano calmi*; 'the car itself was undamaged, but the driver was
hurt' would be rendered with *quanto alla macchina* (not *la macchina
stessa*), *non ha subito danni, ma il guidatore è rimasto ferito*. With the force
of 'as such' *in sè, di per sè* are used: 'the walk itself is not very nice, but the
exercise is good for one' would be rendered with *la passeggiata in sè* (not *la
passeggiata stessa*) *non è molto bella, ma è il moto che fa bene*.

13 Indefinites

We give below examples of the use of indefinite adjectives and pronouns grouped as far as possible according to meaning.

Tutto, tutti 'all', 'every' adjective and pronoun: *ho mangiato tutta
la minestra* 'I have eaten all the soup', *tutti chiedono di te* 'everyone
is asking after you', *li ho visti tutti quanti* 'I saw them all', *sono venuti
tutti e due i ragazzi* 'both boys came'. As well as *tutti e due*, for 'both'
one can also use *entrambi* (*entrambi i ragazzi, entrambe le ragazze*)
and, more rarely, *ambedue* (*ambedue i ragazzi, ambedue le
ragazze*).

Ogni 'every', 'each' invariable adjective, singular only, always
precedes the noun: *mi alzo ogni mattina alle sette* 'I get up every
morning at seven', *bisogna spolverare ogni libro separatamente* 'each
book must be dusted separately', *vado a Roma ogni due settimane* 'I
go to Rome every two weeks', *ogni tanto viene a trovarmi* 'every now
and then he comes to see me'.

Ognuno 'everyone' invariable pronoun, singular only: *ognuno si è comprato questo libro* 'everyone bought this book'.

Ciascuno 'each', 'every' adjective and pronoun, singular only: *ciascuno pensa a sè* 'everyone thinks of himself', *ho fatto un regalo a ciascuna ragazza* 'I gave each girl a present', *ce n'erano tre per ciascuno* 'there were three each'.

Qualche 'some' invariable adjective, singular only, used only with countable nouns (i.e., nouns that can have a plural), always precedes the noun: *mi dai qualche esempio?* 'would you give me some examples?'; *un qualche* corresponds to 'some . . . or other': *si sarà preso un qualche virus* 'he has probably caught some virus or other'. With uncountable nouns *un po' di* is used: *mi dai un po' di latte?* 'would you give me some milk?'.

Pronominally *un poco* can be used: *me ne basta un poco* 'I only need a little', but as the modifier of an adjective *un po'* is normally used: *è un po' dolce* 'it's a bit sweet'. Note also *vuoi un po' di sale?* 'do you want some salt?' and not *un poco di*, but *ne vuoi un altro po'?* or *un altro poco* 'do you want a little more?'. The diminutives *pochino, pochetto, pochettino, pocolino* can replace both *poco* and *po'*. Note the idioms: *è un poco di buono, è una poco di buono* (not *po'*) 'he, she is a bad lot'.

Alcuni 'some' adjective and pronoun, plural only; the singular *alcuno* is only used in negative expressions, see chapter V. 11: *ecco alcune matite* 'here are some pencils', *ne ho visti alcuni* 'I saw some'.

Qualcuno (more rarely *qualcheduno*) 'someone' pronoun, singular only: *è venuto qualcuno a cercarti* 'someone came to look for you';

qualcuno here may be known or not known to the speaker and it may refer to a man or a woman; *è venuto uno* or *è venuta una a cercarti* implies that the speaker does not know the person or is not interested, and so do expressions with the offhand *un tale, una tale, un tizio, una tizia*, etc. *Qualcuno* may also correspond to 'anyone', as in *se viene qualcuno chiamami* 'call me if anyone comes'.

Qualcosa or *qualche cosa* 'something' pronoun, singular only: *vuoi qualcosa da mangiare?* 'do you want something to eat?', *deve essere successo qualcosa* (note the masculine agreement) 'something must have happened', *c'è qualcosa di interessante?* (*di* must be used in these expressions) 'is there anything interesting?'.

Qualunque, qualsiasi 'whatever' invariable adjectives, only with a noun in the singular, if they precede it: *qualunque* or *qualsiasi libro mi interessa* 'any book whatsoever interests me', *dammi un libro qualunque* 'give me any book' (any book at all), *a qualunque tavolo ci si sieda c'è corrente* 'at whatever table one sits there is always a draught', *mi dia un tavolo qualunque* 'give me any table you like'; note the difference in meaning depending on the order. *Qualunque* and *qualsiasi* can go with a plural noun if they follow it: *prendi dei guanti qualsiasi* 'take any old gloves' (or 'buy just ordinary gloves').

Chiunque 'whoever' pronoun, singular only, for people only (for things *qualunque cosa* is used): *chiunque chieda di me, dì che non ci sono* 'whoever asks for me, say I am not in', *chiunque si troverebbe bene qui* 'anyone would like it here', *qualunque cosa ti dicano, non crederci* 'whatever they tell you don't you believe it'.

The forms *checchè* 'whatever' and *chicchessia* 'anyone' are rarely used in modern Italian; they appear in sentences like *checchè ne dica, questo vale di più* 'whatever he may say, this is worth more', *non vuol vedere chicchessia* 'he does not want to see anyone', but the forms *qualunque cosa* 'whatever', *chiunque* (*nessuno* in a negative sentence) 'whoever' are more common.

14 Numerals

We give a list of cardinal and ordinal numbers from which all other numbers can be formed:

(a) Cardinals

1 *uno*, 2 *due*, 3 *tre*, 4 *quattro*, 5 *cinque*, 6 *sei*, 7 *sette*, 8 *otto*, 9 *nove*, 10 *dieci*, 11 *undici*, 12 *dodici*, 13 *tredici*, 14 *quattordici*, 15 *quindici*, 16 *sedici*, 17 *diciassette*, 18 *diciotto*, 19 *diciannove*, 20 *venti*, 21 *ventuno*, 22 *ventidue*, 28 *ventotto*, 30 *trenta*, 31 *trentuno*, 32 *trentadue*, 38 *trentotto*, 40 *quaranta*, 50 *cinquanta*, 60 *sessanta*, 70 *settanta*, 80 *ottanta*, 90 *novanta*, 100 *cento*, 101 *centouno* or *cento e uno*, 108 *cento otto*, 180 *centottanta*, 200 *duecento*, 300 *trecento*, 1000 *mille*, 1001 *mille (e) uno*, 1002 *milledue*, 1003 *milletrè*, 1008 *milleotto*, 1110 *millecentodieci*, 2000 *duemila*, 3000 *tremila*, 1 000 000 *un milione*, 1 000 001 *un milione e uno*, 2 000 000 *due milioni*, 1 000 000 000 *un miliardo*, 2 000 000 000 *due miliardi*.

Italian uses points, not commas, to separate thousands, and commas not points, for decimals.

(b) Ordinals

1st *primo*, 2nd *secondo*, 3rd *terzo*, 4th *quarto*, 5th *quinto*, 6th *sesto*, 7th *settimo*, 8th *ottavo*, 9th *nono*, 10th *decimo*, 11th *undicesimo*, 12th *dodicesimo*, 17th *diciassettesimo*, 21st *ventunesimo*, 23rd *ventitreesimo*.

(i) *uno* has both a masculine and a feminine form (*una*); its morphology is the same as that of the indefinite article, although it is functionally different: *un guanto e uno scialle* 'one glove and one shawl'; the ordinals are adjectives with the regular four endings *-o, -a, -i, -e;*

(ii) there is elision in *ventuno, ventotto*, etc., and in *centottanta* (also *cento ottanta*), rarely in *centouno, cento otto*, and not in *milleotto*; there is also elision of the unstressed vowel before *-esimo* in *undicesimo*, etc. (but no elision when there is a stressed vowel: *ventitreesimo*);

(iii) numbers from *undici* to *sedici* are proparoxytones;

(iv) all cardinal numbers (except of course *uno*) go with plural nouns; this also applies to numbers ending in *uno: ventuno studentesse, ventuno studenti* 'twenty-one students' (avoid *ventuna studentessa* and *ventuno studente*, which are rarely used). But when *uno* is written separately we find both *cento e uno pagine* and *cento e una pagina* '101 pages', *mille e uno persone* and *mille e una persona* '1001 people', cf. the Italian title for the *Arabian Nights, Le mille e una notte*. The elision of *-o* in front of a vowel or single consonant is common: *trentun amici* or *amiche* 'thirty-one friends', *ventun gatti* or *gatte* 'twenty-one cats';

(v) *milione* and *miliardo* are constructed with *di* + plural: *un milione di lire* 'a million lire', but *un milione e duecentomila lire* '1 200 000 lire';

(vi) there are rarer forms: for *duecento* the Tuscanism *dugento*, for *undicesimo* and *dodicesimo* the Latinisms *undecimo* and *duodecimo*; rare in general use, but common to indicate the centuries are *decimoprimo, decimosecondo,* etc., which are also used with names of popes, kings, etc. (in spelling Roman numerals are used): *Luigi XII* (*dodicesimo* or *decimo secondo*), *Giovanni XXIII* (*ventitreesimo* or *ventesimo terzo* or *vigesimo terzo*; also *ventitrè* but note that the cardinal numbers in these designations are limited to familiar usage and are only employed for figures higher than ten)[7];

(vii) the centuries from the thirteenth on are usually called *il Duecento* (= *il secolo tredicesimo*), *il Trecento*, etc. Using figures one normally writes: *il '200, il '300*, etc.;

(viii) in dates the day of the month (except the first: *il primo marzo* '1st March') is indicated by cardinal numbers: *quanti ne abbiamo? – E' il tre* 'what is the date? – It is the third';

(ix) Italians give the expressions *gli anni venti, gli anni trenta*, etc., not only the meaning of 'the Twenties', 'the Thirties', etc., but sometimes also that of the years just before and after 1920, 1930, etc.;

(x) time is indicated as follows (in our examples we use the twelve-hour clock, although the twenty-four-hour one can also be used): *è l'una* 'it's one o'clock', *è mezzanotte* 'it's midnight', *è mezzogiorno* 'it's midday', *è la mezza* 'it's half past twelve', *sono le due*, 'it's two o'clock', *le tre e cinque* 'five past three', *le quattro e un quarto* or *le quattro e quindici* 'a quarter past four', *le cinque e mezzo* or *mezza* or *le cinque e trenta* 'half past five', *le sei e quarantacinque* or *le sei e tre quarti* 'six forty-five', *le sette e cinquantacinque* 'seven fifty-five'. After the half hour one can also say *(sono) le otto meno venti* or *(mancano) venti alle otto* 'it's twenty to eight', *(sono) le nove meno un quarto* or *(manca) un quarto alle nove* 'it's a quarter to nine', etc.;

(xi) *mezzo* is used above as invariable, *mezza* agrees with an implied *ora* 'hour'. Note also the following uses of *mezzo*: *una mezz'ora* 'about half an hour' vs. *mezz'ora* 'half an hour'; *due mezze porzioni di riso* 'two half portions of rice'; *patate mezze sbucciate* 'half-peeled potatoes'; *era mezza morta* 'she was half dead'; in business Italian *mezzo* is sometimes written '$\frac{1}{2}$', even when it does not mean 'half' but 'by means of': *maglietta $\frac{1}{2}$ maniche* (read *mezze maniche*) 'short-sleeved blouse', *spedito a $\frac{1}{2}$ posta* (read *a mezzo posta*) 'sent by post'.

(c) Indefinite numerals

The following are used: *un paio* 'a couple', *una decina* '(about) ten', *una dozzina* 'a dozen' and 'about twelve', *una quindicina* '(about) fifteen', *una ventina* '(about) twenty', etc., *una novantina* '(about) ninety', *un centinaio* '(about) a hundred', *due centinaia* '(about) two hundred', *un migliaio* '(about) a thousand', *due migliaia* '(about) two thousand'. They are all constructed with *di*: *ci sarà stata* or *ci saranno state una ventina di persone* 'there must have been about twenty people'; one can also say *ci saranno state un venti persone*, or *ci saranno state sulle venti persone; c'erano alcune centinaia di studenti* 'there were several hundred students'. Note the difference between *due migliaia di operai* 'about two thousand workers' and *duemila operai* 'two thousand workers'. These indefinite numerals are often used in expressions of age (after the age of thirty): *è sulla trentina* 'she is about thirty', *si avvicina alla quarantina*, 'she is approaching forty'.

15 Verbs

(a) First we set out in full the conjugations of *avere* 'to have', *essere* 'to be', and then of *comprare* 'to buy', *credere* 'to believe', *dormire* 'to sleep', representing the three regular conjugations in *-are, -ere* and

-ire. Some grammars subdivide the *-ere* verbs into two conjugations depending on whether the ending is stressed, as in *temere*, or unstressed, as in *credere*, but in this context this subdivision is not necessary. In the table below, after *avere* and *essere*, the endings of the three conjugations are separated from the stem by a hyphen. As dictionaries give the infinitive forms for verbs, and in regular infinitives the stem is obtained by removing the endings *-are* (1), *-ere* (2), *-ire* (3a and b)[8], this table shows how to conjugate any regular verb found in a dictionary by adding the relevant endings to the stem. Irregular verbs are listed at the end of this section.

Avere

Present	Future	Imperfect	Past historic
ho	avrò	avevo	ebbi
hai	avrai	avevi	avesti
ha	avrà	aveva	ebbe
abbiamo	avremo	avevamo	avemmo
avete	avrete	avevate	aveste
hanno	avranno	avevano	ebbero

Perfect	Future perfect	Pluperfect	Past anterior
ho avuto, etc.	avrò avuto, etc.	avevo avuto, etc.	ebbi avuto, etc.

Present conditional	Past conditional	Present subjunctive	Imperfect subjunctive
avrei	avrei avuto, etc.	abbia	avessi
avresti		abbia	avessi
avrebbe		abbia	avesse
avremmo		abbiamo	avessimo
avreste		abbiate	aveste
avrebbero		abbiano	avessero

Perfect subjunctive	Pluperfect subjunctive	Imperative
abbia avuto, etc.	avessi avuto, etc.	—
		abbi (neg. *non avere*)
		abbia
		abbiamo
		abbiate
		abbiano

Present gerund[9]	Past gerund	Present participle[9]	Past participle	Present infinitive
avendo	*avendo avuto*	*avente*	*avuto, -a, -i, -e*	*avere*

Past infinitive
avere avuto

Essere

Present	Future	Imperfect	Past historic	Perfect	Future perfect
sono	*sarò*	*ero*	*fui*	*sono stato, -a*	*sarò stato, -a*
sei	*sarai*	*eri*	*fosti*	*sei stato, -a*	etc.
è	*sarà*	*era*	*fu*	*è stato, -a*	
siamo	*saremo*	*eravamo*	*fummo*	*siamo stati, -e*	
siete	*sarete*	*eravate*	*foste*	*siete stati, -e*	
sono	*saranno*	*erano*	*furono*	*sono stati, -e*	

Pluperfect	Past anterior	Present conditional	Past conditional
ero stato, -a	*fui stato, -a*	*sarei*	*sarei stato, -a*
etc.	etc.	*saresti*	etc.
		sarebbe	
		saremmo	
		sareste	
		sarebbero	

Present subjunctive	Imperfect subjunctive	Perfect subjunctive	Pluperfect subjunctive
sia	*fossi*	*sia stato, -a*, etc.	*fossi stato, -a*, etc.
sia	*fossi*		
sia	*fosse*		
siamo	*fossimo*		
siate	*foste*		
siano	*fossero*		

Imperative

—

sii (neg. *non essere*)
sia
siamo
siate
siano

Present gerund	Past gerund	Present participle
essendo	*essendo stato, -a, -i, -e*	(*ente*)

Past participle	Present infinitive	Past infinitive
stato, -a, -i, -e	*essere*	*essere stato, -a, -i, -e*

Regular verbs

Present

1	2	3a	3b
compr-o	*cred-o*	*dorm-o*	*fin-isc-o*
-i	*-i*	*-i*	*-isc-i*
-a	*-e*	*-e*	*-isc-e*
-iamo	*-iamo*	*-iamo*	*-iamo*
-ate	*-ete*	*-ite*	*-ite*
-ano	*-ono*	*-ono*	*-isc-ono*

Future

1	2	3
compr-erò	*cred-erò*	*dorm-irò*
-erai	*-erai*	*-irai*
-erà	*-erà*	*-irà*
-eremo	*-eremo*	*-iremo*
-erete	*-erete*	*-irete*
-eranno	*-eranno*	*-iranno*

Imperfect

1	2	3
compr-avo	*cred-evo*	*dorm-ivo*
-avi	*-evi*	*-ivi*
-ava	*-eva*	*-iva*
-avamo	*-evamo*	*-ivamo*
-avate	*-evate*	*-ivate*
-avano	*-evano*	*-ivano*

Past historic

1	2	3
compr-ai	*cred-ei (-etti)*	*dorm-ii*
-asti	*-esti*	*-isti*
-ò	*-è (-ette)*	*-ì*
-ammo	*-emmo*	*-immo*
-aste	*-este*	*-iste*
-arono	*-erono (-ettero)*	*-irono*

Perfect

1	2	3
ho comprato, etc.	*ho creduto,* etc.	*ho dormito,* etc.

Future perfect

1	2	3
avrò comprato, etc.	*avrò creduto,* etc.	*avrò dormito,* etc.

Pluperfect

1	2	3
avevo comprato, etc.	*avevo creduto,* etc.	*avevo dormito,* etc.

Past anterior

1	2	3
ebbi comprato, etc.	*ebbi creduto,* etc.	*ebbi dormito,* etc.

Present conditional

1	2	3
compr-erei	*cred-erei*	*dorm-irei*
-eresti	*-eresti*	*-iresti*
-erebbe	*-erebbe*	*-irebbe*

-eremmo	*-eremmo*	*-iremmo*
-ereste	*-ereste*	*-ireste*
-erebbero	*-erebbero*	*-irebbero*

Past conditional

1	2	3
avrei comprato, etc.	*avrei creduto*, etc.	*avrei dormito*, etc.

Present subjunctive

1	2	3a	3b
compr-i	*cred-a*	*dorm-a*	*fin-isc-a*
-i	*-a*	*-a*	*-isc-a*
-i	*-a*	*-a*	*-isc-a*
-iamo	*-iamo*	*-iamo*	*-iamo*
-iate	*-iate*	*-iate*	*-iate*
-ino	*-ano*	*-ano*	*-isc-ano*

Imperfect subjunctive

1	2	3
compr-assi	*cred-essi*	*dorm-issi*
-assi	*-essi*	*-issi*
-asse	*-esse*	*-isse*
-assimo	*-essimo*	*-issimo*
-aste	*-este*	*-iste*
-assero	*-essero*	*-issero*

Perfect Subjunctive

1	2	3
abbia comprato, etc.	*abbia creduto*, etc.	*abbia dormito*, etc.

Pluperfect subjunctive

1	2	3
avessi comprato, etc.	*avessi creduto*, etc.	*avessi dormito*, etc.

Imperative

1	2
–	–
compr-a (neg. *non comprare*)	cred-i (neg. *non credere*)
-i	-a
-iamo	-iamo
-ate	-ete
-ino	-ano

3a	3b
–	–
dorm-i (neg. *non dormire*)	fin-isc-i (neg. *non finire*)
-a	-isc-a
-iamo	-iamo
-ite	-ite
-ano	-isc-ano

Present gerund

1	2	3
compr-ando	cred-endo	dorm-endo

Past gerund

1	2	3
avendo compr-ato	avendo cred-uto	avendo dorm-ito

Present participle

1	2	3
compr-ante	cred-ente	dorm-ente (dorm-iente)

Past participle

1	2	3
compr-ato	cred-uto	dorm-ito

Present infinitive

1	2	3
compr-are	*cred-ere*	*dorm-ire*

Past infinitive

1	2	3
avere compr-ato	*avere cred-uto*	*avere dorm-ito*

For 3b, past historics in *-etti*, present participles in *-ente, -iente*, see below. Past participles have forms in *-o, -a, -i, -e* like adjectives.

(b) The following forms are stressed on the root (on which syllable of the root depends on the individual verb, e.g., *abit-* [ábit-] 'to live', but *invit-* [invít-] 'to invite'): first, second, third persons singular and third person plural of the present indicative and subjunctive, second person singular of the imperative (also third persons singular and plural, which are the same as in the subjunctive), and some infinitives in *-ere*. In all other cases the stress is on the ending, and the resulting forms are paroxytones apart from the following: (i) first, second, third persons singular of the future, first and third persons singular of the past historic and present conditional, which are oxytones (except for the forms in *-ii*)[10]; (ii) third person plural of the imperfect indicative and subjunctive, and of the past historic, and first person plural of the imperfect subjunctive, which are proparoxytones. When there is *-isc-* it is always stressed.

(c) Inchoative verbs. The verbs of the third conjugation which insert *-isc-* in the singular and in the third person plural of the present indicative and subjunctive and in the imperative are traditionally known as inchoative because in Latin the verb endings *-asco, -esco, -isco* indicated the beginning of an action. The label inchoative may be used even though the infix no longer has this force in Italian. Common inchoative verbs are *agire* 'to act', *capire* 'to understand', *costruire* 'to build', *ferire* 'to wound', *finire* 'to finish', *obbedire* 'to obey', *preferire* 'to prefer', *pulire* 'to clean', *sparire* 'to disappear'. Common *-ire* verbs without the infix are *aprire* 'to open', *coprire* 'to cover', *dormire* 'to sleep', *fuggire* 'to flee', *offrire* 'to offer', *partire* 'to leave', *pentirsi* 'to repent', *seguire* 'to follow', *sentire* 'to feel', *servire* 'to serve', *soffrire* 'to suffer', *vestire* 'to dress'. Some have both forms: *apparire* 'to appear', *applaudire* 'to applaud', *assorbire* 'to absorb', *avvertire* 'to warn', *comparire* 'to appear', *convertire* 'to convert', *cucire* 'to sew', *mentire* 'to lie'; but the forms without -*isc*- are more common.

(d) Verbs in -*iare* which in the first person singular of the present indicative have a stem-final stressed *i*, like *invio* 'I send', have -*ii* only in the second person singular of the present, *tu invii*, but *noi inviamo*, etc. Verbs in -*iare* which in the first person singular of the present indicative have an unstressed *i*, like *macchio* 'I stain', have a single *i* throughout, *tu macchi*, *noi macchiamo*, etc.

(e) First conjugation verbs in -*care* and -*gare* retain throughout the velar sound at the end of the stem: *gioco* 'I play', *giochi, giocherà; pago* 'I pay', *paghi, pagherà*, etc. Verbs in –*ciare*, –*giare* and -*sciare* retain the palatal sound: *comincio* 'I begin', *cominci, comincerà; mangio* 'I eat', *mangi, mangerà; lascio* 'I leave', *lasci, lascerà*, etc. The *i* of the stem is omitted in the spelling if the ending begins with *e* or *i*. Verbs in -*gnare* retain the *i* when it is part of the ending: *sogniamo* 'we dream' is the first person plural of the present indicative and subjunctive, *sogniate* is the second person plural of the present subjunctive, *sognate* is the second person plural of the present indicative.

(f) Second conjugation verbs in -*cere*, -*gere*, -*scere* retain the palatal sound at the end of the stem before *e* or *i*, but if the ending begins with *a* or *o* the preceding sound is a velar: *vinco* 'I win', *vinci, vincono; leggo* 'I read', *leggi, leggono; conosco* 'I know', *conosci, conoscono*; this also applies to the third conjugation verb *fuggire* 'to flee': *fuggo, fuggi, fuggono*. A few -*cere* verbs retain the palatal sound throughout: *cuocere* 'to cook', *giacere* 'to lie', *nuocere* 'to harm', *piacere* 'to please', *tacere* 'to be silent', and so does the third conjugation *cucire* 'to sew'. *Cuocere* and *cucire* have a single palatal throughout (present indicative *cuocio, cuoci, cuoce, cuociamo, cuocete, cuociono*; present subjunctive *cuocia, cuocia, cuocia, cuociamo, cuociate, cuociano*), whereas the other verbs (and those forms of *fare* which have a palatal) alternate single and double palatals according to the following pattern: present indicative:

piaccio, piaci, piace, piacciamo, piacete, piacciono; present subjunctive: *piaccia, piaccia, piaccia, piacciamo, piacciate, piacciano*. Note however that the following forms are equally common for *nuocere* and *tacere*: present indicative *nuociamo, taciamo*, and present subjunctive *nuociamo, nuociate, taciamo, taciate; giacere* may have the form *giaciate* in the present subjunctive. Similarly in *dovere* 'must' and *sapere* 'to know' we find double consonants in the present indicative *dobbiamo, sappiamo*, and *debbono* (alongside *devono*), and in the subjunctive *debba* (alongside *deva*), *dobbiamo, dobbiate, debbano* (alongside *devano*), and *sappia, sappiamo, sappiate, sappiano*. Note that for *dovere*, as for *avere*, the double consonant is *b* and the single one is *v*.

(g) Some verbs (which we list with the irregulars) introduce a *g* between the stem and the ending (in *trarre* 'to draw' a double *gg: traggo*), in the first person singular and in the third person plural of the present indicative, in the first, second, third persons singular and third person plural of the present subjunctive, and in the third persons singular and plural of the imperative. The other persons in these tenses have the stem of the present (which may or may not be the same as the stem of the infinitive) without the *g: porre* 'to place': *pongo, poni, pone, poniamo, ponete, pongono*. A *gl* at the end of the stem becomes *l* in front of the *g: togliere* 'to take off': *tolgo*. The main verbs which introduce this *g* are: *cogliere* 'to pick', *dolere* 'to ache', *porre* 'to place', *rimanere* 'to remain', *salire* 'to go up', *scegliere* 'to choose', *sciogliere* 'to melt', *tenere* 'to hold', *togliere* 'to take off', *trarre* 'to draw', *valere* 'to be worth', *venire* 'to come', and their compounds.

(h) Verbs in *-rere* and *-rire*. Owing to the Tuscan development of [rj]>[j] we have the following present indicatives and subjunctives: *morire* 'to die', indicative *muoio, muori, muore, muoiamo* or *moriamo, morite, muoiono*; subjunctive *muoia, muoia, muoia, muoiamo* or *moriamo, muoiate* or *moriate, muoiano* (for the movable diphthongs see (i) below); *parere* 'to seem', indicative *paio, pari, pare, paiamo* or *pariamo, parete, paiono*; subjunctive *paia, paia, paia, paiamo* or *pariamo, paiate* or *pariate, paiano*.

(i) Movable diphthongs. In some present tenses the diphthong *ie* alternates with the simple vowel *e* and the diphthong *uo* with the simple vowel *o*. This has a historical reason in that stressed Latin short *e* and short *o* in a free syllable diphthongized, whereas vowels in a checked syllable or unstressed vowels did not (see chapter III, p. 46); cf. *vengo* 'I come', *voglio* 'I want': no diphthong because the syllable is checked; *viene, vuole*: with a diphthong because there is a stressed vowel in a free syllable; *venite, volete*: no diphthong because the vowel is unstressed. In many verbs this distinction has been eliminated by analogy: *nego* 'I deny', *neghi, nega, neghiamo, negate, negano; suono* 'I play', *suoni, suona, suoniamo, suonate, suonano* (the forms *soniamo, sonate* are disappearing).

This is the present indicative with a movable diphthong of *sedere* 'to sit': *siedo, siedi, siede, sediamo, sedete, siedono*. The other forms with the diphthong are: all persons of the future (*siederò*, etc.), conditional (*siederei*, etc.), the first, second, third persons singular and third person plural of the present subjunctive (*sieda*, etc.), and the second and third persons singular and third person plural of the imperative (*siedi, sieda, siedano*). The same applies to its compound *possedere* 'to possess', to *commuovere* 'to move' (emotionally) and *promuovere* 'to promote' (but not to *muovere* 'to move' which, like *suonare* 'to ring', has generalized the diphthong). *Morire* 'to die' does not have the diphthong in the future and the conditional.

A different pattern is followed by *tenere* 'to hold'; present indicative: *tengo, tieni, tiene, teniamo, tenete, tengono*; the other form with the diphthong is the second person singular of the imperative: *tieni*. The same applies to the compounds of *tenere (appartenere* 'to belong', *astenersi* 'to abstain', *contenere* 'to contain', *mantenere* 'to keep', *ottenere* 'to obtain', *ritenere* 'to maintain', *sostenere* 'to uphold', *trattenere* 'to withold'), to *venire* 'to come' and its compounds (*avvenire* 'to happen', *convenire* 'to be convenient', *intervenire* 'to intervene', *pervenire* 'to reach', *prevenire* 'to prevent', *rinvenire* 'to find', *svenire* 'to faint'), and to *potere* 'to be able', *volere* 'to want', *dolere* 'to ache', *solere* 'to be used to'. Any other irregularities of these verbs are described in other sections.

(j) Past historic in *-etti*. The alternative forms in the second conjugation *temetti* 'I feared' for *temei, temette* for *temè, temettero* for *temerono*, are avoided if the stem of the verb ends in *t*: *potei* 'I was able' is preferred to *potetti*.

(k) Present participles in *-ente* and *-iente*. *Dormire* 'to sleep' has alternative forms *dormente* and *dormiente*. Other verbs have a present participle only in *-ente*, like *fuggente* 'fleeing', *partente* 'leaving', *seguente* 'following', *uscente* 'going out'; others have a form in -*iente*: *esordiente* 'starting', *nutriente* 'nourishing', *saliente* 'salient', *ubbidiente* 'obedient', *veniente* 'coming'. Some of these forms are used only as adjectives or nouns. *Avere* has a rarely used participle *avente,* as in *gli aventi diritto* 'those entitled', and an alternative form *abbiente* which is used as an adjective or noun: *gli abbienti* 'the well off'.

(l) The auxiliary. As a rule transitives take the auxiliary *avere,* intransitives *essere.* Here is a list of common verbs which take the auxiliary *essere: accadere* 'to happen', *andare* 'to go', *arrivare* 'to arrive', *bastare* 'to be enough', *bisognare* 'to be necessary', *cadere* 'to fall', *comparire* 'to appear', *costare* 'to cost', *dipendere* 'to depend', *diventare* 'to become', *entrare* 'to enter', *essere* 'to be', *morire* 'to die', *nascere* 'to be born', *parere* 'to seem', *partire* 'to leave', *piacere* 'to please', *restare* 'to remain', *rimanere* 'to remain', *riuscire* 'to succeed', *scappare* 'to escape', *sembrare* 'to seem', *sparire* 'to disappear', *spiacere* 'to displease', *stare* 'to stay', *succedere* 'to happen', *uscire* 'to go out', *venire* 'to come'.

Impersonal verbs normally take the auxiliary *essere: è capitato, è successo* 'it happened', but impersonal verbs referring to the weather take either auxiliary: *è piovuto* or *ha piovuto* 'it rained', *era nevicato* or *aveva nevicato* 'it had snowed'.

So-called reflexive or pronominal verbs (i.e., those with a reflexive pronoun) take the auxiliary *essere: mi sono sbagliato* 'I made a mistake', *si è stancato* 'he got tired', *si è lavato le mani* 'he washed his hands', *si sono scritti* 'they wrote to each other'. So we have *si è messo la matita in tasca,* but *ha messo la matita in tasca* 'he put the pencil in his pocket'; *si è scritto un appunto* but *ha scritto un appunto* 'he wrote a note'; *si sono mangiati la torta* but *hanno mangiato la torta* 'they ate the cake'.

If a verb taking the auxiliary *essere* is constructed with *dovere* 'must', *potere* 'can', *volere* 'will', these three verbs in a compound tense usually take the auxiliary *essere: è dovuto partire* or *ha dovuto partire* 'he had to leave', *non è potuto arrivare* or *non ha potuto arrivare* 'he could not arrive', *è voluto venire* or *ha voluto venire* 'he wanted to come'.

In a construction with verb + infinitive, if the infinitive is a reflexive and the reflexive pronoun is attached to the main verb (cf. chapter V. 8(d)), the latter takes the auxiliary *essere: si è cominciato a spostare* or *ha cominciato a spostarsi* 'it started moving' (with a non-reflexive pronoun the auxiliary, of course, does not change: *lo ha cominciato a spostare* or *ha cominciato a spostarlo* 'he started moving it'), *si è dovuto portare la valigia alla stazione* or *ha dovuto portarsi la valigia alla stazione* 'he had to take his case to the station'; *se l'è potuto mangiare* or *ha potuto mangiarselo* 'he was able to eat it'; *se n'è voluto andare* or *ha voluto andarsene* 'he wanted to go away'. In constructions with a modal + a reflexive infinitive, the modal tends to take the auxiliary *essere* only when the reflexive pronoun goes with the modal itself: *è voluto andarsene* is avoided.

Note the past infinitive in *deve essersi portato la valigia alla stazione* 'he must have taken his case to the station', indicating probability (*si è dovuto portare la valigia alla stazione* cannot indicate probability). With non-reflexives too there is the same difference between *può essere partito* 'he may have left' and *è* or *ha potuto partire* 'he was able to leave'; *deve essere sceso* 'he must have gone down' and *è* or *ha dovuto scendere* 'he had to go down'.

Some verbs take the auxiliary *avere* when used (i) transitively and the auxiliary *essere* when used (ii) intransitively: *aumentare* (i) *quel negoziante ha aumentato il prezzo* 'that shopkeeper has put up the price', (ii) *gli aranci sono aumentati di prezzo* 'oranges have gone up in price'; *avanzare* (i) *ha avanzato un'ipotesi interessante* 'he put forward an interesting hypothesis', (ii) *la marea è avanzata fino alle capanne* 'the tide rose as far as the huts'; *cessare* (i) *ha cessato i versamenti* 'he stopped the payments', (ii) *il vento è cessato* 'the wind stopped'; *cominciare* (i) *ho cominciato il mio libro* 'I have started my book', (ii) *lo spettacolo è cominciato* 'the show has begun'; *continuare* (i) *ha continuato il lavoro* 'he went on with his work', (ii) *è continuato il lavoro* 'the work went on'; *diminuire* (i) *mi hanno diminuito lo stipendio* 'they have lowered my salary', (ii) *la febbre gli è diminuita* 'his temperature has gone down'; *esplodere* (i) *ha esploso una raffica di mitra* 'he fired a volley with his machine gun', (ii) *è esplosa una bomba* 'a bomb exploded'; *finire* (i) *hanno finito le pulizie* 'they have finished doing the cleaning', (ii) *la commedia è finita alle dieci* 'the play ended at ten'; *guarire* (i) *il dottore l'ha guarito in tre giorni* 'the doctor cured him in three days', (ii) *è guarito due mesi fa* 'he recovered two months ago'; *invecchiare* (i) *la malattia mi ha invecchiato* 'the illness aged me', (ii) *è invecchiato da un momento all'altro* 'he got old very suddenly'; *migliorare* (i) *ha migliorato la sua situazione* 'he improved his position', (ii) *la sua situazione è migliorata* 'his position has improved'; *passare* (i) *mi ha passato il suo libro* 'he passed his book to me', (ii) *è passato un anno* 'a year has passed'; *salire* (i) *ha salito le scale* 'he went up the stairs', (ii) *è salito in fretta* 'he went up in a hurry'; *scendere* (i) *ha sceso le scale* 'he went down the stairs', (ii) *è sceso in fretta* 'he went down in a hurry'; *seguire* (i) *ha seguito la ragazza* 'he followed the girl', (ii) *è seguito un discorso* 'a speech followed'; *servire* (i) *ha servito il partito* 'he served the party', (ii) *è servito al partito* 'it was useful to the party'; *sfilare* (i) *ti ha sfilato il portafoglio dalla tasca* 'he slipped your wallet from your pocket', (ii) *sono sfilati in corteo* 'they filed past in a procession'; *terminare* (i) *ha terminato il suo racconto* 'he ended his story', (ii) *la guerra è terminata da due anni* 'the war ended two years ago'; *vivere* (i) *ha vissuto dei brutti momenti* 'he went through some bád moments', (ii) *quando è vissuto il Crivelli?* 'when did Crivelli live?'.

Convenire with the meaning 'to agree' takes *avere*: *hanno convenuto che era meglio* 'they agreed it was better', otherwise it takes *essere*: *erano convenuti in piazza* 'they had gathered in the square', *non gli è convenuto accettare* 'it wasn't in his interest to accept'. *Correre* 'to run' is found intransitively with both auxiliaries: *essere* is used with reference to the direction or goal, as in *è corso via* 'he ran away', *è corso a casa* 'he ran home', but *ha corso tanto* 'he ran a lot', *ha corso due chilometri* 'he ran two kilometres', *quando ha corso deve riposarsi* 'when he has been running he has to rest'; with objects like *rischio, pericolo* the auxiliary is *avere*: *non abbiamo corso nessun rischio* 'we ran no risk'. *Durare* with *avere* indicates durability, *queste scarpe hanno durato molto* 'these shoes have lasted a long time', and with *essere* duration, *la commedia è durata due ore* 'the play lasted two hours'. *Mancare* with the meaning 'to be lacking', 'to fail', 'to be missing' takes the auxiliary *essere*: *gli è mancato il coraggio* 'his courage failed him', *è mancato all'appello* 'he was not present at roll-call'; with the meaning 'to lack', 'to neglect' it takes *avere*: *ha mancato di coraggio* 'he lacked courage', *ha mancato di parola* 'he didn't keep his word', *ha mancato ai suoi doveri* 'he neglected his duties', *ha mancato all'appuntamento* 'he missed his appointment'. *Procedere* with the meaning 'to progress' takes the auxiliary *essere*: *è proceduto notevolmente* 'he has progressed considerably'; with the meaning 'to behave' it takes *avere*: *ha proceduto da persona onesta* 'he acted honestly'. *Appartenere* takes either auxiliary: *questo libro ha* or *è appartenuto a Ugo* 'this book belonged to Ugo'.

(m) The uses of the imperfect, perfect and past historic will be discussed in chapter VI. 12. Here are some notes on other tenses.

The present is often used in Italian for imminent action where English uses the future: *resto a casa nel pomeriggio* 'I'll stay at home in the afternoon', *vengo subito* 'I'll come at once'. When the time is defined the present may also be used for a future action: *parto domani* 'I am leaving tomorrow', *fra un anno mi trasferisco a Milano* 'in a year's time I shall move to Milan'.

There are usages in which a modal appears in English but not in Italian: 'from the window you can see the mountains': *dalla finestra si vedono le montagne*; this does not apply only to the present: in the same example we can have 'one could see': *si vedevano*, 'one will be able to see': *si vedranno*.

The future and future perfect are often used to express scepticism, possibility or probability: *mi dici che è intelligente; sarà* 'you tell me he is intelligent; maybe'; *suonano; sarà Ugo* 'there is the bell; it must be Ugo'; *hai idea dove siano? – Saranno tornati a casa* 'have you any idea where they are? – They have probably gone home'.

The past anterior is used in literary Italian as an antecedent to the past historic, where more colloquial Italian uses the pluperfect as an antecedent to the perfect after *quando, dopo che, appena,* etc.: *quando fu arrivato in fondo alla strada rallentò il passo* 'when he got to the end of the street he slowed down', *dopo che lo ebbero visto telefonarono alla polizia* 'after they had seen him they rang the police', *appena furono arrivati scrissero a casa* 'as soon as they had arrived they wrote home'. When a habitual action is being described the pluperfect is used: *quando aveva finito di mangiare andava sempre a riposare* 'when he had finished eating he always rested'.

The past participle is normally passive, but in a few cases it may also have an active value: *ammirato* may mean 'admiring' as in *restai ammirato* 'I was struck with admiration', *con aria ammirata* 'with an admiring look'; *deciso* may be someone 'decided' not someone who has been 'convinced'; *saputo* may mean 'knowing': *con tono saputo* 'with a knowing tone'; *bevuto* may mean, dialectally or jocularly, 'drunk', as in *è un po' bevuto* 'he is a bit drunk'.

(n) The present gerund refers to time contemporary to that of the main clause; the past gerund to time previous to that of the main clause; the present gerund may however be anterior and not simultaneous to a future of the main clause: *se ne andò sbattendo la porta* 'he went out slamming the door', *avendo aspettato due ore gli la-*

sciammo un biglietto 'after waiting two hours we left him a note', *studiando molto quest'estate l'anno prossimo potrai far l'esame* 'if you work a lot this summer you can take the exam next year'.

The subject of the gerund is normally the same as that of the main clause except in cases where a different subject is specified: *essendo malato l'insegnante la lezione fu sospesa* 'as the teacher was ill the lesson was cancelled', *essendo finito il ballo tornarono a casa* 'when the dance was over they went home', *avendo scritto due romanzi i soldi non gli mancano* 'as he has written two novels he is not short of money', and in the case of proverbs: *l'appetito vien mangiando* 'the more you have the more you want'. More commonly however in the case of different subjects a subordinate clause is found: *lo abbiamo visto che attraversava la strada* 'we saw him crossing the road'; *lo abbiamo visto attraversando la strada* means 'we saw him as we crossed the road'; *la guardavo mentre scriveva la cartolina* 'I watched her writing the card'; *la guardavo scrivendo la cartolina* means 'I watched her as I wrote the card'.

The gerund cannot have the adjectival function of the present participle: *piangendo non mi commuovi* 'your crying will not move me' but *il salice piangente* 'the weeping willow'; *sorridendo ottiene tutto quello che vuole* 'she gets all she wants by smiling' but *mi guardava con un'espressione sorridente* 'she was looking at me smilingly'. The gerund may be used with *stare* as a duration form, although it is far less common than the equivalent in English: *sto mangiando* 'I am eating', *stava lavorando quando entrai* 'he was working when I came in', *starà facendo la spesa* 'she is probably out shopping'. This construction is not possible with any past tense except the imperfect: to 'I have been reading all night' corresponds *ho letto tutta la notte* or *sono stato tutta la notte a leggere*, etc., but not *sono stato leggendo tutta la notte*; with this construction the passive too is avoided and is replaced either by a *si* construction or by the active: 'the grass is being cut' corresponds not to *l'erba sta essendo tagliata* but to *si sta tagliando l'erba* or *stanno tagliando l'erba*.

Andare and *venire* + gerund suggest a repetition of action: *va dicendo che sei stata licenziata* 'he goes round saying you were sacked', *negli ultimi anni è venuto pubblicando importanti contributi sull'alienazione* 'in the last few years he has been publishing important works on alienation'.

(o) The infinitive can be used as a noun: *lavorare stanca* 'it's tiring to work'. It can be used with a variety of values: (i) *averne!* 'if only one had plenty!', *riuscirci!* 'if only one could make it!'; (ii) *pensare che erano qui ieri!* 'to think that they were here yesterday'; (iii) *scivolare e rompersi una gamba è un momento* 'it's only too easy to slip and break one's leg'; (iv) *venire, viene* 'he's coming all right'; it can be preceded by *per: per accettare, accetta* 'he's accepting all right'; (v) *che fare?* 'what's to be done?', *che dire?* 'what can one say?'; (vi) *i quattrini? Spenderli!* 'money? Spend it!'; (vii) the infinitive can also have a use close to that of the imperative: *circolare!* 'pass along please', *provare per credere* 'it has to be tried to be believed'.

(p) Passive form. Transitive verbs can be changed from active to passive by the use of the auxiliary *essere* with the past participle, as follows: *Ugo ha corretto le bozze* 'Ugo has corrected the proofs', *le bozze sono state corrette da Ugo* 'the proofs have been corrected by Ugo'. The passive is however less commonly used in Italian than in English, the *si* construction being preferred: *Ada non si è vista* is more common than *Ada non è stata vista* 'Ada hasn't been seen'; even when one wants to put the object of a verb at the beginning of a sentence one normally uses an inverted active construction instead of a passive: *gli avanzi li mangerà il gatto* rather than *gli avanzi saranno mangiati dal gatto* 'the scraps will be eaten by the cat'.

Most commonly the passive is used when the agent is not expressed: *è stato derubato sull'autobus* 'he was robbed on the bus', *è stato eletto presidente* 'he was elected president', *è stato ucciso in battaglia* 'he was killed in battle'. The passive is preferred when the active would make the agent at the beginning of the sentence into the theme of the statement: *purtroppo questo quadro è stato rovinato dall'umidità* 'unfortunately this picture has been spoilt by damp' is the normal sentence when we want to talk about the picture, whereas in *purtroppo l'umidità ha rovinato questo quadro* 'unfortunately damp has spoilt this picture' we would be talking primarily about the damp (see the distinction between theme and rheme in chapter VI. 1).

In some cases the verbs *venire* (in its simple tenses) and *andare* can replace *essere*. *Venire* indicates action: *la finestra viene chiusa* 'the window is being shut'; *la finestra è chiusa* is the regular passive of *chiude la finestra*, but it is more spontaneously interpreted as copula + adjective: 'the window is shut'. This also applies to *la finestra era chiusa*, but not to *la finestra fu chiusa* which is interpreted as a passive.

Andare is less widely used but it is found with verbs like *perdere, disperdere, smarrire* 'to lose': *il pacco è andato smarrito* 'the parcel went astray'. Except in these cases, *andare* introduces an element of obligation: *questo va finito per domani* 'this must be finished by tomorrow', *questo film va visto senz'altro* 'this film is a must', *va fatto così* 'this is how it should be done'. Note also the use of *rimanere*: *è rimasto ferito nell'incidente* 'he was injured in the accident'.

In Italian only the direct object of a verb can become the subject of a passive construction, so to English sentences like 'he was given a present', 'I was taught Sanskrit' correspond *gli è stato fatto un regalo, mi è stato insegnato il sanscrito.*

In constructions with *fare, lasciare* + infinitive, Italian, unlike English, prefers not to passivize the infinitive: *si è lasciato convincere* 'he let himself be persuaded', *gli dispiaceva essersi lasciato convincere* 'he was sorry he had let himself be persuaded', *è stato fatto visitare da un dottore* 'a doctor was called in to see him'.

(q) **Irregular verbs**　We give a list of common irregular verbs preceded by a few observations.

(i) Irregularities are mostly found in the past historic and past participle of second conjugation verbs. The verb *prendere* 'to take' for instance in the past historic has three 'strong' forms (i.e., forms with stress on the stem) *presi, prese, presero* and three 'weak' forms (i.e., forms with the stress on the ending) *prendesti, prendemmo, prendeste*. This alternation of strong and weak forms originated in the Vulgar Latin development of verbs like *nocere* where three persons, *nòqui, nòquit, nòquerunt* kept the velar sounds (Italian *nocqui, nocque, nocquero*) and three, *noquìsti, noquèmus, noquìstis*, lost the pretonic *u* and therefore palatalized the velar, thus acquiring the same stem as the infinitive (Italian *nocesti, nocemmo, noceste*). All verbs which have a strong past historic retain weak forms in the second person singular and plural and in the first person plural, except *dare, stare* and *essere* which have strong forms throughout.

The strong past historics mainly go back to three kinds of Latin perfects: the sigmatic ones, i.e., with an *s*: *accesi* 'I lit', *decisi* 'I decided', *presi* 'I took', *risi* 'I laughed', *vinsi* 'I won', *dissi* 'I said', *scossi* 'I shook'; the apophonic ones, i.e., with a change in the stem vowel: *feci* 'I did' vs. *fare, vidi* 'I saw' vs. *vedere*; those in *-ui*, cf. *nocqui* quoted above: *giacqui* 'I lay', *piacqui* 'I was liked'; note that the *-u-* of Vulgar Latin *-ui* causes the doubling of the preceding consonant and it usually falls unless preceded by a velar: *caddi* 'I fell'<*cadui* (Classical Latin *cecidi*); *ebbi* 'I had'<*habui; ruppi* 'I broke'<*rupui* (Classical Latin *rupi*); *seppi* 'I knew'<*sepui* (Classical Latin *sapivi*); *tenni* 'I kept'<*tenui; venni* 'I came'<*venui* (Classical Latin *veni*); *volli* 'I wanted'<*volui*.

Strong past participles can also be sigmatic: *acceso* 'lit', *deciso* 'decided', *mosso* 'moved', *preso* 'taken', *riso* 'laughed', *scosso* 'shaken'; or end in *-to*: *assolto* 'absolved', *detto* 'said', *letto* 'read', *risposto* 'answered', *scritto* 'written', *vinto* 'won', *visto* 'seen'.

Other common irregularities are historically caused by the fall of a vowel (syncope): *andrò* 'I will go' for *anderò, andrei* 'I would go' for *anderei;* or by syncope and assimilation: *verrò* 'I will come' for *venirò, porre* 'to put' for *ponere, terrò* 'I will keep' for *tenerò, vorrò* 'I will want' for *volerò* (*volerò* is in fact the future of *volare* 'to fly').

In the following list only the irregular forms are given. For tenses which have the same irregularities throughout and also for past historics which follow the pattern of strong and weak forms described above only the first person is given. As the future and conditional always have the same stem, where they are irregular only the future is given. The present subjunctive is only given when its form is not based on the present indicative.

We indicate the first person singular in *-go* for the present indicative when it is not predictable from the infinitive (the only persons formed in the same way are the third plural of the present indicative, and the first, second, third singular and third plural of the present subjunctive, as stated above in (g)).

Some verbs, like *dire* 'to say', *porre* 'to place', use one stem (*dir-, porr-*) in the infinitive, future and conditional, and a different stem (*dic-, pon-*) in the rest of the conjugation; they are listed under the infinitive, but the different stem is in each case indicated; they are all of the second conjugation, so we do not state this in the list.

All irregularities concerning the movable diphthong are discussed above in (i).

(ii) The following abbreviations are used: PI=present indicative, F=future, II=imperfect indicative, PH=past historic, PS=present subjunctive, IS=imperfect subjunctive, I=imperative, PP=past participle, G=gerund, MD=movable diphthong (see (i) above).

In impersonal verbs the third person instead of the first is given. When there are alternative forms, the one which appears to us most advisable for a foreign student to use is given first, and then the others are added in brackets.

accadere 'to happen', F *accadrà*, PH *accadde*
accendere 'to light', PH *accesi*, PP *acceso*
accludere 'to enclose', PH *acclusi*, PP *accluso*
accogliere 'to welcome', PI *accolgo*, PH *accolsi*, PP *accolto*
accorgersi 'to notice', PH *mi accorsi*, PP *accorto*
affliggere 'to afflict', PH *afflissi*, PP *afflitto*
aggiungere 'to add', PH *aggiunsi*, PP *aggiunto*
alludere 'to allude', PH *allusi*, PP *alluso*
ammettere 'to admit', PH *ammisi*, PP *ammesso*
andare 'to go', PI *vado, vai, va, andiamo, andate, vanno*, F *andrò*,
    PS *vada, vada, vada, andiamo, andiate, vadano*, I *va (vai, va')*,
    andate
apparire 'to appear', PI *appaio (apparisco)*, PH *apparvi (apparii,*
    apparsi), PP *apparso*
appartenere 'to belong', PI *appartengo*, F *apparterrò*, PH *appartenni*
    (MD)
appendere 'to hang', PH *appesi*, PP *appeso*
apprendere 'to learn', PH *appresi*, PP *appreso*
aprire 'to open', PH *aprii (apersi)*, PP *aperto*
assalire 'to assault', PI *assalgo (assalisco)*, PH *assalii (assalsi)*
assistere 'to assist', PP *assistito*
assolvere 'to absolve', PH *assolsi (assolvei, assolvetti)*, PP *assolto*
assumere 'to engage', PH *assunsi*, PP *assunto*
attendere 'to wait', PH *attesi*, PP *atteso*
avere 'to have', PI *ho, hai, ha, abbiamo, avete, hanno*, F *avrò*, PH
    ebbi, PS *abbia*, I *abbi*
avvenire 'to happen', PI *avviene, avvengono* PH *avvenne* (MD)
avvolgere 'to wrap', PH *avvolsi*, PP *avvolto*
bere 'to drink' (stem *bev-*), F *berrò*, PH *bevvi*
cadere 'to fall', F *cadrò*, PH *caddi*
chiedere 'to ask', PH *chiesi*, PP *chiesto*
chiudere 'to shut', PH *chiusi*, PP *chiuso*
cogliere 'to pick', PI *colgo*, PH *colsi*, PP *colto*
comparire 'to appear', PI *compaio (comparisco)*, PH *comparvi (com-*
    parii, comparsi), PP *comparso*
comprendere 'to understand', PH *compresi*, PP *compreso*
concedere 'to concede', PH *concessi (concedei, concedetti)*, PP *con-*
    cesso (conceduto)
concludere 'to conclude', PH *conclusi*, PP *concluso*

condurre 'to lead' (stem *conduc-*), PH *condussi*, PP *condotto*

confondere 'to confuse', PH *confusi*, PP *confuso*

conoscere 'to know', PH *conobbi*

convincere 'to convince', PH *convinsi*, PP *convinto*

coprire 'to cover', PH *coprii (copersi)*, PP *coperto*

correggere 'to correct', PH *corressi*, PP *corretto*

correre 'to run', PH *corsi*, PP *corso*

costringere 'to force', PH *costrinsi*, PP *costretto*

crescere 'to grow', PH *crebbi*

cuocere 'to cook', PH *cossi*, PP *cotto*

dare 'to give', PI *do, dai, dà, diamo, date, danno*, F *darò*, PH *diedi* or
   detti, desti, diede or *dette, demmo, deste, diedero* or *dettero*, PS *dia*,
   IS *dessi*, I *dà (dai, da')*

decidere 'to decide', PH *decisi*, PP *deciso*

dedurre 'to deduce' (stem *deduc-*), PH *dedussi*, PP *dedotto*

deludere 'to disappoint', PH *delusi*, PP *deluso*

descrivere 'to describe', PH *descrissi*, PP *descritto*

difendere 'to defend', PH *difesi*, PP *difeso*

diffondere 'to spread', PH *diffusi*, PP *diffuso*

dipendere 'to depend', PH *dipesi*, PP *dipeso*

dipingere 'to paint', PH *dipinsi*, PP *dipinto*

dire 'to say' (stem *dic-*), PH *dissi*, I *dì (di')*, PP *detto*

dirigere 'to direct', PH *diressi*, PP *diretto*

discutere 'to discuss', PH *discussi*, PP *discusso*

disfare 'to undo' (stem *disfac-*), PI *disfo* or *disfaccio*, F *disferò* or
   disfarò, II *disfavo* or *disfacevo*, PH *disfeci*, PP *disfatto*, G *dis-
   facendo* or *disfando*

dispiacere 'to displease', PI *dispiaccio*, PH *dispiacqui*

disporre 'to dispose' (stem *dispon-*), PI *dispongo*, PH *disposi*, PP
   disposto

distendere 'to stretch out', PH *distesi*, PP *disteso*

distinguere 'to distinguish', PH *distinsi*, PP *distinto*

distrarre 'to distract' (stem *distra-*), PI *distraggo*, PH *distrassi*, PP
   distratto

distruggere 'to destroy', PH *distrussi*, PP *distrutto*

dividere 'to divide', PH *divisi*, PP *diviso*

dolere 'to ache', PI *dolgo*, F *dorrò*, PH *dolsi*

dovere 'must', PI *devo (debbo), devi, deve, dobbiamo, dovete, devono
   (debbono)*, F *dovrò*

eleggere 'to elect', PH *elessi*, PP *eletto*

emergere 'to emerge', PH *emersi*, PP *emerso*

erigere 'to erect', PH *eressi*, PP *eretto*

escludere 'to exclude', PH *esclusi*, PP *escluso*

esigere 'to demand', PP *esatto*

esistere 'to exist', PP *esistito*

espellere 'to expel', PH *espulsi*, PP *espulso*

esplodere 'to explode', PH *esplosi*, PP *esploso*

esporre 'to expound' (stem *espon-*), PI *espongo*, PH *esposi*, PP
  esposto

esprimere 'to express', PH *espressi*, PP *espresso*

essere 'to be', PI *sono, sei, è, siamo, siete, sono*, F *sarò*, II *ero, eri, era,
  eravamo, eravate, erano*, PH *fui, fosti, fu, fummo, foste, furono*, PS
  sia, IS *fossi*, I *sii*, PP *stato*

estendere 'to extend', PH *estesi*, PP *esteso*

estinguere 'to extinguish', PH *estinsi*, PP *estinto*

estrarre 'to extract' (stem *estra–*), PI *estraggo*, PH *estrassi*, PP *estratto*

fare 'to make' (stem *fac-*), PI *faccio, fai, fa, facciamo, fate, fanno*,
  PH *feci*, I *fa (fai, fa')*, PP *fatto*

fingere 'to pretend', PH *finsi*, PP *finto*

fondere 'to melt', PH *fusi*, PP *fuso*

friggere 'to fry', PH *frissi*, PP *fritto*

fungere 'to act', PH *funsi*, PP *funto*

giacere 'to lie', PI *giaccio*, PH *giacqui*

giungere 'to arrive', PH *giunsi*, PP *giunto*

godere 'to enjoy', F *godrò*

illudere 'to delude', PH *illusi*, PP *illuso*

immergere 'to immerse', PH *immersi*, PP *immerso*

imporre 'to impose' (stem *impon-*), PI *impongo*, PH *imposi*, PP
  imposto

imprimere 'to impress', PH *impressi*, PP *impresso*

incidere 'to engrave', PH *incisi*, PP *inciso*

indurre 'to induce' (stem *induc-*), PH *indussi*, PP *indotto*

infliggere 'to inflict', PH *inflissi*, PP *inflitto*

infrangere 'to break', PH *infransi*, PP *infranto*

insistere 'to insist', PP *insistito*

intendere 'to mean', PH *intesi*, PP *inteso*

interrompere 'to interrupt', PH *interruppi*, PP *interrotto*

introdurre 'to introduce' (stem *introduc-*), PH *introdussi*, PP *intro-
  dotto*

invadere 'to invade', PH *invasi*, PP *invaso*

iscrivere 'to enroll', PH *iscrissi*, PP *iscritto*

leggere 'to read', PH *lessi*, PP *letto*

mettere 'to put', PH *misi*, PP *messo*

mordere 'to bite', PH *morsi*, PP *morso*

morire 'to die', PI *muoio*, PP *morto* (MD)

muovere 'to move', PH *mossi*, PP *mosso* (MD)

nascere 'to be born', PH *nacqui*, PP *nato*

nascondere 'to hide', PH *nascosi*, PP *nascosto*

occorrere 'to be necessary', PH *occorse*, PP *occorso*

offendere 'to offend', PH *offesi*, PP *offeso*

offrire 'to offer', PH *offrii (offersi)*, PP *offerto*

opporre 'to oppose' (stem *oppon-*), PI *oppongo*, PH *opposi*, PP *opposto*

ottenere 'to obtain', PI *ottengo*, F *otterrò*, PH *ottenni* (MD)

parere 'to seem', PI *paio*, F *parrò*, PH *parvi (parsi)*, PP *parso*

perdere 'to lose', PH *persi (perdei, perdetti)*, PP *perso (perduto)*

permettere 'to allow', PH *permisi*, PP *permesso*

persuadere 'to persuade', PH *persuasi*, PP *persuaso*

piacere 'to please', PI *piaccio*, PH *piacqui*

piangere 'to cry', PH *piansi*, PP *pianto*

piovere 'to rain', PH *piovve*

porgere 'to hand', PH *porsi*, PP *porto*

porre 'to place' (stem *pon-*), PI *pongo*, PH *posi*, PP *posto*

potere 'to be able', PI *posso, puoi, può, possiamo, potete, possono*, F *potrò* (MD)

prendere 'to take', PH *presi*, PP *preso*

pretendere 'to demand', PH *pretesi*, PP *preteso*

prevedere 'to foresee', F *prevedrò*, PH *previdi*, PP *previsto*

produrre 'to produce' (stem *produc-*), PH *produssi*, PP *prodotto*

promettere 'to promise', PH *promisi*, PP *promesso*

proporre 'to propose' (stem *propon-*), PI *propongo*, PH *proposi*, PP *proposto*

proteggere 'to protect', PH *protessi*, PP *protetto*

pungere 'to prick', PH *punsi*, PP *punto*

raccogliere 'to gather', PI *raccolgo*, PH *raccolsi*, PP *raccolto*

radere 'to shave', PH *rasi*, PP *raso*

raggiungere 'to reach', PH *raggiunsi*, PP *raggiunto*

reggere 'to bear', PH *ressi*, PP *retto*

rendere 'to return', PH *resi*, PP *reso*

resistere 'to resist', PP *resistito*

respingere 'to repel', PH *respinsi*, PP *respinto*

ridere 'to laugh', PH *risi*, PP *riso*

ridurre 'to reduce' (stem *riduc-*), PH *ridussi*, PP *ridotto riflettere* 'to reflect' (of light), PH *riflessi*, PP *riflesso* (but the verb is regular when the meaning is 'to consider')

rimanere 'to remain', PI *rimango*, F *rimarrò*, PH *rimasi*, PP *rimasto*

rincrescere 'to grieve', PH *rincrebbe*

risolvere 'to resolve', PH *risolsi*, PP *risolto*

rispondere 'to answer', PH *risposi*, PP *risposto*

ritenere 'to believe', F *riterrò*, PH *ritenni* (MD)

riuscire 'to succeed', PI *riesco, riesci, riesce, riusciamo, riuscite, riescono*

rivolgere 'to turn', PH *rivolsi*, PP *rivolto*

rompere 'to break', PH *ruppi*, PP *rotto*

salire 'to go up', PI *salgo*

sapere 'to know', PI *so, sai, sa, sappiamo, sapete, sanno*, F *saprò*, PH *seppi*, PS *sappia*, I *sappi*

scalfire 'to scratch', PP *scalfitto* and *scalfito*

scegliere 'to choose', PI *scelgo*, PH *scelsi*, PP *scelto*

scendere 'to go down', PH *scesi*, PP *sceso*

sciogliere 'to melt', PI *sciolgo*, PH *sciolsi*, PP *sciolto*

scommettere 'to bet', PH *scommisi*, PP *scommesso*

sconfiggere 'to defeat', PH *sconfissi*, PP *sconfitto*

scoprire 'to discover', PH *scoprii (scopersi)*, PP *scoperto*

scorgere 'to catch sight of', PH *scorsi*, PP *scorto*

scrivere 'to write', PH *scrissi*, PP *scritto*

scuotere 'to shake', PH *scossi*, PP *scosso* (MD)

seppellire 'to bury', PP *seppellito* or *sepolto*

smettere 'to stop', PH *smisi*, PP *smesso*

soddisfare 'to satisfy' (stem *soddisfac-*), PI *soddisfo*, F *soddisferò*, PH *soddisfeci*, PP *soddisfatto*

soffrire 'to suffer', PH *soffrii (soffersi)*, PP *sofferto*

sorgere 'to rise', PH *sorsi*, PP *sorto*

sorprendere 'to surprise', PH *sorpresi*, PP *sorpreso*

sorridere 'to smile', PH *sorrisi*, PP *sorriso*

sospendere 'to suspend', PH *sospesi*, PP *sospeso*

sostenere 'to maintain', PI *sostengo*, F *sosterrò*, PH *sostenni* (MD)

spandere 'to spill', PP *spanto*

spargere 'to scatter', PH *sparsi*, PP *sparso*

spegnere 'to put out', PH *spensi*, PP *spento*

spendere 'to spend', PH *spesi*, PP *speso*

spiacere 'to displease', PI *spiaccio*, PH *spiacqui*

spingere 'to push', PH *spinsi*, PP *spinto*

stare 'to stay', PI *sto, stai, sta, stiamo, state, stanno*, F *starò*, PH *stetti*, *stesti, stette, stemmo, steste, stettero,* PS *stia,* IS *stessi,* I *sta (stai, sta')*

stendere 'to spread out', PH *stesi,* PP *steso*

stringere 'to tighten', PH *strinsi,* PP *stretto*

succedere 'to happen', PH *successe,* PP *successo* (but the verb is regular when the meaning is 'to succeed' (to a position))

supporre 'to suppose' (stem *suppon-*), PI *suppongo,* PH *supposi,* PP *supposto*

svenire 'to faint', PI *svengo,* PH *svenni* (MD)

svolgere 'to unfold', PH *svolsi,* PP *svolto*

tacere 'to be silent', PI *taccio,* PH *tacqui*

tendere 'to stretch', PH *tesi,* PP *teso*

tenere 'to hold', PI *tengo,* F *terrò,* PH *tenni* (MD)

tingere 'to dye', PH *tinsi,* PP *tinto*

togliere 'to take off', PI *tolgo,* PH *tolsi,* PP *tolto*

tradurre 'to translate' (stem *traduc-*), PH *tradussi,* PP *tradotto*

trarre 'to draw' (stem *tra-*), PI *traggo,* PH *trassi,* PP *tratto*

trascorrere 'to spend time', PH *trascorsi,* PP *trascorso*

uccidere 'to kill', PH *uccisi,* PP *ucciso*

udire 'to hear', PI *odo, odi, ode, udiamo, udite, odono,* F *udirò (udrò)*

ungere 'to grease', PH *unsi,* PP *unto*

uscire 'to go out', PI *esco, esci, esce, usciamo, uscite, escono*

valere 'to be worth', PI *valgo,* F *varrò,* PH *valsi,* PP *valso*

vedere 'to see', F *vedrò,* PH *vidi,* PP *visto (veduto)*

venire 'to come', PI *vengo,* F *verrò,* PH *venni* (MD)

vincere 'to win', PH *vinsi,* PP *vinto*

vivere 'to live', F *vivrò,* PH *vissi,* PP *vissuto*

volere 'to want', PI *voglio, vuoi, vuole, vogliamo, volete, vogliono,* F *vorrò,* PH *volli* (MD)

volgere 'to turn', PH *volsi,* PP *volto*

(iii) Defective verbs. These are verbs which do not have a full conjugation. Although some of them are not common, it may be of interest to have a list of the main ones. We give examples for the forms which are most frequently used. Brackets are used for rare infinitives.

(*consumere*) 'to consume': the only existing forms are the PP *consunto* and three persons of the PH, *consunsi, consunse, consunsero; era consunto dalle sofferenze* 'he was wasted by suffering'.

delinquere 'to commit an offence': only used in the infinitive, as in *associazione a delinquere* 'conspiracy to commit a crime'; *delin-*

quente 'criminal' is used as noun and adjective.

divergere 'to diverge': no PP, no compound tenses; *le loro opinioni divergevano radicalmente* 'their opinions were radically opposed'.

esimere 'to exempt': no PP, no compound tenses; *non si esime mai dai suoi doveri* 'he never shirks his duties'.

(*lucere*) 'to shine': no PP, no compound tenses; *lucevano le stelle* 'the stars were shining'.

prudere 'to itch': no PP, no compound tenses; *gli prudeva il naso* 'his nose was itching'.

solere 'to be used to': no F, conditional, PP, present participle (MD); for the missing tenses *esser solito* is used; *come soleva dire Ugo* 'as Ugo used to say'.

stridere 'to creak': no PP, no compound tenses; *bisogna ungere quei cardini perchè stridono* 'we must oil those hinges because they are creaking'.

urgere 'to urge': no PH, PP, compound tenses; the present participle *urgente* is very common as an adjective; *urge la tua presenza* (telegraphic style) 'your presence urgently required'.

vertere 'to be about': no PH, PP, compound tenses; *su cosa verte la questione?* 'what is the question about?'.

vigere 'to be in force': no PH, PP, compound tenses; *qui vigono severe leggi fiscali* 'here strict tax laws are in force'.

Notes

[1] The use of northern Italian phonology in the teaching of Italian as a foreign language has been advocated with strong arguments by BRESSAN, D., in *International Review of Applied Linguistics*, 7, 1969, pp. 1–10. On our proposal see LEPSCHY, G., in *Studi Italiani di Linguistica Teorica e Applicata*, 4, 1975, pp. 201–9.

[2] *Microbi*, plural of *microbio*, was pronounced with the stress on the antepenultimate, in place of the expected one on the penultimate, and on this proparoxytonic *microbi*, a new singular *microbo*, also proparoxytonic, was formed.

[3] Note that traditionally the cluster [stʃ] is not supposed to exist in Italian, and cannot be rendered by Italian spelling. But by adding the prefix [s] to words beginning with [tʃ] one gets [stʃ], and words such as *scervellato* 'scatterbrained', *scentrato* 'off-centre' for which dictionaries give an initial [ʃ] are often pronounced with [stʃ]. A word like *sciabattare* 'to shuffle' (not given by standard dictionaries, but used in colloquial Italian instead of

ciabattare and *acciabattare;* a literary example: *la sentivamo sciabattare e brontolare per i corridoi* 'we heard her shuffling and grumbling along the corridors', from CALVINO, I., 'Le notti dell' UNPA' in *I racconti,* Turin, 1958, p. 304) would be comic with [ʃ] instead of [stʃ]. In words such as *sgelare* 'to unfreeze', *disgiungere* 'to separate' the cluster [zdʒ] is accepted (intervocalically purists also suggest [zz]).

[4] Purists accept as correct, although less common, a pronunciation with [i] or [j] (depending on the syllable boundary) for words in which the *i* goes back to a Latin vowel (as in *scienza* 'science', *religione* 'religion', *società* 'society') or is morphologically justified (*mangiamo* 'we eat', *usciate* 'that you go out') but not in words like *mangio* 'I eat', *uscio* 'door', *ragione* 'reason'. A pronunciation without [i] or [j] between the palatal consonant and the following vowel is however more common.

[5] This limitation to appositive clauses was suggested to us by G. Cinque.

[6] This observation was suggested to us by G. Cinque.

[7] Cf. on this point the note by G. FOLENA in *Lingua Nostra,* 19, 1958, pp. 120–121.

[8] The *-ire* verbs in 3b are inchoatives: cf. point (c) below.

[9] The terms 'gerund' and 'present participle' are used here to correspond to the Italian terms *gerundio* and *participio presente,* with reference to the *-ndo* and *-nte* forms respectively.

[10] The *-ii* ending is bisyllabic and stressed on the first vowel; the forms with the monosyllabic endings *-ai, -ei* are considered oxytones.

VI Fifteen Points of Syntax

1 Some notes on word order

This section opens with some points on intonation, a topic which must be taken into account in the discussion on word order, as their functions are closely linked. The following three notions will be used:[1]

Tonality: the subdivision of the sentence into tone groups, treated as minimal intonational units, each corresponding to one information unit. Tone group boundaries are marked in transcription by double slants: //.

Tonicity: the positioning of the tonic nucleus (or tonic) within the tone group; a tonic corresponds to the focus of information in the tone group. It is marked in transcription by small capitals.

Tones: the meaningful pitch movements centred on the tonic. A primary system of five tones can be used: 1 falling, 2 rising, 3 level-rising, 4 falling-rising, 5 rising-falling. They are marked in transcription by digits at the beginning of the tone group. They can for instance be contrasted in one-word sentences like *lui* 'him', *no* 'no', *sicuro* 'sure', etc.: //1 LUI// (statement); //2 LUI// (question), //3 LUI// (non committal answer, suspensive or enumerative), //4 LUI// (emphatically suspensive, or, with more marked fall, unbelieving question), //5 LUI// (committal answer, or contradiction, or exclamation).

A sentence like *non lo fa per te* 'he is not doing it for you' can have different meanings, depending on its intonation, such as for example: //1 non lo fa per TE// (he is doing it, but not for you); //1 non lo FA//1 per TE// (it is because of you that he is not doing it); //1 non lo FA per te// (he won't do it for you).

In a sentence one can normally distinguish two parts: in the first the speaker establishes what he is talking about and in the second he says something about it. We shall call the former 'theme' and the latter 'rheme'; their order is always theme + rheme.

The tonic element is the part of the sentence which carries 'new' information (the information focus); the rest is 'given', i.e., provided by what has already been said or by the situational context. The unmarked order (i.e., the one which is most normal, the one which can be expected in ordinary circumstances) is given + new.

In many languages (among them Italian) the unmarked order of the elements of a sentence is subject + predicate. Consequently it is normal in Italian for the subject to be thematic (what the speaker talks about) and given (what is assumed to be accessible to the hearer from the context), and for the predicate to be rhematic (what the speaker says about the subject) and new (what the hearer is not expected to know already).

In other terms, an unmarked sentence in Italian usually answers the implicit question 'what did the subject do?', and not 'who did the action expressed by the predicate ?' For instance, in

(a) //1 Ugo si è ADDORMENTATO// 'Ugo fell asleep', the speaker talks about Ugo (theme), who is supposed to be recognized by the hearer (given), and says that he fell asleep (rheme), which the hearer is supposed not to know (new).

But it is not necessary for the subject to be thematic and given, and for the predicate to be rhematic and new. It is possible to make the subject rhematic and the predicate thematic, by inverting their order, as in

(b) //1 si è addormentato UGO//, where the speaker talks about someone falling asleep, and says it was Ugo who fell asleep; 'falling asleep' is given in the context, and 'Ugo' is new.

It is also possible for the theme to carry the tonic, so that it becomes new while the rheme becomes given. Thus one obtains

(c) //1 UGO si è addormentato//, where the speaker talks about Ugo (theme) and says what he did (rheme), assuming that it was a question of people falling asleep (given), but that the hearer did not know it was Ugo who fell asleep (new);

(d) //1 si è ADDORMENTATO Ugo//, where the speaker talks about someone falling asleep (theme), and says who fell asleep (rheme), assuming that Ugo is present in the hearer's mind (given), but that the hearer did not know that he had fallen asleep (new).

In comparison with unmarked (a), we can say that (b) is marked with regard to theme, (c) is marked with regard to tonic, and (d) is marked both with regard to theme and to tonic.

The four sentences may be taken to correspond to the following implicit questions: (a) 'what did Ugo do?', (b) 'who fell asleep?', (c) 'who was it who fell asleep?', (d) 'what was it that Ugo did?'.

Taking sentence (a) as unmarked, we find that to answer question (b) Italian leaves the rheme tonic and changes the order of subject and predicate, while English makes the theme tonic and leaves the order of subject and predicate unchanged: the English counterpart to (b) is '*Ugo* fell asleep'. To make it clear in (c) that Ugo is not only new but also thematic, Italian makes the theme tonic, while English may keep (b) '*Ugo* fell asleep', or change the sentence to 'it was Ugo who fell asleep'. To answer question (d) Italian both changes the order of subject and predicate and makes the theme tonic (i.e., makes *si è addormentato* both thematic and new), while English puts an emphatic stress on the rheme: 'Ugo fell *asleep*', or, to make the predicate thematic, uses the colloquial 'he fell asleep, Ugo did'.

Different devices are preferred to produce marked sentences: changes in word order for Italian, and changes in intonation for English. What corresponds to sentences like '*I* did this', '*Ugo* told me' etc. (with marked tonicity and the usual order, i.e., subject + predicate) is in Italian *l'ho fatto io, me l'ha detto Ugo,* etc. (with marked order, i.e., predicate + subject and the usual tonicity). But these sentences differ because in English it is the subject which is thematic, while in Italian it is the predicate.

In Italian it is normal with some verbs for the predicate to be thematic: for instance, whereas with *partire* 'to leave' the unmarked order is *Ugo è partito* 'Ugo has left', with *arrivare* 'to arrive' it is *è arrivato Ugo* 'Ugo has arrived'. In fact the normal interpretation of *Ugo è arrivato* is that he has arrived somewhere else: we are not being told who has arrived here, but what Ugo did, i.e., that he reached his destination. In Fellini's *La strada* Anthony Quinn is angered when Giulietta Masina tamely says that he has got there: *Zampanò è arrivato* //1 Zampanò è ARRIVATO//, instead of announcing, to the accompaniment of her drum, that it is the great man himself who has arrived: *è arrivato Zampanò* //3 è ARRIVATO//5 ZAMPANÒ//.

In a sentence like *il gatto ha mangiato la carne* 'the cat ate the meat' the unmarked order is subject + verb + object, and the unmarked intonation consists of one tone group with tonic on the object. It is possible to mark the subject or the verb as new by making them tonic. The subject is here thematic. The traditional way to make the object thematic, in the literary language, is to use the passive: *la carne è stata mangiata dal gatto.* But in colloquial language a different construction is preferred, with the object at the beginning, in a tone group of its own with tone 3 (suspensive) 'as for the meat . . .', or tone 4 (contrastive) 'as for the *meat* . . .', and the verb in the active with an unstressed object pronoun: *la carne, l'ha mangiata il gatto.* Note that when the verb with the object pronoun (*l'ha mangiata*) and the object (*la carne*) are in the same tone group, the latter cannot be tonic.

We can also find other parts of the sentence, including the subject, in this initial, thematic tone group; //4 il GATTO//1 ha mangiato la CARNE//, //4 il GATTO//1 l'ha MANGIATA la carne//, //4 ha mangiato la CARNE//1 il GATTO// etc.

It would seem that the following combinations are possible, with different values according to the changes in theme and tonic ('S' is used for 'subject', 'V' for 'verb', 'O' for 'object', comma for tone group boundary, and bold print for the tonic):

with   *il   gatto   ha   mangiato   la   carne:*   S,V**O**   S,**V**O
S,**O**V   O,S**V**   S**V**,O   **O**V,S   V**O**,S   **V**O,S

and, when there is an unstressed object pronoun with the verb (e.g., *la carne, l'ha mangiata il gatto*): S,   **V**O   S,O**V**   O,S**V**   O,S**V**
O,V**S**   O,**V**S   S**V**,O   S**V**,O   V**S**,O   **V**S,O   O**V**,S   **V**O,S.

If S, V, and O are assigned one tone group each, all combinations are possible, but their meanings become ambiguous. It is fairly common on the literary level to find the construction V, S, O where the subject is felt to be inserted, as a parenthesis, in the VO clause: *scrisse, il nostro autore, diversi romanzi* 'our author wrote several novels' //3 SCRISSE//3 il nostro AUTORE//1 diversi ROMANZI//. These are, however, rhetorical devices not normally employed in colloquial Italian.

2 The use of the article[2]

(a) Definite and indefinite articles with common nouns

(i) In Italian as in English the definite article indicates something known (given), and the indefinite something new. Accordingly the definite article is used with a noun indicating an object already referred to: (*Ecco un libro e un disco. Quale vuoi?*) *Prendo il disco*

'(Here is a book and a record. Which do you want?) I'll take the record'; and the indefinite article is used with a noun indicating an object that has not yet been referred to: *ho comprato un disco* 'I bought a record'. This distinction can also be linked with word order: (A) *allora la ragazza entrò* 'then the girl came in' and (B) *allora entrò una ragazza* 'then in came a girl' are the unmarked expressions with theme/given first followed by rheme/new (see chapter VI. 1); in (A) we are being told what the girl did, the presupposition being that she had already been mentioned; in (B) we are being told who came in, the presupposition being that we did not expect anyone in particular to enter; in (C) *allora una ragazza entrò* 'then a girl came in' the presupposition would be that she, as yet unidentified, is one of several people already mentioned, and in (D) *allora entrò la ragazza* 'then in came the girl' the presupposition would be that we were expecting someone to come in, either that girl or someone else who was not a girl.

(ii) The definite article is used with a noun that is defined by an adjective or a relative clause, and also when it has the value of a demonstrative: *prendo la biro verde* 'I'll take the green biro', implying that there is only one green biro, vs. *prendo una biro verde* 'I'll take a green biro', implying that there are several biros but not necessarily more than one green one; *compra il libro che hai visto ieri* 'buy the book which you saw yesterday', where the fact that the book is known is indicated by the relative clause, vs. *ecco un libro che mi ha dato ieri Ugo* 'here is a book that Ugo gave me yesterday', where the book is presented as a new element by *un*: the relative clause is not enough to make it into a known element but just adds more information; *tornerà entro la settimana* 'he will come back some time this week'.

(iii) The definite article is used with nouns referring to objects of which only one exists: *il sole* 'the sun', *la luna* 'the moon', *la terra* 'the earth' (but *un sole, una luna* in an astronomical context).

(iv) The definite article is used with reference to habitual action, or action expected in the context, whereas the indefinite refers to a rarer or unexpected event: *prendi l'autobus o prendi un taxi?* 'are you going by bus or taking a taxi?'; *legge il giornale* 'he is reading the paper' vs. *legge un giornale* 'he is reading a paper'; *prendiamo il tè?* 'shall we have tea?' vs. *prendiamo un tè?* 'shall we have a cup of tea?'.

(v) The definite article is used with a noun indicating a species or category: *l'elefante è una bestia paziente* 'the elephant is a patient animal'. The indefinite article may also refer to the species, as represented by any one individual: *un elefante non dimentica niente* 'an elephant never forgets'.

(vi) The definite article (and sometimes the indefinite) can be used to turn words belonging to other parts of speech into nouns: *il perchè e il percome* 'the why and the wherefore', *senza nè un perchè nè un percome* 'without a why or a wherefore'.

In (iv), (v), and (vi) the definite article seems to be more widely used in Italian than in English:

(iv–A) *fa il bagno* 'he is having a bath', *fa la doccia* 'he is having a shower', *fa i compiti* 'he is doing his homework', *è pronta la colazione?* 'is breakfast ready?', *ci vuole il passaporto* 'one needs a passport', *ha la macchina* 'he has a car', *ha la televisione a colori* 'he has colour television', *ha la tosse* 'he has a cough'. With illnesses the definite article in Italian may correspond to the indefinite article, as above, or to no article in English: *ha l'influenza* 'he has flu', *ha il morbillo* 'he has measles', but *ha un* or *il raffreddore* 'he has a cold'.

(v–A) *l'uomo è traditore* 'men are traitors', *la donna è mobile* 'woman is fickle', *'Casa dello Studente'* 'Student Hostel'; the singular with a definite article to indicate a category (*lo studente, lo straniero* 'the foreigner', *l'italiano* 'the Italian') often has a more rhetorical or bureaucratic connotation than the singular with an indefinite article or the plural: *lo straniero è soggetto alle leggi del paese in cui vive* 'foreigners are subject to the laws of the country in which they live' vs. *uno straniero* and *gli stranieri*, etc.

(vi–A) *il bello e il brutto* 'beauty and ugliness', *il leggere e lo scrivere* 'reading and writing', *il nero gli sta bene* 'black suits him'.

(vii) (A) Whilst both in English and in Italian singular countable nouns normally have to be accompanied by an article (*il*, or *un libro è sul tavolo* 'the (or: a) book is on the table', *vedo il* or *un libro* 'I see the (or: a) book'), uncountable nouns in English do not have to take the article even when they are at the beginning of a sentence, whereas in Italian they do (as the examples in (v–A) and (vi–A) reveal; in those groups the nouns are uncountable: with those meanings they do not have plurals). This covers many of the cases normally listed in grammars as differing from English in the use of the article.

The definite article is hence used in Italian with

(B) nouns indicating matter: *l'argento* 'silver', *il fuoco* 'fire', *l'ossigeno* 'oxygen', *il carbone è un minerale* 'coal is a mineral', *il carbone non mi piace* 'I don't like coal', but cf. *voglio carbone* 'I want coal' vs. *voglio il carbone* 'I want the coal'. One can say *neve, ne abbiamo avuta tanta* 'we had a lot of snow', *carbone, non ne vogliono* 'they don't want coal', where *ne* indicates that the initial noun is used for *di neve, di carbone.*

(C) abstract nouns: *l'arte* 'art', *la virtù* 'virtue', *la pazienza* 'patience', *la bellezza* 'beauty'; *la pittura non gli interessa* 'painting does not interest him', *non capisce la musica* 'he does not understand music', but *è una bellezza* 'it's a beauty', where the concept has become concrete.

(D) names of languages: *studia il russo* 'he is studying Russian', *insegno l'italiano* 'I teach Italian', *capisco il francese* 'I understand French'; but when a recognized subject of study (and this applies to any subject, not just a language) is being referred to, the article may be omitted: *studia russo all'università* 'he is studying Russian at the university', *insegna tedesco in un liceo* 'he teaches German in a lycée'. The article is also omitted after *parlare* with reference to a speech act: *l'ho sentito parlare inglese* 'I heard him speak English', but not with reference to someone's ability to speak a language: *non sa parlare l'italiano* 'he cannot speak Italian' (*non sa parlare italiano* is also possible, but refers to someone's performance in individual speech acts rather than to his competence). The article is not used in certain constructions with *di* and *in*: *non sa una parola di francese* 'he does not know a word of French', *scrivo in tedesco* 'I am writing in German' but: *le difficoltà del francese* 'the difficulties of French', *si è immerso nel tedesco* 'he has plunged into German'.

(viii) The definite article is used in Italian with numerical expressions

(A) of time: *sono le due* 'it is two o'clock', *alle undici* 'at eleven o'clock', *nel 1956* 'in 1956', and with other expressions of time: *il mese scorso* 'last month', *il sabato va dalla nonna* 'on Saturdays he goes to his grandmother's' vs. *è venuto a trovarci sabato* 'he came to see us on Saturday'.

(B) of age: *sarà fra i trenta e i quaranta* 'he is probably between thirty and forty', *sarà sulla cinquantina* 'he must be about fifty' (cf. chapter V. 14 (c)), but *ha vent'anni, ha trent'anni,* etc. 'he is twenty', 'he is thirty', etc.

(C) with a distributive value: *100 lire l'uno* '100 lire each', *200 lire al* or *il chilo* '200 lire a kilo', *100 chilometri all'ora* or *l'ora* '100 km an hour', *50 lire la parola* '50 lire a word', but not after *per*: *50 lire per parola* '50 lire a word' (no article also in *50 lire a parola* '50 lire a word', *50 lire a testa*, or *a persona* '50 lire each').

(D) with a collective sense: *entrambi* (or *ambedue, tutti e due*) *i ragazzi* 'both boys', *entrambe* (or *ambedue, tutte e due*) *le ragazze* 'both girls', *tutte e tre le ragazze* 'all three girls'.

(ix) The definite article is used with possessive adjectives: *la nostra casa* 'our house'; for the use of article and possessive with nouns denoting family relationships cf. chapter V. 9.

(x) The definite article is used with reference to something belonging to the subject. In this context English uses a possessive adjective.

(A) It is used with parts of the body: *scuote la testa* 'he shakes his head', *arriccia il naso* 'he wrinkles his nose' (cf. *ha il naso lungo* 'he has a long nose', but *ha un naso da calmucco* 'he has a nose like a Kalmuck' [i.e., flat], because it is a type of nose), *si dipinge le unghie* 'she paints her nails', *devo farmi tagliare i capelli* 'I must have my hair cut', but *muove una mano, un piede* 'he moves his hand, his foot' with the indefinite article because it is one out of two: cf. *muove le mani, i piedi* 'he moves his hands, his feet'.

(B) It is used with possessions: *mi presti la penna?* 'would you lend me your pen?', *hai la borsa aperta* 'your bag is open', *ho dimenticato il portamonete* 'I forgot my purse', *si mette la cravatta* 'he is putting on his tie' vs. *si mette una cravatta* 'he is putting on a tie' (see above (a)(iv)).

(C) It is used with relatives: *ha il padre inglese e la madre russa* 'his father is English and his mother is Russian', *è arrivato lo zio* 'our (or: your, etc.) uncle has arrived'.

(b) Omission of article with common nouns

(i) Plural nouns are often used without an article, even those which in the singular have to take one: *ha pesche?* 'do you have peaches?' (which differs from both *ha le pesche?* 'have you got the peaches?', plural of *la pesca* indicating a notion already mentioned, and *ha delle pesche?* 'have you any peaches?', plural of *una pesca* indicating a new notion), *ci sono scoiattoli in questo paese?* 'are there squirrels in this country?', *abbiamo uova in casa?* 'have we got any eggs in the house?', *ci vogliono donne in gamba per questo* 'you need able women for this', *dovete comprare libri?* 'have you got to buy books?', *non fare storie, scherzi, sciocchezze,* etc. 'do not make a fuss, play tricks, do anything silly', etc.

(ii) Nouns in a negative sentence are often used without an article, whereas they would take one in a corresponding positive sentence: *non c'erano libri sul tavolo* 'there were no books on the table' corresponds to the positive *c'erano dei libri sul tavolo*, while *non c'erano dei libri sul tavolo* is not the negative but the denial of the preceding sentence, i.e., the former just states that there were no books, whereas the latter implies that someone suggested there were, and states that on the contrary there were not. More rarely even the singular of a countable noun may be used without an article in a negative sentence: *non c'era anima viva* 'there was not a soul', *non c'è avvenimento su cui lui non metta bocca* 'he has his say about everything'.

(iii) Uncountable nouns (or nouns which in the context do not go into the plural), may be used without an article unless they occupy first place in the sentence (cf. above (a)(vii)(A)): *c'è latte (burro, formaggio)* 'there is milk (butter, cheese)', *abbiamo avuto pioggia (neve, grandine)* 'we had rain (snow, hail)', *cercar casa (lavoro)* 'to look for a house (for work)', *prender moglie (marito)* 'to take a wife (a husband)', *sentir compassione (tenerezza)* 'to feel compassion (tenderness)', *far pena (pietà)* 'to be pathetic (pitiful)', *far piacere (dispiacere)* 'to make one pleased (sorry)', *prender paura* 'to take fright', *prender sonno* 'to fall asleep', *gli vien male (sonno)* 'he feels faint (sleepy)', *sentir caldo (freddo)* 'to feel hot (cold)', *aver caldo (freddo, sonno, fame, sete, paura)* 'to be hot (cold, sleepy, hungry, thirsty, afraid)', *aver bisogno* 'to need', *aver mal di testa (mal di denti, mal di gola)* 'to have a headache (toothache, a sore throat)'.

Note: *ha comprato latte (invece di birra)* 'he bought milk (instead of beer)', *ha comprato il latte* 'he bought the milk' (cf. above (a)(iv)); *sta cercando lavoro* 'he is looking for work', *ha trovato lavoro* 'he has found work', *ha trovato un lavoro* 'he has found a job'; *sento caldo* 'I feel hot', *sento il caldo* 'I feel the heat', *il caldo mi dà fastidio* 'heat bothers me', *fa caldo* 'it is hot', *fa un caldo . . .* 'it's so hot'; *mi fa piacere* 'I'm pleased', *mi fa un piacere . . .* 'I'm so pleased'; *mi vien rabbia solo a pensarci* 'the mere thought makes me angry', *mi è venuta una rabbia . . .* 'I got so angry'.

(iv) No article is used after prepositions in many (A) noun complements, (B) verb complements. As this would seem to depend on the individual expression, we limit ourselves to listing some examples:

(A)   *una specie di casa* 'a kind of house', *un vestito di seta* 'a silk dress', *un litro di latte* 'a litre of milk', *un uomo di valore* 'a man of worth', *un bicchiere di cristallo* 'a cut glass tumbler', *un bicchiere di vino* 'a glass of wine', *carte da gioco* 'playing cards', *camera da letto* 'bedroom', *sala da pranzo* 'dining room', *vestito da sera* 'evening dress', *camicia da notte* 'night dress'; for constructions like *un diavolo d'uomo* 'a devil of a man', *questo straccio di vestito* 'this rag of a dress' cf. chapter VI. 8(c).

(B)   *è in cima* 'he is at the top', *in fondo* 'at the bottom', *in acqua* 'in the water', *in montagna* 'in the mountains', *in città* 'in town', *in casa, a casa* 'at home', *a casa sua* 'in his own home', *in cucina* 'in the kitchen'; *va in treno* 'he goes by train', *in aereo* 'by plane', *in macchina* 'by car', *a teatro,* but *al cinema* 'to the theatre, to the cinema'; *sta senza cappello,* but *con il cappello* 'he is wearing no hat, a hat'; *è in pigiama* 'he is in his pyjamas', *è in costume da bagno* 'he is wearing a bathing costume'; *si comporta con sicurezza* 'he behaves confidently', *con giudizio* 'sensibly', *con coraggio* 'bravely'; *lo farò con piacere* 'I'll do it with pleasure'; *fallo con tuo comodo* 'do it at your convenience'; *lo scrivo a modo mio* 'I write it my own way'.

Note that *da una parte . . . dall'altra* corresponds to the English 'on the one hand . . . on the other', but whereas in English the second element can be used on its own: 'on the other hand . . .', in Italian one has in this case to say *d'altra parte . . .* and not *dall'altra parte . . .*

Expressions for playing games also come under this category: *giocare a mosca cieca* 'to play blind man's buff', *a rimpiattino* 'hide and seek', *a palla* or *alla palla* 'ball', *a ping pong* 'ping-pong', *a tennis* 'tennis', *a domino* 'dominoes', *a poker* 'poker', *a dama* 'draughts', *a scacchi* 'chess', but *a calcio* and *al calcio, al pallone* 'football'.

(v) The article may be omitted in nominal predicates:

(A) If a nominal predicate is without an article it describes the subject in the same way as an adjective would: *Ada è pianista* 'Ada is a pianist' (by profession); if it is with an indefinite article it gives the category to which the subject belongs: *Ada è una pianista* 'Ada is a pianist' (belongs to the category of pianists); if it is with the definite article it identifies the subject in the context: *Ada è la pianista* 'Ada is the pianist'.

(B) When the predicate follows verbs of choosing, nominating, electing, etc., no article is used: *fu eletto deputato* 'he became an MP', *lo hanno proclamato presidente* 'they proclaimed him president'.

(C) When the predicate is a noun in apposition, there may be no article: *Gadda, (l') autore del Pasticciaccio* 'Gadda, the author of the *Pasticciaccio*', *Felice Brusasorzi, (il) pittore veronese* 'Felice Brusasorzi, the Veronese painter'. There is a tendency to use the article when the apposition is considered sufficient for identification:[3] in *Cinque, il linguista veneziano*, we are being reminded, while in *Cinque, linguista veneziano*, we are being informed that he is a Venetian linguist. *Cinque, il linguista veneziano* corresponds to 'the Venetian linguist Cinque', while *Cinque, linguista veneziano* corresponds to 'a Venetian linguist, Cinque'. This explains why the apposition is normally without an article when it is directly relevant to what is being said: *Cinque, linguista veneziano, non si occupa di dialetti veneti* corresponds to 'Cinque', (although he is) a Venetian linguist, does not work on Venetian dialects'.

(vi) In lists the article need not be used: *ha preso bicchiere, libro, scarpe e lampada* 'he took glass, book, shoes and lamp'. Otherwise, when two or more coordinated nouns are not felt to constitute a list, the article is usually repeated: *ha preso i fiori e l'ombrello* 'he took the flowers and his umbrella', but it may be omitted if the objects are felt to be habitually linked: *ho preso carta e matita* 'I took paper and pencil', *ho preso impermeabile e ombrello* 'I took my raincoat and umbrella', *ho preso libri e riviste* 'I took books and magazines'.

If the presence of the article is required by a following specification, the article may nevertheless be omitted in the plural with the second and subsequent nouns if they have the same gender as the first: *i libri e giornali che hanno portato* 'the books and newspapers that they brought', but *il libro e la rivista che hanno portato* 'the book and the magazine that they brought'.

Note that *il segretario e tesoriere della società* 'the secretary and treasurer of the society' refers to one person only, whilst *il segretario e il tesoriere della società* 'the secretary and the treasurer of the society' refers to two separate people (unless the context indicates otherwise).

(vii) The article is often omitted for brevity in telegrams and advertisements: *confermo mio arrivo per inaugurazione corso* is short for *confermo il mio arrivo per l'inaugurazione del corso* 'I confirm my arrival for the opening of the course'; also in proverbs: *cosa fatta capo ha* 'what is done is done', *paese che vai usanza che trovi* 'when in Rome do as the Romans do', *gallina vecchia fa buon brodo* 'experience counts'; and in expressions which are created to be brief or striking, such as titles of books, periodicals, etc.: *Guerra e pace* 'War and Peace', *Rinascita.*

(viii) In comparative expressions there is a distinction between comparative, with no article, and superlative, with the definite article, as we have seen in chapter V. 6.

(ix) No article is used in vocatives and exclamations: *scusi, signore* 'excuse me, sir', *ehi, ragazzo* 'hey there, boy', *peccato!* 'pity!', *che peccato!* 'what a pity!', *porco!* 'pig!', *che porco!* 'what a swine!'.

(c) Note on the sequence of articles

In a group consisting of noun + complement, various combinations of definite and indefinite and no article are found: (i) *il proprietario dell'albergo* 'the hotel proprietor', (ii) *il proprietario di un albergo* 'the proprietor of a hotel', (iii) *il proprietario d'albergo* 'a hotel proprietor' (generic), 'hotel proprietors', (iv) *un proprietario di un albergo* 'a hotel proprietor, a proprietor of a hotel', (v) *un proprietario dell'albergo* 'one of the proprietors of the hotel', (vi) *un proprietario d'albergo* 'a hotel proprietor'.

In normal circumstances the types represented by (i) and (vi) are the most commonly used, they are the unmarked expressions; they show a correspondence between the definite article in the first part and the definite article in the second, and between the indefinite in the first and no article in the second. Another example is *dammi il mazzo delle carte* 'give me the pack of cards', but, buying in a shop, *mi dia un mazzo di carte* 'could I have a pack of cards?'. In *il mazzo di carte che è nel cassetto* 'the pack of cards which is in the drawer' it is not necessary to have *delle*, because the identifying element after *il* is represented by the relative clause.

(d) Use of the definite article with proper names

(i) The article is not normally used with first names: *chiamo Ugo* 'I'll call Ugo', *arriva Ada* 'Ada is coming', but in familiar language the article is frequently used with feminine names: *ho visto l'Ada* 'I have seen Ada', and more rarely with masculine names: *dov'è l'Ugo?*

'where is Ugo?'. With famous figures who are known by their first
names, and with names from classical antiquity, the article is never
used: *Dante, Leonardo, Michelangelo, Aristotele, Cicerone.* If these
names are used with an article they refer to the person's work, or, in
the case of writers, to a volume of their work: *mi presti il tuo Virgilio?*
'would you lend me your Virgil?', *hai visto il Raffaello di quel
museo?* 'did you see the Raphael in that museum?'.

The article must be used when a name is accompanied by an
adjective or a restrictive relative clause: *ho visto la povera Ada* 'I
saw poor Ada', *non pareva più l'Ugo che conosciamo* 'he no longer
seemed the Ugo we knew'.

(ii) With surnames the use of the article is optional in referring to
men: *ho visto Zanco* or *ho visto lo Zanco* 'I saw Zanco', but it is often
used if the figure is well-known: *il Manzoni parlava milanese* 'Manzoni spoke Milanese'; (it would seem to be rarely used with names
of musicians: *un'opera di Verdi, di Mozart, di Vivaldi* 'a work (or: an
opera) by Verdi, Mozart, Vivaldi'). It is not used with very famous
modern figures: *Picasso* rather than *il Picasso.* Some authors follow
the convention of never using the article with the name of a living
person.

If a woman is referred to only by her surname, the article must be
used: *la Corti*, but *Maria Corti* (or also *la Maria Corti*; whereas if a
man is referred to, the article with name and surname, as in *il Mario
Baratto*, implies greater familiarity).

When a nickname or an adjective from a place-name is used as a
surname, the article is optional: *(il) Tintoretto, (il) Veronese.*

As with first names, the article must be used when a surname is
accompanied by an adjective or a restrictive clause.

(iii) No article is used with titles such as *don, donna, frate (fra): Don
Abbondio, Fra Cristoforo;* with *Santo, San: San Giorgio (il San
Giorgio di Carpaccio* refers to a painting), and with ordinals after
names: *Papa Giovanni XXIII.*

With other titles the article is used, both with surnames: *il professor Rossi, il dottor Bruni, il signor Marchi, l'ingegner Zanco* (note
the fall of *-e* before the proper name) and with first names: *la signorina Anna, la signora Bianca*, except when used in direct
address: *buon giorno dottor Bruni*, which is in keeping with all vocatives. It is common to use these titles on their own without names
both with the third person and as vocatives: *cosa prende la signora?*
'what is the lady having?', *cosa ne pensa, ingegnere?* 'what do you

think about it, (literally) engineer?'.

In the plural the article with a surname indicates the whole family: *gli Sforza*; in the feminine it refers to the female members of the family, often of the same generation. It may also indicate, as in English, 'people like – ': *dove sono i Tiziano e i Tintoretto di oggi?* 'where are the Titians and Tintorettos of today?'.

Note that with name and surname the surname normally comes second: *Gianni Scarabello*, not *Scarabello Gianni*. It comes first in bureaucratic communications and alphabetical lists. In other circumstances the sequence surname + name is considered to be uneducated and as such is often used in literature for stylistic characterization. When introducing oneself or identifying oneself over the phone, often only the surname is given. In official documents paternity used to be indicated with the name of the father preceded by *di*, or if the father was dead by *di fu, del fu*, or just *fu: Ada Brambilla di Ugo*, or *(del) fu Ugo. Fu* (preceded by the definite article) can be used with the value of 'late', as in Pirandello's novel *Il fu Mattia Pascal*. Married women may use both their maiden name and their married name: there is no fixed order. When the married name comes second it may be preceded, in documents, by *in* (or more rarely *nei*): *Ada Brambilla in Biffi*; also *Ada Biffi nata Brambilla*. If a married woman prefers to use her maiden name she would still be called *signora* rather than *signorina: la signorina Brambilla* after marrying *il signor Biffi* becomes *la signora Biffi*, or *la signora Brambilla*, unlike the English custom of calling her Miss Brambilla or Mrs. Biffi.

(e) Use of the article with place-names

(i) The definite article is used with names of mountains, seas, oceans, rivers, and lakes: *il Cervino* 'the Matterhorn', *le Ande* 'the Andes', *il Mediterraneo* 'the Mediterranean', *il Pacifico* 'the Pacific', *il Tevere* 'the Tiber', *il Garda* 'lake Garda'.

(ii) It is also used with regions, countries, continents, large islands (which are presumably considered like countries or regions) and groups of islands: *il Piemonte, l'Italia, l'Europa, la Sardegna, le Antille.*

After the preposition *in* these names do not take an article: *andare in Australia* 'to go to Australia', *vivere in Corsica* 'to live in Corsica', but with masculine names in the singular the article is optional: *vado nel* or *in Belgio* 'I am going to Belgium', *vivo nel* or *in Canadà* 'I live in Canada'.

As for Italian regions, there would seem to be no clear rule: the article tends not to be used with feminine singular names (*in Calabria, in Lombardia, in Toscana)*, and to be used with masculine or plural names (*nel Veneto, negli Abruzzi, nelle Marche*), but: *in Piemonte*, and *in* or *nel Trentino*.

After the preposition *di* place-names do not take the article when *di* indicates a national characterization or a *de iure* relationship, but they do take it when *di* indicates a more neutral geographical characterization or a *de facto* relationship: *i vini di Francia* 'French wines' are a national category appreciated by connoisseurs, whereas *i vini della Francia* 'the wines of France' are the wines produced in France; *i laghi d'Italia* 'Italian lakes' belong to the country's 'image', whereas *i laghi dell'Italia* 'the lakes of Italy' is a more objective geographical designation; *il re di Grecia* 'the king of Greece' is not *il re della Grecia* if he is in exile. With other values of *di* the article is retained: *la Russia è piu grande della Polonia* 'Russia is bigger than Poland'.

With masculine names however the article is used after *di: il governo del Cile* 'the government of Chile', *i cittadini del Portogallo* 'the citizens of Portugal', *le città del Brasile* 'the cities of Brazil'; (but the article is not used in *Alessandria d'Egitto* nor in the idiom *d'Egitto*, expressing derogatory disbelief, as in *ha un impegno. – Ma che impegno d'Egitto!* 'he has an engagement. – What engagement, my foot!').

With a qualified name, or plural name, or a name that has a fixed attribute the article is normally used after *in* and *di: viaggiare negli Stati Uniti* 'to travel in the United States', *il governo dell'Unione Sovietica* 'the government of the Soviet Union', *vivere nell'Italia settentrionale* (but also *in Italia settentrionale*) 'to live in northern Italy'.

With prepositions other than *in* and *di* the article is used: *passare per l'Austria* 'to cross Austria', *tornare dalla Spagna* 'to return from Spain'.

(iii) No article is used with names of towns and small islands (perhaps considered like towns): *Torino* 'Turin', *Venezia* 'Venice', *Livorno* 'Leghorn', *Ischia, Capri, Malta* (also *Cuba, Cipro* 'Cyprus' in spite of their size), unless they are qualified: *la bella Firenze* 'beautiful Florence', *la Firenze di vent'anni fa* 'Florence of twenty years ago', or the article forms part of the name: *L'Aquila, La Spezia, L'Aia* 'The Hague'. In this case two articles are avoided: *l'orgogliosa Spezia* 'proud La Spezia', *la* (or *La*) *Spezia di vent'anni fa* 'La Spezia of twenty years ago'. With preposition + article in spelling one may find *di La Spezia* (perhaps preferable), *de La Spezia, della Spezia. Il Torino, il Vicenza, la Roma,* etc., are football teams.

(iv) The article may or may not be used with names of avenues, streets or squares: *(il) corso Italia sbocca in piazza Gramsci* 'corso Italia leads into piazza Gramsci'; generally no article is used after prepositions: *passare per Corso Italia* 'to go along Corso Italia' (but *passeggiare per il Corso* 'to stroll up and down the avenue'), *sta in via Giuseppe Verdi* 'he lives in via Giuseppe Verdi', *andiamo in Piazza San Marco* 'let's go to St Mark's Square' (and also *andiamo in Piazza*); with *palazzo* the article is omitted if a family name follows: *c'incontriamo a Palazzo Pitti?* 'shall we meet at Palazzo Pitti?', *hai visitato Palazzo Doria?* 'have you visited Palazzo Doria?', but it is used if an adjective or a complement follows: *dov'è il Palazzo Ducale?* 'where is the Doge's Palace?', *ecco il Palazzo della Ragione* 'here is the Palazzo della Ragione'.

3 Evaluative suffixes

Italian is particularly rich in suffixes which can be attached to nouns and adjectives. In Italian grammars these suffixes are traditionally subdivided into four groups: *diminutivi, accrescitivi, vezzeggiativi,* and *peggiorativi* or *spregiativi,* roughly with the value of 'small', 'large', 'nice', and 'nasty' respectively. In practice it is difficult to attribute one or more of these values to a particular suffix, as the effect is influenced by the word which is modified, for example *poverello* from *povero* 'poor' is normally *diminutivo* and *vezzeggiativo,* whereas *miserello* from *misero* 'wretched' is *diminutivo* and *peggiorativo,* or by the context: for example *alberello* may be *diminutivo* and *vezzeggiativo* 'a nice little tree', or *diminutivo* and *peggiorativo* 'a stunted little tree'.

These suffixes sometimes express none of the above set of values but simply the emotive involvement of the speaker, for example *vestitino* (from *vestito* 'dress'), *cenetta* (from *cena* 'supper'), *mammina* (from *mamma* 'mother'), *zietta* (from *zia* 'aunt').

In time the force of the suffix may be lost, and so the word becomes neutral: *cucchiaino* 'teaspoon', *figliolo* 'son', *scarponi* 'boots', *violoncello* 'cello'; in this respect one is reminded of the familiar Late Latin into Italian development of words like *genu – ginocchio* 'knee', *auris – orecchia* 'ear', *avis – uccello* 'bird', *soror – sorella* 'sister', *frater – fratello* 'brother' which takes place through the expressive use of the diminutive suffixes as in *genuculum, auriculam,* etc.

Many suffixes are productive, that is, can be attached to a wide number of words as the need arises, creating perfectly acceptable forms often not documented in dictionaries. However this mechanism does not work indiscriminately and some combinations of nouns or adjectives + suffix seem to be excluded. As no satisfactory account exists of how this pairing mechanism functions, we shall limit ourselves to giving a list of suffixes (which does not aim at being complete). The list is not subdivided into the four categories mentioned above, because so many suffixes do not fit them, but is ordered alphabetically with examples and approximate translations or with explanations from which the force of the suffix emerges. We have put a † by the most common suffixes, and have put in brackets those which are least productive. Wherever possible we give examples of both nouns and adjectives. The suffixes we list are stressed on the penultimate syllable, except for *–ercolo, -iciattolo, -ognolo, -onzolo, -ottolo, -ucolo, -uncolo, -upola* which are stressed on the antepenultimate. In *-accio, -iccio, -occio, -uccio* the stress is on the vowel preceding the *cc* (the following *i* is there only to indicate the palatal sound of the preceding consonant).

-acchione: furbacchione 'crafty so-and-so', *mattacchione* 'joker'
-acchiotto: lupacchiotto 'wolf cub', *orsacchiotto* 'bear cub'; *fessacchiotto* 'a bit of a fool'
†*-accio: ragazzaccio* 'rough boy', *topaccio* 'great big rat', *vitaccia* 'rotten life'; *golosaccio* 'greedy fellow', (*-accio, -occio, -uccio* also have phonologically different forms *-azzo, -ozzo, -uzzo,* but are not freely interchangeable with them)
-astro: giovinastro 'young lout', *poetastro* 'poetaster'; *furbastro* 'crafty', *rossastro* 'reddish'
(*-atto): cerbiatto* 'fawn', *lupatto* 'wolf cub', *orsatto* 'bear cub'
-azzo: amorazzo 'love affair' (pejorative)
-ello: paesello 'little village'; *cattivello* 'little rascal'
(*-ercolo): libercolo* 'booklet'
-erello: fatterello 'incident', *fuocherello* 'little fire'; *scioccherello* 'silly

little thing'

†*-etto: libretto* 'little book', *ometto* 'little man'; *furbetto* 'cunning little thing'

-iccio: attaccaticcio 'sticky', *malaticcio* 'sickly', *rossiccio* 'reddish'

-icciolo: porticciolo 'small port', *stradicciola* 'lane'

-icello: botticella 'cask', *campicello* 'plot of land', *fiumicello* 'stream', *pianticella* 'small plant', *solicello* 'weak sun', *venticello* 'breeze'; *grandicello* 'big', 'growing up' (of children)

-iciattolo: febbriciattola 'low fever', *mostriciattolo* 'little horror', *omiciattolo* 'stunted little man'

-icino: corpicino 'slight figure', *cuoricino* 'little heart'

(-igno): asprigno 'sourish'

†*-ino: piedino* 'little foot'; *bellino* 'pretty' (feminine nouns in acquiring this suffix may become masculine in gender: *donna* 'woman', *donnino* 'a grown up little girl' vs. *donnina* 'a little woman'; *penna* 'pen', *pennino* 'nib' vs. *pennina* 'a little pen'; the reverse may happen: *palazzo* 'building, palace', *palazzina* 'villa' vs. *palazzino* (rarer) 'small palace')

-occio: bamboccio 'plump child, doll', *fantoccio* 'puppet'; *belloccio* 'quite attractive' (in a plump sort of way), *grassoccio* 'plump'

-ognolo: amarognolo 'slightly bitter', *verdognolo* 'greenish'

-olino: cagnolino 'little dog', *pesciolino* 'small fish', *topolino* 'little mouse'; *verdolino* 'greenish'

-(u)olo: montagnola 'hillock', *notiziola* 'small piece of information', *poesiola* 'little poem', *faccenduola* 'small job', *ragazzuolo* 'young boy'

-ona: bisteccona 'large steak'; *grassona* (adjective and noun) 'fat (woman)'

†*-one: librone* 'big book'; *simpaticone* 'an easy-going hearty person' (this suffix normally changes the gender of feminine nouns to which it is affixed: *donna* 'woman', *donnone* 'large woman' (less frequently *donnona*), *barba* 'beard', *barbone* 'tramp', 'big beard' (with the latter meaning, also *barbona*), *cassa* 'box', *cassone* 'chest', *febbre* 'temperature', *febbrone* 'high temperature', *faccia* 'face', *faccione* 'big face' (less frequently *facciona*), *forca* 'pitch fork', 'gallows', *forcone* 'pitch fork', *scala* 'stairs', *scalone* 'monumental staircase', *strada* 'road', *stradone* 'main country road')

(-onzolo): mediconzolo 'second rate doctor', *pretonzolo* 'unpleasant little priest' or 'unctuous person'

-otto: aquilotto 'young eagle', *leprotto* 'levret', *ragazzotto* 'sturdy boy', *anzianotto* 'elderly', *bassotto* 'rather short', 'dachshund'.

(-ottolo): viottolo 'lane'

(-ozzo): predicozzo 'little sermon'

(-scello): arboscello 'sapling', *ramoscello* 'twig'

†*-uccio: cappelluccio* '(cheap) little hat'; *caruccio* 'rather expensive', 'pet', *deboluccio* 'rather weak'

-ucolo: paesucolo 'little village', *poetucolo* 'second rate poet', *scrittorucolo* 'hack writer'

(-uncolo): ladruncolo 'petty thief', *omuncolo* 'dwarfish man'

(-upola): casupola 'hut'

(-uzzo): avvocatuzzo 'undistinguished little lawyer', *pietruzza* 'little pebble'

It is useful to note the following points:

(a) One may find a suffix used as an independent word: *è proprio accio?* or *è proprio accio accio?* 'is it really bad?'

(b) Words in *-one, -ona* acquire *-c-* before a suffix: *bastone* 'stick', *bastoncino* 'little stick, rod', *cannone* 'cannon', *cannoncino* 'little cannon', *furgone* 'van', *furgoncino* 'small van', *leone* 'lion', *leoncino* 'lion cub', *persona* 'person', *personcina* 'slight figure'. Similarly *camion* 'lorry', *camioncino* 'van', *paltò* 'coat', *paltoncino* 'little coat'. There is also modification of the stem in other cases: *cane* 'dog', *cagnolino, cagnetto* 'little dog', *cagnaccio* 'nasty big dog', *città* 'town', *cittadina* 'small town'.

(c) Suffixes may combine with each other (but again not all combinations are possible). Some of the suffixes listed above are, from a diachronic point of view, combinations (e.g., *-acchione*). We now give some examples of suffixes which are synchronically felt to be combined:

-acchione + -ello: furbacchioncello 'crafty creature'

-accio + -one: libraccione 'great big book', *omaccione* 'hulking fellow'

-erello + -ino: fuocherellino 'little fire'

-etto + -accio: cagnettaccio 'nasty little dog'

-etto + -ino: librettino 'little book', *omettino* 'little man'

-one + -ino: cartoncino 'small card', *cordoncino* 'thin cord', *scarponcini* 'climbing boots' (mostly when *-one* is no longer felt as an augmentative suffix)

-otto + -ino: leprottino 'levret'

(d) Adverbs may sometimes be modified by suffixes: *bene* 'well', *benino* 'quite well', *benone* 'very well' (cf. *benissimo* 'very well'); *male* 'badly', *malino, maluccio* 'rather badly', *malaccio*, limited to expressions like *non c'è malaccio* 'not too bad' (cf. *malissimo* 'very badly'); *presto* 'early', *prestino* 'rather early' (cf. *prestissimo* 'very early'); *tardi* 'late', *tarduccio* 'rather late' (cf. *tardissimo* 'very late').

(e) Verbs too may be modified by certain suffixes (such as *-acchiare, -erellare, -icchiare, -occhiare, -ottare, -ucchiare, -ucolare, -uzzare*) usually indicating repetition of the action on a smaller or inferior scale: *baciare* 'to kiss', *sbaciucchiare* 'to kiss repeatedly', 'to slobber over', *bruciare* 'to burn', *bruciacchiare* 'to scorch', *cantare* 'to sing', *canterellare, canticchiare* 'to hum, to sing to oneself', *dormire* 'to sleep', *dormicchiare* 'to snooze', *fischiare* 'to whistle', *fischierellare, fischiettare* 'to whistle cheerfully', *girare* 'to go around', *girellare* 'to mooch about', *gironzolare* 'to wander around', 'to hover about', *lavorare* 'to work', *lavoricchiare* 'to do a bit of work', *leggere* 'to read', *leggiucchiare* 'to read half-heartedly', *mangiare* 'to eat', *mangiucchiare* 'to nibble', *parlare* 'to speak', *parlucchiare, parlottare* 'to chatter', *piangere* 'to cry', *piagnucolare* 'to whine', *ridere* 'to laugh', *ridacchiare* 'to cackle', *rubare* 'to steal', *rubacchiare* 'to pilfer', *scrivere* 'to write', *scribacchiare, scrivucchiare* 'to scribble', *sgranare* 'to shell' (peas), 'to tell' (one's rosary), *sgranocchiare* 'to crunch', *sputare* 'to spit', *sputacchiare* 'to splutter', *studiare* 'to study', *studiacchiare* 'to study half-heartedly', *tagliare* 'to cut', *tagliuzzare* 'to chop up', *vivere* 'to live', *vivacchiare* 'to rub along', *volare* 'to fly', *svolazzare* 'to flutter'.

(f) Personal names can also be modified by suffixes; sometimes the modified name becomes a name in its own right and the suffix loses all emotive value, in other cases the suffix may be used sporadically and so retain its expressiveness. Suffixation in this case is often connected with hypocoristic shortening (cf. English 'William', 'Bill', 'Billy'; 'Robert', 'Bob', 'Bobby'; 'Margaret', 'Meg', 'Maggie', etc.): *Antonia, Antonietta; Antonio, Tonio, Toni* (mainly northern), *'Ntoni* (mainly southern), *Tonino; Carla, Carlotta; Carlo, Carlino, Carletto; Donata, Donatella; Giovanni, Giovannino, Nanni, Vanni, Gianni, Giannino; Giuseppe, Beppe, Beppino, Peppe, Peppino; Lina, Linetta, Linuccia; Luigi, Luigino, Gigi, Gigino, Gigetto; Maria, Marietta, Mariuccia, Mariù, Mariolina; Pietro, Piero, Pierino, Pieretto; Simona, Simonetta.*

In many cases a dialectal diminutive is the form habitually used in all circumstances (apart from official ones), for instance in Venice *Bepi* for *Giuseppe, Gegia* for *Teresa, Nane* for *Giovanni*. The use of nicknames is also common; they may become semi-official, for instance for Venetian gondoliers: Sergio Tagliapietra, a famous competitor in regattas, is always known as *Ciaci*.

(g) The word with the suffix often has an independent meaning, not predictable from the original word: *braccio* 'arm', *bracciolo* 'arm of a chair'; *busta* 'envelope', *bustarella* 'bribe money'; *canna* 'rod', *cannone* 'cannon'; *capello* 'hair', *capellone* 'hippy'; *carro* 'cart', *carrozza* 'carriage'; *pane* 'bread', *panettone* 'panettone' (a special cake, commonly eaten at Christmas); *spago* 'string', *spaghetti* 'spaghetti'; *verme* 'worm', *vermicelli* 'vermicelli'.

(h) Although we are not dealing with suffixation in general, in a discussion on evaluative suffixes one should mention the following, which have expressive connotations:

- *-aglia*, to form derogatory collectives, as in *accozzaglia* 'jumble' (a term introduced into the literary language by Manzoni), *anticaglia* 'old junk', *canaglia* 'rabble', 'wretch', *marmaglia* 'riffraff', *plebaglia* 'common herd', *ragazzaglia* 'a noisy band of boys', *soldataglia* 'band of soldiers'; the force of the suffix has been obliterated in *battaglia* 'battle', *boscaglia* 'underwood'
- *-ame*, to form collectives, as in *bestiame* 'live-stock', *fogliame* 'foliage', *pollame* 'poultry', *ossame* 'heap of bones', but it may have derogatory implications which are taken up in occasional creations: *bambiname* 'horde of children'; the politician M. Scelba in 1949 referred to Italian intellectuals hostile to his party as *culturame* 'cultural scum'
- *-ardo*, to form pejorative adjectives and nouns, as in *testardo* 'stubborn', *vecchiardo* 'nasty old man' (cf. *bastardo* 'bastard', *bugiardo* 'liar', *codardo* 'coward', *infingardo* 'slacker')
- *-io*, to form nouns indicating repeated intensive action, as in *borbottio* 'muttering', *brontolio* 'grumbling', *calpestio* 'stamping', *formicolio* 'swarming', 'tingling', *lavorio* 'constant working', *mormorio* 'murmuring'
- *-one*, to form nouns indicating someone who indulges excessively in an action, as in *beone* 'drinker', *brontolone* 'grumbler', *chiacchierone* 'chatterer', *fannullone* 'idler', *imbroglione* 'cheat', *mangione* 'glutton'

-ume, to form derogatory collectives, or to indicate a substance derogatorily, as in *forestierume* 'foreign muck' or 'foreign scum', *biancume* 'whitish stuff'. It is appended to words which already have unpleasant connotations: *sudiciume* 'filth', *untume* 'grease'.

(i) It may be interesting to note that a variety of suffixes can be added to one and the same stem, for instance from *carta* 'paper', *cartina* '(cigarette) paper', *carticino* 'signature' (a typographic term), *cartella* 'brief-case', *cartellina* 'folder', *cartaccia* 'waste paper', *cartoccio* 'wrapping', *cartone* 'cardboard', *cartoncino* 'card', *cartonaccio* 'cheap cardboard', *cartuccia* 'cartridge', *cartello* 'poster', *cartellino* 'tag', *cartellone* 'wall poster', *cartolina* 'postcard' (and other words are formed with suffixes we have not listed above, as they are not evaluative, such as *cartiera* 'paper mill', *cartiglio* 'scroll', *cartoleria* 'stationer's', etc.).

4 Compound and juxtaposed nouns

(a) Compounds

A purely diachronic classification would be inappropriate in this context, because in many cases the mechanism of the composition has no relation to contemporary grammatical structure (e.g., *terremoto* 'earthquake', *ferragosto* 'August bank holiday', *pettirosso* 'redbreast'). A purely synchronic classification would be hindered by the large number of cases where it is difficult to establish whether the word is felt to be a compound by present day speakers, or how the components are felt to be related to each other (e.g., *capolavoro* 'masterpiece', *girasole* 'sunflower'); it would have to limit itself to listing certain differences (such as *capostazione* 'station master' plural *capistazione* vs. *capogiro* 'dizziness' plural *capogiri* vs. *capomastro* 'master builder' plural *capimastri*) which fall into place not in terms of our present day awareness of the relationship between the components, but rather with a diachronic consideration of their original relationship.

We offer a classification of compounds based on the grammatical categories to which the components belong, and the grammatical function (as head or modifier) which the components fill in the compound; in the analysis of individual compounds we follow the etymology if the structure is not synchronically recognizable. Both the singular and plural of the words are given, with a comment at the end of each section on the formation of the plural.

(i) *Noun + noun*

(A)(I)Modifier (complement) + head: *l'acquedotto* 'aqueduct' *gli acquedotti, la banconota* 'banknote' *le banconote, il capogiro* 'dizziness' *i capogiri, la ferrovia* 'railway' *le ferrovie, la filovia* 'trolley-bus line' *le filovie, il fruttivendolo* 'greengrocer' *i fruttivendoli, il manoscritto* 'manuscript' *i manoscritti, il manrovescio* 'back handed slap' *i manrovesci, il pescivendolo* 'fishmonger' *i pescivendoli, il terremoto* 'earthquake' *i terremoti.*

As one would expect only the head goes into the plural.

(II) Modifier (attribute)+head: *il capocomico* 'actor manager' *i capicomici* or *capocomici, il capocuoco* 'head cook' *i capicuochi* or *capocuochi, il capoluogo* 'main town' *i capiluoghi* or *capoluoghi, il capomastro* 'master builder' *i capimastri* or *capomastri.*

As the relationship between the components has been obscured, we get two forms of the plural. Otherwise the normal form is with both components in the plural. When a feminine can exist, *capo* is felt to be a prefix: *la capocuoca, le capocuoche.*

(B) (I) Head + modifier (complement): *l'acquavite* 'eau de vie' *le acqueviti, il capobanda* 'ringleader' *i capibanda, il capofamiglia* 'head of the family' *i capifamiglia, il capolavoro* 'masterpiece' *i capolavori, il capolinea* 'terminus' *i capilinea, il capopopolo* 'popular leader' *i capipopolo, il caporeparto* 'foreman' *i capireparto, il caposezione* 'head clerk' *i capisezione, il capostazione* 'station master' *i capistazione, il capotreno* 'guard' *i capitreno, la cartapecora* 'parchment' *le cartapecore, il crocevia* 'cross-road' *i crocevia, il cruciverba* 'crossword' *i cruciverba, il ferragosto* 'August bank holiday' *i ferragosti, la madreperla* 'mother of pearl' *le madreperle, il nerofumo* 'dark grey' *i nerifumo, il verderame* 'verdigris' *i verdirame.*

Only the head goes into the plural (although it is the first element in the compound), except for the cases where the relationship has been obscured as in *ferragosto, acquavite, capolavoro, cartapecora, crocevia, cruciverba, madreperla,* when the word is treated as a unit (*crocevia* and *cruciverba* are invariable). Alternative plurals are found, such as *acquaviti, capilavori, nerofumo* and *verderame.*

(II) Head + modifier (attribute): *l'arcobaleno* 'rainbow' *gli arcobaleni, la cassapanca* 'chest' *le cassepanche, il cavolfiore* 'cauliflower' *i cavolfiori, il grillotalpa* 'mole-cricket' *i grillitalpa, il pe-scecane* 'shark' *i pescecani* or *pescicani, il pescespada* 'swordfish' *i pescispada, il porcospino* 'porcupine' *i porcospini.*

If both components have the same gender as the compound they both go into the plural, but if the word is felt to be a unit only the last component goes into the plural: *arcobaleni*; if the last component has a different gender from the compound only the head goes into the plural.

(ii) *Noun + adjective*

(A) Head + modifier: *l'acquaforte* 'etching' *le acqueforti, il camposanto* 'cemetery' *i camposanti, il caposaldo* 'stronghold' *i capisaldi, la cassaforte* 'safe' *le casseforti, il granturco* 'maize' *i gran-turchi, il palcoscenico* 'stage' *i palcoscenici, la terracotta* 'terracotta' *le terrecotte, la terraferma* 'mainland' *le terreferme.* In this context one can add what was originally noun (head) + preposition + noun (modifier): *il pomodoro* 'tomato' *i pomidoro, i pomidori* or more commonly *i pomodori*; and also a group of invariable words which can be used to modify or to replace a noun or personal name: *bar-banera* 'black beard', *barbarossa* 'red beard', *denti d'oro* 'gold teeth', *gambacorta* 'short leg', *manolesta* 'light-fingered', *occhitorti* 'squint eyed', *piedipiatti* 'flat footed', *spadalunga* 'long sword', etc.

As one might expect both components go into the plural (even *pomidori*, where if the composition is taken into account one gets the rarer *pomidoro*); but if the awareness of the composition has been obscured the word is treated as a unit: *camposanti, palco-scenici,* and the alternative plurals *cassaforti, terracotte.*

(B) Modifier + head: *la capinera* 'black cap' *le capinere, il pet-tirosso* 'redbreast' *i pettirossi.*

One can also add literary adjectives like *biancovestito* 'white clad' = *vestito di bianco* and *fededegno* 'trustworthy' = *degno di fede.* As one might expect the head goes into the plural.

(iii) *Adjective + noun*

Modifier + head: *l'altopiano* (or *altipiano*) 'plateau' *gli altopiani* (or *altipiani*), *il bassorilievo* 'basrelief' *i bassorilievi* (or, rarer, *bas-sirilievi*), *il belvedere* 'observation point' *i belvederi, il biancospino* 'hawthorn' *i biancospini, la buonalana* 'rascal' *le buonelane, il fran-cobollo* 'stamp' *i francobolli, il galantuomo* 'gentleman' *i galan-*

tuomini, la grancassa 'big drum' *le grancasse, il granduca* 'grand duke' *i granduchi, la mezzaluna* 'crescent' *le mezzelune, la mezzanotte* 'midnight' *le mezzenotti, la mezzatinta* 'half tone' *le mezzetinte, il mezzogiorno* 'midday' *i mezzogiorni*. One can also add *purosangue* 'thoroughbred' which is invariable and can be used nominally or adjectivally: *ha due purosangue* 'he has two thoroughbreds'.

If the word is felt to be a unit, the head alone goes into the plural (*francobolli*), otherwise both the head and the modifier have plural endings (*mezzetinte*).

(iv) *Adjective + adjective*

(A) *agrodolce, -i* 'bittersweet', *grigioverde, -i* 'grey green', *pianoforte, -i* 'piano', *sordomuto, -i* 'deaf and dumb', *verdazzurro, -i* 'greenish blue'.

As far as the plural is concerned, these compounds are treated as units.

(B) There are many compounds which are created as the need arises and are not usually given in dictionaries. Only the last component agrees in gender and number with the noun it refers to; the preceding components often end in an *-o-* which takes the place of their normal ending; sometimes they have a shorter form without an adjectival suffix: *abitudini piccolo-borghesi* 'petty bourgeois habits', *questioni economico-sociali* or *socio-economiche* 'socio-economic questions', *anarco-sindacalista* 'anarcho-syndicalist'. This *-o-* has been widely used in learned terminology in the European languages since the sixteenth century when it was taken from Greek models. It is now particularly frequent at the end of 'prefixoids' (cf. chapter IV. 2(d)(vi)), as in *aero-, radio-,* etc.; it is not the *-o* of the Italian masculine singular ending, as is apparent from cases like *bucco-laringale* 'bucco-laryngeal', *vegeto-minerale* 'vegeto-mineral', *radico-socialista* 'radical-socialist', and from the fact that it is also used in other languages, like English, where *-o* is not the normal masculine ending. In some cases the 'connective' vowel is not the *-o-* common in Greek but the *-i-* which was common in Latin: cf. *centimetro* 'centimetre', *funivia* 'cableway' with *-i-*, as against *chilometro* 'kilometre', *filovia* 'trolley-bus' with *-o-*. The components may have different values: *italo-americani* may mean 'Americans who are of Italian origin', or 'involving Italy and America' as in *accordi italo-americani* 'Italo-American agreements'. Adjectives in *-ale* usually drop the final vowel (or the whole suffix) when they are used as non-final components: *radical-socialista* or *radico-socialista* 'radical-socialist'. These compounds would seem to suggest a unity rather than a split: one therefore expects *alleanza liberal-socialista* 'liberal-socialist alliance', but *polemica liberale-socialista* 'polemic between liberals and socialists'. In *social-comunista* 'socialist-communist' the first component stands of course for *socialista*.

(v) *Verb + noun*

(A) When the noun is the object: *l'asciugamano* 'towel' *gli asciugamani*, *l'attaccapanni* 'clothes hanger' *gli attaccapanni*, *il baciamano* 'handkissing' *i baciamani*, *il battimano* 'clapping' *i battimani*, *il beccafico* 'garden warbler' *i beccafichi*, *il beccamorto* 'sexton' *i beccamorti*, *il bucaneve* 'snowdrop' *i bucaneve*, *il cacciavite* 'screwdriver' *i cacciavite* or *cacciaviti*, *il cavalcavia* 'flyover' *i cavalcavia*, *il cavatappi* 'corkscrew' *i cavatappi*, *il coprifuoco* 'curfew' *i coprifuochi*, *il girarrosto* 'spit' *i girarrosti*, *il grattacielo* 'skyscraper' *i grattacieli*, *il guardaboschi* 'forester' *i guardaboschi*, *il guardaroba* 'wardrobe' *i guardaroba*, *la lavastoviglie* 'washing-up machine' *le lavastoviglie*, *il mangiadischi* '(a kind of) record player' *i mangiadischi*, *il mangiapane* 'loafer' *i mangiapane*, *il parabrezza* 'windscreen' *i parabrezza*, *il paracadute* 'parachute' *i paracadute*, *il parafango* 'mudguard' *i parafanghi*, *il parafulmine* 'lightening conductor' *i parafulmini*, *il paralume* 'lampshade' *i paralumi*, *il paravento* 'screen' *i paraventi*, *il piantagrane* 'troublemaker' *i piantagrane*, *il portabandiera* 'standard bearer' *i portabandiera*, *il portacenere* 'ashtray' *i portacenere* or *portaceneri* (the latter is not found in standard dictionaries but is used), *il portafoglio* 'wallet' *i portafogli*, *il portafortuna* 'mascot' *i portafortuna*, *il portalettere* 'postman' *i portalettere*, *il portamonete* 'purse' *i portamonete*, *il portaombrelli* 'umbrella stand' *i portaombrelli*, *il rompiscatole* 'pain in the neck' *i rompiscatole*, *il salvagente* 'life buoy' *i salvagente* or *salvagenti*, *lo scansafatiche* 'shirker' *gli scansafatiche*, *lo spartiacque* 'watershed' *gli spartiacque*, *lo spazzacamino* 'chimney sweep' *gli spazzacamini*, *lo stuzzicadente* (or *stuzzicadenti*) 'tooth pick' *gli stuzzicadenti*, *il tergicristallo* 'windscreen wiper' *i tergicristalli*, *il tirapiedi* 'sidekick' *i tirapiedi*, *il tritacarne* 'mincer' *i tritacarne*, *il tritatutto* 'mincer' *i tritatutto*.

These compound nouns, if masculine, and if the noun component is masculine, or is a feminine ending in -*o* or in -*e*, usually have a plural ending in -*i*: *i grattacieli, gli asciugamani, i cacciaviti;* but they are invariable if the noun component is feminine ending in -*a*: *i cavalcavia*. If the noun component is already in the plural then naturally the word is invariable: *il/i cavatappi*. These rules apply also to (v) (B) and (C).

(B) When the noun is the subject: *il battibecco* 'squabble' *i battibecchi, il batticuore* 'palpitation' *i batticuori, il battiscopa* 'skirting board' *i battiscopa, il crepacuore* 'heart break' *i crepacuori, il marciapiede* 'pavement' *i marciapiedi, il saltamartino* 'jack-in-the-box' *i saltamartini*.

(C) Other combinations: *il cascamorto* 'spoon' *i cascamorti*, and (with a preposition) *il saltimbanco* 'acrobat' *i saltimbanchi, il saltimbocca* 'saltimbocca' (a Roman meat dish) *i saltimbocca*.

(vi) *Verb + verb*

l'andirivieni 'coming and going' *gli andirivieni, il dormiveglia* 'doziness' *i dormiveglia, il fuggi-fuggi* 'flight' *i fuggi-fuggi, il pappataci* 'sandfly' *i pappataci, il parapiglia* 'confusion' *i parapiglia, il saliscendi* 'latch' *i saliscendi, il tiramolla* 'wavering' *i tiramolla, il va e vieni* 'coming and going' *i va e vieni*.

As one might expect these compounds are invariable.

(vii) *Preposition + noun*

il dopopranzo 'afternoon' *i dopopranzi, il doposcuola* 'after school activities' *i doposcuola, il fuoribordo* 'outboard motorboat' *i fuoribordo, il Lungarno* 'the Lungarno' *i Lungarni, il lungomare* 'the promenade' *i lungomari* or *lungomare, il retroterra* 'hinterland' *i retroterra, il senzatetto* 'homeless' *i senzatetto, il sottaceto* 'pickle' *i sottaceti, il sottopassaggio* 'underground passage' *i sottopassaggi*.

There is a plural ending if the compound has the same gender as the noun component (*i dopopranzi*, but *i doposcuola*), unless the word is felt to be an invariable modifier of a noun which is understood: *i senzatetto* are 'people who are *senza tetto'*.

(b) Juxtapositions

With terms of colour one finds phrases like *rosa pastello* 'pastel pink', *viola scuro* 'dark mauve', *verde bottiglia* 'bottle green', *rosso fuoco* 'flame red', *giallo oro* 'golden yellow', *grigio perla* 'pearl grey', etc. They may be used as masculine nouns; the form taken by the plural depends on the nature of the juxtaposition: *il giallo oro, i gialli oro, il viola scuro, i viola scuri, il rosa pastello, i rosa pastello.* As adjectives they are invariable: *guanti grigio perla* 'pearl grey gloves'.

We also find constructions like *delle sciarpe color verde bottiglia* 'bottle green scarves', with four nouns juxtaposed. This brings us to a phenomenon which is gaining ground in modern Italian, i.e. nominal juxtaposition.

(c) (i) Whilst in English in a typical juxtaposition of noun + noun the function of the juxtaposed items is modifier + head, in Italian the function is always head + modifier ('restaurant car' vs. *vagone ristorante*). The origin of this widespread use of juxtapositions is probably the telegraphic style of technical and commercial communications. Expressions like *calze filo* and *filo calze* are not used in ordinary language but there are contexts in which they could easily be found, for example, in a shop window, the former advertising *calze di filo* 'cotton socks' and the latter labelling a type of thread, *filo per calze* 'cotton for socks'.

The juxtaposition of head and modifier can cover different relationships which may be grouped into two main categories:
(A)   in the first group the modifier is like a noun complement: *treno merci* 'goods train' which is *un treno per le merci; stile impero* 'Empire style', that is *stile dell'impero; piazzale ovest* 'West yard', that is *il piazzale a ovest; formato cartolina* 'postcard format', that is *formato di una cartolina;*
(B)   in the second group the modifier is more like a predicate: the head is like, or shares qualities with, the modifier: *discorso fiume* is a speech that goes on and on like a river; *donna cannone* is a woman as large as a cannon; *valigia armadio* is a suitcase that also has the function of a wardrobe; *chiusura lampo* 'zip' is a fastener which can be closed as fast as lightning.

(ii) Some of these juxtaposed pairs can in turn be used as modifiers of a preceding head: *un vestito stile impero* 'an Empire style dress', *una fotografia formato cartolina* 'a postcard sized photo', *guanti tipo cameriere* 'waiter style gloves'.

(iii) In these pairs which can be juxtaposed as modifiers to other nouns, we frequently get as head words like *formato* 'size' (*fotografia formato tessera* 'passport sized photo'), *genere* 'type' (*dei film genere Cinecittà* 'Cinecittà type films'), *marca* 'brand' (*un prodotto marca Zeta* 'a Zeta brand product'), *misura* 'measure' (*canottiere misura bambino* 'children's size vests'), *stile* 'style' (*un tavolo stile Luigi XIV* 'a Louis XIV table'), *tipo* 'type' (*sigari tipo magnate* 'tycoon type cigars'), *uso* 'imitation' or 'in the manner of' (*una borsa uso pelle* 'an imitation leather briefcase', *una natura morta uso Braque* 'a still-life in the manner of Braque'); on the other hand, in ordinary juxtapositions, we frequently get as modifiers words like *base* 'basic' (*idea base* 'basic idea'), *chiave* 'key' (*concetto chiave* 'key concept'), *tema* 'theme' (*parola tema* 'theme word'), *fiume* 'river' (*romanzo fiume* 'endless novel', 'saga'), *modello* 'model' (*impiegato modello* 'model employee'), *tipo* 'typical' (*famiglia tipo* 'typical family'). One consequence of this is that certain juxtapositions are ambiguous: *formato chiave* may mean either 'key size' or 'key sized'.

The productive use of juxtapositions is very common in English, whereas in Italian it is more limited, and is felt to be a bold innovation often retaining the harshness of a telegraphic style and not very satisfactorily integrated into Italian syntactic patterns.

5 Position of adjectives

(a) The basic rule concerning the position of adjectives[4] is that

(i) they follow the noun they qualify when they have a distinguishing, restrictive function, i.e., when the quality they express is contrasted to others which might refer to the same noun: *si sedette sulla poltrona vecchia* 'he sat down in the old armchair' implies a contrast with at least another armchair which is not old.

(ii) they precede the noun they qualify when they have a purely descriptive, non-restrictive value: *si sedette sulla vecchia poltrona* 'he sat down in the old armchair' also tells us that the armchair is old, but does not contrast it with newer ones.

The restrictive use of the postnominal position is particularly clear when there is a definite article: a choice is implied. But even when the indefinite article is used, the difference between the two functions is still clear, although the postnominal position does not imply a choice between armchairs: *si sedette su una poltrona vecchia* tells us that the chair is old and not new, whereas *si sedette su una vecchia poltrona* merely tells us that the chair happens to be old, i.e., in the second sentence the contrast old/new is only a lexical feature of the word *vecchia*, in the first it is brought out by the syntax.

Most adjectives can have both these functions: *prendiamo un po' di buon vino* 'let's have some good wine' implies that we appreciate wine; *prendiamo un po' di vino buono* 'let's have some good wine', or 'wine which is good' implies we are choosing good wine; *ha preso il pacco grosso* 'he took the big parcel' (and not the smaller one); *ha preso il grosso pacco* 'he took the big parcel' (a parcel which happened to be big); *dall'altra parte si vedevano delle scogliere bianche* 'on the other side we could see some white cliffs'; *dalla nave traghetto avvistammo le bianche scogliere di Dover* 'from the ferryboat we sighted the white cliffs of Dover'.

(b) An adjective which precedes is often weakened in its descriptive function, so that it becomes almost a cliché, as in *pallida luna* 'pale moon', *teneri affetti* 'tender feelings', *dura necessità* 'harsh necessity', *gentile invito* 'kind invitation'. This may even lead to a change of meaning: *un buon uomo* 'a good fellow' is different from *un uomo buono* 'a man who is good'. The difference in meaning may become even more pronounced: *un grand' uomo* 'a great man', but *un uomo grande* 'a big man'; *un pover'uomo* 'an unfortunate man' is not necessarily *un uomo povero* 'a poor man' (i.e., not rich). Usually the adjective has a literal sense when it follows the noun, and a metaphorical one when it precedes.

There are also adjectives which have a more radical difference in meaning according to position: *certe notizie* 'some news', *notizie certe* 'news which are certain'; *diversi libri* 'several books', *libri diversi* 'different books'; *un nuovo vestito* 'a new dress', in the sense of a different dress; *un vestito nuovo* 'a new dress', in the sense of a dress worn for the first time; *numerose famiglie* 'many families', *famiglie numerose* 'large families'; *è un semplice furto* 'it is simply a theft', *è un furto semplice* 'it is an easy theft', *un unico libro* 'one book only', *un libro unico* 'a unique book'; *un vecchio amico* 'an old friend' (of long standing), *un amico vecchio* 'an elderly friend'.

(c) Certain adjectives normally precede the noun: cardinal numbers (but not in commercial usage: *lire 1000, metri 2* '2 metres', *scatole 5* '5 boxes'), ordinal numbers and *ultimo* 'last' (but in books we have *capitolo primo* 'chapter one', *parte seconda* 'part two', *libro terzo* 'book three', etc.), possessives (unless they are contrastive: *voglio il cappello mio* 'I want *my* hat') and indefinites. Examples, in the above order: *voglio due caffè* 'I want two coffees', *mi metto in prima (seconda, ultima) fila* 'I'm going to sit in the first (second, last) row', *dov'è il mio libro?* 'where is my book?', *fra pochi minuti* 'in a few minutes', *ha molte qualità* 'he has many qualities'.

(d) There are other adjectives which normally follow the noun, for instance adjectives of nationality, past participles used as adjectives, and those adjectives which, on account of their meaning, are almost always used with a restrictive function: *il popolo italiano* 'the Italian people', *ecco le camicie stirate* 'here are the ironed shirts', *ci sono mele cotte?* 'are there any stewed apples?', *c'erano degli uomini armati* 'there were armed men', *si era messo un vestito scuro* 'he had put on a dark suit'.

(e) When a noun is followed by a specification, the adjective often precedes, and when an adjective is followed by a specification it follows the noun: *gli ampi risvolti della giacca* 'the wide lapels of the jacket' (but also *i risvolti ampi della giacca* and *i risvolti della giacca ampi), un uomo lesto di mano* 'a light-fingered man', *una ragazza scura di carnagione* 'a girl with a dark complexion'.

An adjective modified by an adverb almost inevitably has a restrictive function and therefore follows the noun: *una passeggiata molto lunga* 'a very long walk' modifies the notion of *una passeggiata lunga*, not of *una lunga passeggiata*. (But if the adverb is *più* 'more' or *bene* 'well', one may have, with the expected descriptive function, *una ben triste vicenda* 'a very sad event', *un più facile successo* 'an easier success'.) Adjectives modified by a suffix similarly tend to follow the noun: *una valigia pesantuccia* 'a heavyish case', *un pacco grossetto* 'a biggish parcel', etc.

If there are several adjectives, they are usually restrictive, and so they follow the noun: *vini buoni, secchi, leggeri* 'good, light, dry wines'. Similarly a double adjective with the value of a superlative will follow the noun: *scrivimi una lettera lunga lunga* 'write me a long long letter', but a double adjective with the function of an adverb has greater freedom of position: *seria seria la bambina mi guardò* or *la bambina seria seria mi guardò* or *la bambina mi guardò seria seria* 'the little girl looked at me very seriously'.

(f) For reasons of emphasis there may be inversion, that is a restrictive adjective may precede and a descriptive adjective may follow, the appropriate intonation being used to show that the restrictive adjective, although preceding, has not acquired a descriptive function, and vice versa; the adjective is then in a tone group of its own; there are two tone groups in *ha preso il pacco grosso* //3 ha preso il PACCO//1 GROSSO// (= *ha preso il grosso pacco*, descriptive); and there are three tone groups in *ha preso il grosso pacco* //3 ha PRESO//3 il GROSSO//1 PACCO// (= *ha preso il pacco grosso*, restrictive). These inversions, however, belong to a rhetorical style and not to everyday language.

6 Agreement of adjectives

As stated in chapter V. 5 an adjective agrees in gender and number with the noun it qualifies. When an adjective refers to two or more nouns and follows them, the simplest and least ambiguous rule of agreement is that if the nouns to which it refers are feminine, the adjective is feminine plural, and in all other cases it is masculine plural: (a) *cerco una gonna e una camicetta gialle* 'I am looking for a yellow skirt and a yellow blouse', (b) *cerco un cappotto e un cappello neri* 'I am looking for a black coat and a black hat', (c) *porta cravatta e cappello neri* 'he is wearing a black tie and a black hat', (d) *porta cappello e scarpe neri* 'he is wearing a black hat and black shoes', (e) *porta guanti e scarpe gialli* 'she is wearing yellow gloves and yellow shoes'.

There is also the possibility of making the adjective agree with the nearest noun, using *gialla* in (a), *nero* in (b) and (c), *nere* in (d) and *gialle* in (e). This form of agreement is particularly frequent when the nouns refer to a single notion, as in *lingua e letteratura italiana* 'Italian language and literature': the name of a discipline. This agreement is inevitably ambiguous as the adjective could be taken to refer to the last noun only.

When one of the nouns is in the masculine plural, it is possible to make the two rules coincide, by putting it last, but if instead of (e) one says *porta scarpe e guanti gialli*, one avoids the clash between *scarpe* and *gialli*, but one reintroduces an ambiguity.

If the adjective precedes, it agrees with the nearest noun: *buonissime paste e dolci* 'very good cakes and sweets', *completa pace e silenzio* 'complete peace and silence'.

When an adjective referring to several nouns is used as a predicate, the agreement must be in the plural, in the feminine if all nouns are feminine, in the masculine in all other cases: (a) *la gonna e la camicetta erano gialle*, (b) *il cappotto e il cappello erano neri*, (c) *la cravatta e il cappotto erano neri*, (d) *il cappello e le scarpe erano neri*, (e) *i guanti e le scarpe erano gialli*.

We saw in chapter V. 5(c) (x)–(xi) that adjectives of foreign origin (*blu, beige, marron*) and adjectives such as *rosa* and *viola* are invariable; complex expressions indicating colour are also invariable (they are in the masculine singular): *una sciarpa rosso fuoco* 'a flame red scarf', *delle giacche verde bottiglia* 'bottle-green coats', *una maglia giallo pallido* 'a pale yellow jersey', *una vestaglia arancione cupo* 'a dark orange dressing-gown'.

Some noun complements can be used in a similar way to *aggettivi sostantivati* (i.e., adjectives used as nouns), but are normally invariable. Just as one says *le grandi* 'the big girls', *i piccoli* 'the little ones', so one can also have *è una second'anno* 'she is a second year', *i quart'anno* 'the fourth years', etc., instead of *è una studentessa di second'anno, gli studenti di quart'anno*.

7 Position of adverbs

(a) If an adverb modifies an adjective or another adverb, it precedes it: *è piuttosto bravo* 'he is rather good', *si può fare molto facilmente* 'it can be done very easily'.

(b) If it modifies a verb, it usually immediately follows, or comes at the end of the clause: *ha finito presto* 'he finished early', *parlava forte* 'he was talking loudly', *legge raramente testi che non siano tecnici* 'he rarely reads non-technical works', *viene sempre a trovarmi* 'he always comes to see me', *me l'ha detto di nuovo* 'he told me again', *l'ho visto solo due volte* 'I only saw him twice', *ha accettato volentieri la mia proposta* 'he gladly accepted my proposal', *ha chiuso silenziosamente la porta* 'he quietly shut the door', *ha chiuso la porta silenziosamente* 'he shut the door quietly'. Note that 'he speaks Italian well' corresponds to *parla bene l'italiano; parla l'italiano bene* has an emphatic collocation of the adverb.

The position of the adverb may change the meaning of a sentence: *stranamente ha parlato di questo argomento* and *ha stranamente parlato di questo argomento* both correspond to 'strangely he talked about this subject', whilst *ha parlato stranamente di questo argomento* and *ha parlato di questo argomento stranamente* both correspond to 'he talked about this subject strangely' (all with unmarked intonation); *mi ha detto subito di venire* 'he at once told me to come', *mi ha detto di venire subito* 'he told me to come at once'.

(c) As will be noticed in the example *ha stranamente parlato di questo argomento* the adverb may come between the first auxiliary and the past participle. There are some adverbs for which this is the normal position: *è già venuto* 'he has already come', *è già stato preso* 'he has already been caught', *non l'ho ancora letto* 'I have not read it yet', *non l'avevo più visto* 'I had not seen him again', *l'ha sempre fatto* 'he has always done it', *non l'ho mai visto* 'I have never seen him', *non aveva affatto detto questo* 'he had not said that at all', *ti ha forse parlato di me?* 'did he perhaps mention me to you?', *ti ha poi raccontato quella storia?* 'did he in the end tell you that story?', *te ne avevo ben parlato* 'I had surely told you about it' (cf. *te ne avevo parlato bene* 'I had spoken well of it to you').

In constructions with more than one verb, the adverb follows the verb it modifies (or its auxiliary): *ha già cercato di imparare ad andare in bicicletta* 'he has already tried to learn to ride a bicycle', *ha cercato di imparare rapidamente ad andare in bicicletta* 'he has tried to learn to ride a bicycle in a short time', *ha cercato di imparare ad andare dappertutto in bicicletta* 'he has tried to learn to cycle everywhere'.

(d) The adverbial positions we have given above are the neutral, normal ones; it is of course possible to convey greater emphasis by changing the position: *molto facilmente si può fare* 'very easily it can be done', *di nuovo me l'ha detto* 'again he told me', *già è venuto* or *è venuto già* 'already he has come'.

Instead of changing the position of the adverb, a similar effect may be achieved by changing the normal intonation, as shown in the following example by the use of commas: *ha parlato, stranamente, di questo argomento* //3 ha PARLATO//3 STRANAMENTE//1 di questo ARGOMENTO// = *stranamente ha parlato di questo argomento*.

(e) *Anche* 'also', *neanche* 'not even', *solo, solamente, soltanto* 'only' precede the word they modify: *è venuto anche lui* 'he came too', *non è venuto neanche lui* 'not even *he* came', *ho anche visto Ugo* 'I also saw Ugo' (as well as doing other things), *ho visto anche Ugo* 'I saw Ugo too' (as well as seeing other people), *ho visto Ada e anche Ugo* 'I saw Ada and also Ugo', *io ho visto Ada e Ugo anche* 'I saw Ada and so did Ugo' (where *anche* suggests that a following *l'ha vista* is understood), *ho solo comprato una matita* 'I only bought a pencil' (and did nothing else), *ho comprato solo una matita* 'I only bought a pencil' (and nothing else).

(f) *Ci* 'there' which is commonly used with *essere* (*c'è, ci sono* 'there is, there are') is frequently used with *avere* at a colloquial level: *ci avresti un fiammifero?* (= *avresti un fiammifero?*) 'would you have a match on you?', and often indicates greater involvement of the subject: *hai un bel paio di scarpe* 'you've got a nice pair of shoes' vs. *ci hai un bel paio di scarpe* 'that's a nice pair of shoes you've got'. The spelling may be *ci avresti, ci hai,* or *c'avresti, c'hai*; the normal pronunciation is in any case [tʃavrèsti], [tʃài].

8 Some constructions with/without prepositions

(a) We give examples of constructions with verb + verb and verb + noun, to show which prepositions, if any, are used. We try to give productive constructions, and to avoid purely idiomatic ones. A semicolon separates verb constructions from noun constructions.

ABITUARSI: si è abituato a fumare la pipa 'he has got used to smoking a pipe'; *si è abituato alla pipa* 'he has got used to a pipe', *lo hanno abituato alla pipa* 'they have accustomed him to a pipe'

ACCENNARE: non accenna ad entrare 'he shows no sign of coming in', *mi accenna di entrare* 'he beckons me to come in'; *ha accennato un gesto di rifiuto* 'he made a slight sign of refusal', *ha accennato a un episodio spiacevole* 'he hinted at an unpleasant episode'

ACCETTARE: accetto di venire 'I agree to come'; *accetto l'invito* 'I accept the invitation'

ACCONDISCENDERE: ha accondisceso a fermarsi 'he agreed to stop'; *accondiscendono alla tue esigenze* 'they agree to your demands'

ACCONSENTIRE: ha acconsentito a parlare 'he consented to speak'; *hanno acconsentito alla nostra richiesta* 'they agreed to our request'

ACCUSARE: lo accusava di essere un pedante 'he accused him of being pedantic'; *lo accusavano di pedanteria* 'they accused him of pedantry'

AFFRETTAR(SI): si è affrettato a partire 'he hastened to leave'; *ha affrettato la partenza* 'he hastened his departure'

AIUTARE: l'aiuterò a scendere 'I'll help him get down'; *aiutavo Ada* 'I helped Ada'

AMARE: ama cantare 'he loves singing'; *ama la discussione* 'he loves arguing'

AMMETTERE: ammette di averlo fatto 'he admits he has done it'; *non ammette obiezioni* 'he admits no objections'

ANDARE: vado a prenderlo 'I'm going to get it'; *vado in Italia* 'I'm going to Italy', *vado a Milano* 'I'm going to Milan', *vado da Ugo* 'I'm going to Ugo's', *vado dal macellaio* 'I'm going to the butcher's'

ARRIVARE: è arrivato a insultarmi 'he got to the point of insulting me'; *è arrivato all'esasperazione* 'he got to the point of exasperation', *è arrivato in Italia* 'he got to Italy', *è arrivato a Roma* 'he got to Rome', *è arrivato da Roma* 'he has arrived from Rome', *è arrivato da Ugo* 'he got to Ugo's'

ARRISCHIAR(SI): mi arrischio a parlare 'I venture to speak'; *si è arrischiato in un progetto difficile* 'he ventured upon a difficult project', *arrischio una grossa somma* 'I risk a large sum'

ASPETTARE: aspetta di partire 'he is waiting to leave', *aspetta a partire!* 'don't leave yet!', *aspetto a partire che arrivi Ugo* or *aspetto che arrivi Ugo per partire* 'I am waiting for Ugo to arrive before I leave'; *aspetta il treno* 'he is waiting for the train'

ASPETTARSI: non mi aspettavo di riuscirci 'I did not expect to succeed', *mi aspetto che arrivi Ugo* 'I am expecting Ugo to arrive'; *mi aspetto una telefonata* 'I am expecting a telephone call' (vs. *aspetto una telefonata* 'I am waiting for a telephone call')

ASPIRARE: aspira a diventar papa 'he is aspiring to become pope'; *aspira al pontificato* 'he is aspiring to the pontificate', and, with a different meaning, *non dovresti aspirare il fumo* 'you shouldn't inhale smoke', *aspira le consonanti* 'he aspirates his consonants'

ASSICURAR(SI): mi ha assicurato di saperlo fare 'he assured me he could do it', *assicurati di non avere impegni* 'make sure you have no engagements'; *ha assicurato la casa contro gli incendi* 'he insured his house against fire', *quell'impiego gli assicura la tranquillità economica* 'that job guarantees him freedom from financial worries'

ASTENERSI: si astiene dal bere 'he is abstaining from drinking'; *si astiene dal vino* 'he is abstaining from wine'

AUGURARE: gli auguro di star bene and *gli auguro buona salute* 'I wish him good health'

AVERE: ho da far questo 'I must do this', *ho da fare* 'I am busy', *ho da leggere un libro* 'I have to read a book' (less commonly *ho a* instead of *ho da*); *ho un libro da leggere* 'I have a book to read' (in the past: *ebbe a dirmi che l'aveva fatto lui* 'he happened to tell me he had done it himself')

BADARE: bada a fare il tuo lavoro 'you just get on with your work', *bada di finire il tuo lavoro* 'mind you finish your work', *bada di non cadere* 'mind you don't fall' (specific), *bada a non cadere* 'be careful you don't fall' (general); *bada ai fatti tuoi* 'mind your own business', *bada alla minestra* 'look after the soup', or 'careful with the soup'

CAPIRE: capì di essere responsabile 'he understood he was responsible'; *ha capito il ragionamento* 'he understood the argument'

CERCARE: cerca di finire 'he is trying to finish'; *cercavano te* 'they were looking for you', *cercavano di te* 'they were asking for you'

CESSARE: *ha cessato di parlare* 'he stopped talking'; *ha cessato le sue attività* 'he gave up his activities'

CHIEDERE: *ha chiesto di parlarti* 'he asked to speak to you'; *ha chiesto un libro a Ada* 'he asked Ada for a book', *ha chiesto di Ugo* 'he asked after Ugo'

COMANDARE: *ha comandato ai soldati di marciare* 'he ordered the soldiers to march'; *comanda l'esercito* 'he commands the army'

COMBINARE: *hanno combinato d'incontrarsi al Museo Britannico* 'they arranged to meet at the British Museum'; *hanno combinato dei pasticci* 'they've got themselves into a mess', *hanno combinato un matrimonio* 'they have arranged a marriage', *hanno combinato un affare* 'they did a deal', *non combinano niente* 'they don't get anything done'

COMINCIARE: *ha cominciato a leggere* 'he has begun to read'; *ha cominciato col leggere* 'he began with reading', *ha cominciato il libro* 'he has begun the book', *ha cominciato col libro* or *dal libro* 'he began with the book', *è una parola che comincia per vocale* 'it's a word that begins with a vowel'

COMPIACERSI: *si compiace di vestirsi bene* 'he takes pleasure in dressing well'; *si compiace nel parlare di sè* 'he enjoys talking about himself', *si compiace della sua posizione* 'he is pleased with his position'

CONCEDERE: *gli concedo di partire* 'I allow him to leave'; *gli concedo una vacanza* 'I am allowing him a holiday'

CONDANNARE: *lo condanna a tacere* 'he condemns him to be silent'; *lo condanna al silenzio* 'he condemns him to silence', *lo hanno condannato a due anni per furto* 'he was sentenced to two years' imprisonment for theft'

CONSENTIRE: *ha consentito a parlare* 'he agreed to speak', *ha consentito a venire* 'he agreed to come' (he came of his own accord), *ha consentito di venire* 'he agreed to come' (he said he would come), *questa borsa gli consentirà di andare a Parigi* 'this scholarship will enable him to go to Paris'; *non posso consentire con voi* 'I cannot agree with you', *ha consentito al mio suggerimento* 'he agreed to my suggestion'

CONSIGLIARE: *lo consiglio a partire* or *gli consiglio di partire* or *gli consiglio la partenza* 'I advise him to leave'

CONTINUARE: *continuo a scrivere* 'I'm going on writing'; *continuo la lettera* 'I'm going on with the letter'

CONTRIBUIRE: *contribuisce a renderlo infelice* 'it contributes to making him unhappy'; *contribuisce alla sua infelicità* 'it contributes to his unhappiness'

CONVENIRE: *a Ugo conviene (di) partire* 'it's better for Ugo to leave', *gli è convenuto (di) partire* 'it was better for him to leave', *ha convenuto di partire* 'he agreed to leave'; *a Ugo conviene questo* 'this is better for Ugo'

CONVINCERE: *lo ha convinto a partire* 'he persuaded him to leave', *lo hanno convinto di essere onesti* 'they convinced him they were honest'; *lo hanno convinto del suo sbaglio* 'they convinced him of his mistake'

COSTRINGERE: l'ha costretto ad accettare 'he forced him to accept'

CREDERE: crede di essere ricco 'he thinks he is rich'; *crede tutte le bugie che gli dicono* 'he believes all the lies they tell him', *non crede a questo racconto* 'he does not believe this story', *non credo nella sua onestà* 'I do not believe in his honesty', *non ci credo* 'I do not believe it', *non lo credo* 'I do not think it is true', *credo a Ugo* 'I believe Ugo', *gli credo* 'I believe him'

CURARSI: non si cura di nascondersi 'he does not trouble to hide'; *non si cura delle apparenze* 'he does not care about appearances'

DAR(SI): mi dà da fare 'he keeps me busy', *gli ha dato ad intendere che aveva finito* 'he gave him to understand that he had finished', *non me la dà a bere* 'he won't make me swallow that', *si diede a cantare* (literary) 'he started to sing' or 'he took up singing'; *ho dato un libro a Ugo* 'I gave Ugo a book', *gli do del tu, del lei* 'I address him as *tu*, as *lei*', *gli ho dato del ladro* 'I called him a thief', *si è dato al canto* 'he has taken up singing', *questa finestra dà sul cortile* 'this window faces onto the courtyard'

DECIDER(SI): ha deciso di partire 'he decided to leave', *si è deciso a partire* 'he has made up his mind to leave' or 'he has finally left'; *ha deciso la data della partenza* 'he has fixed the date of departure'

DEGNAR(SI): non si degna di venire 'he does not deign to come'; *non mi ha degnato di un saluto* 'he did not even bother to greet me'

DESIDERARE: desidera (di) partire 'he wants to go away'; *desidera un aumento* 'he wants a rise'

DESTINARE: questo è destinato a finire 'this is destined to finish'; *è destinato al fallimento* 'it is doomed to failure'

DETERMINARE: ha determinato di vincere 'he has decided to win', *questo mi determina ad accettare* 'this makes me decide to accept'; *ha determinato la nostra sorte* 'it determined our fate'

DICHIARAR(SI): ha dichiarato di esser pronto 'he stated he was ready'; *ha dichiarato le sue intenzioni* 'he declared his intentions', *si è dichiarato a favore* 'he declared himself in favour'

DIFFIDARE: l'hanno diffidato ad or *dall'aumentare i prezzi* 'they warned him not to put up the prices'; *diffido di Ugo* 'I do not trust Ugo'

DIMENTICAR(SI): ha dimenticato (or *si è dimenticato*) *di scrivere* 'he forgot to write'; *ha dimenticato* (or *si è dimenticato*) *a casa il libro* 'he left the book at home by mistake', *ha dimenticato* (or *si è dimenticato*) *tutte quelle date* 'he forgot all those dates', *si è dimenticato del libro* 'he forgot about the book'

DIMOSTRAR(SI): ha dimostrato di saperlo 'he has shown he knows it'; *ha dimostrato un teorema* 'he has proved a theorem', *si è dimostrato abile* 'he has proved skilful'

DIRE: ci dice di venire 'he tells us he is coming' or 'he tells us to come'; *dice qualche parola a Ugo* 'he is saying a few words to Ugo', *dire di sì o di no* 'to say yes or no'

DISPERAR(SI): dispera di arrivarci 'he despairs of getting there', *si dispera di essere in ritardo* 'he is very upset at being late'; *dispera della vittoria* 'he has given up all hope of victory', *si dispera del ritardo* 'he is very upset at the delay,

DISPIACERE: *gli dispiace di non sapere il tedesco* 'he is sorry he doesn't know German'; *questo mi dispiace* 'I am sorry about this'

DISPOR(SI): *ho disposto di partire* 'I decided to leave', *si dispone a partire* 'he is preparing to leave'; *dispone di grandi ricchezze* 'he has great riches at his disposal', *si dispone alla partenza* 'he is preparing for his departure', *ha disposto tutto per la partenza* 'he has prepared everything for his departure'

DISSUADERE: *li ha dissuasi dal bere* 'he persuaded them not to drink'; *li ha dissuasi dal tabacco* 'he persuaded them not to smoke'

DIVERTIRSI: *si diverte a giocare* 'he enjoys playing'; *si diverte agli scherzi* 'he enjoys jokes'

DOMANDARE: *le domanda di partire* 'he asks her if he can leave' or 'he asks her to leave'; *domanda un favore* 'he asks a favour', *domanda di te* 'he asks after you'

DOVERE: *deve leggere* 'he has to read'; *gli deve mille lire* 'he owes him 1000 lire'

DUBITARE: *dubita di riuscire* 'he doubts whether he will succeed'; *dubita dell'esito* 'he is doubtful about the outcome'

ECCITAR(SI): *si eccita a cantare* 'he gets excited singing', *il suo senso della giustizia lo eccita a ribellarsi* or *alla ribellione* 'his sense of justice moves him to rebel' or 'to rebellion'; *si eccita alle canzoni* 'the songs excite him'

ESASPERAR(SI): *si esaspera di* (or *ad*) *esser chiamato Fufi* 'it maddens him to be called Fufi'; *la musica lo esaspera* 'music exasperates him'

ESCLUDERE: *ha escluso di venire* 'he has excluded the possibility of coming'; *ha escluso questa ipotesi* 'he has ruled out this hypothesis', *hanno escluso quel candidato dalla gara* 'they have barred that contestant from the race'

ESERCITAR(SI): *si esercita a correre* 'he practises running', *si esercita correndo* 'he keeps in practice by running'; *si esercita alla corsa, al nuoto* 'he practices running, swimming', but with non-sporting activities *in* is used instead of *a*: *si esercita nel canto e nel disegno* 'he practises singing and drawing', *esercita la professione di avvocato* 'he practises the profession of lawyer', *esercitano pressioni su Ugo* 'they are exerting pressure on Ugo', *lo hanno esercitato ai combattimenti* 'they trained him for battle', *questo gioco esercita la memoria* 'this game exercises one's memory'

ESITARE: *esita a entrare* 'he hesitates to come in'; *esita nell'entrare* 'he hesitates as he comes in', *esita nel canto* 'he hesitates as he sings'

FARE: *fa di venire* 'try and come', *fa fare un tavolo* 'he is having a table made', *far vedere un cieco* 'to make a blind man see' or 'to exhibit a blind man' (cf. chapter VI. 10(c)), *questo fa (da) ridere* 'this is ridiculous'; *faresti meglio a venire* 'you had better come', *gli fa piacere (di) venire* 'he is pleased to come', *puoi fare a meno di venire* 'you needn't bother to come', *Ugo fa da mangiare* 'Ugo is cooking', *Ugo fa la minestra* 'Ugo is making the soup',

Ugo fa il furbo 'Ugo is trying to be clever', *Ugo fa il dottore* 'Ugo is a doctor'

FIGURARSI: *si figura di essere furbo* 'he thinks he is clever'; *figurati la sua soddisfazione* 'just imagine his satisfaction'

FINGER(SI): *finge di non sentirlo* 'he is pretending not to hear him'; *finge la sordità* or *si finge sordo* 'he pretends to be deaf'

FINIRE: *ha finito di scrivere* 'he has finished writing', *è finito a scrivere* 'he has ended up writing', *ha finito per scrivere* or *ha finito collo scrivere solo due righe* 'he has ended up by only writing a note'; *ha finito la lettera* 'he has finished the letter', *è finito in tragedia* 'it ended in a tragedy', *Ugo è finito a Londra* 'Ugo ended up in London', *l'autostrada finisce a Mestre* 'the motorway ends at Mestre'

FORZARE: *lo ha forzato a partire* and *lo ha forzato alla partenza* 'he forced him to leave'; *hanno forzato la porta* 'they forced the door'

GIOCAR(SI): *giocano a nascondersi* 'they are playing hide-and-seek'; *giocano a scacchi* 'they are playing chess', *giocano una partita di calcio* 'they are playing a game of football', *si è giocato quel posto* 'he has lost that job', *ci giocherei un milione* 'I bet you a million'

GIURARE: *ha giurato di aiutarlo* 'he swore he would help him'; *giurò vendetta* 'he swore revenge'

GODER(SI): *godo a* or *di* or *nel sentirlo* 'I am gratified to hear it'; *godo (di) buona salute* 'I enjoy good health', *si gode la vita* 'he enjoys life'

GUARDAR(SI): *guarda di coprirti* 'mind you put on some warm clothes'; *guardati dal prender freddo* 'mind you don't get cold', *guarda lo spettacolo* 'he is watching the show', *si guarda allo specchio* 'she is looking at herself in the mirror', *guardati dalle correnti d'aria* 'be careful of draughts', *quella finestra guarda sul* or *verso il* (or, less common, *nel*, or *il*) *giardino* 'that window looks onto the garden'

ILLUDER(SI): *si illude di riuscirci* 'he has the illusion that he is going to succeed'; *molte speranze lo illudevano* 'he nourished vain hopes', *ha illuso un po' tutti con la sua vivacità* 'everyone was a bit taken in by his liveliness'

IMMAGINAR(SI): *(s') immagina di esser povero* 'he thinks he is poor'; *te la immagini a ballare?* 'can you see her dancing?', *s'immagina la povertà* 'he imagines what poverty is like', *ha immaginato una complessa vicenda* 'he thought up a complicated story'

IMPARARE: *impara a leggere* 'he is learning to read'; *impara l'alfabeto* 'he is learning the alphabet', *impara a memoria una poesia* 'he is learning a poem by heart', *l'ho imparato da lui* 'I learnt it from him'

IMPEDIRE: *le impedisce di scrivere* 'he is preventing her from writing'; *gli impedisci il riposo* 'you are preventing him from resting'

IMPEGNAR(SI): *si è impegnato a ottenerlo* 'he undertook to get it' or 'he went all out to get it', *si è impegnato di partire* 'he undertook to leave', *è impegnato a comporre* 'he is engaged in composing'; *ha impegnato un capitale* 'he has pledged a large sum', *questo lavoro lo impegna molto* 'this work makes heavy demands on him'

IMPORRE: *gli ha imposto di venire* 'he ordered him to come'; *ci hanno* *imposto quest'obbligo* 'they imposed this duty on us'

INCARICARE: ha incaricato Ugo di controllare 'he told Ugo to do the checking'; *lo ha incaricato di questo* 'she entrusted this to him'

INCITARE: lo ha incitato a ribellarsi 'he incited him to rebel'; *lo ha incitato alla ribellione* 'he incited him to rebellion'

INCORAGGIARE: lo ha incoraggiato a studiare 'he encouraged him to study'; *lo ha incoraggiato alla pazienza* 'he encouraged him to be patient'

INDURRE: lo ha indotto a venire 'he induced him to come'; *lo ha indotto a un delitto* 'he induced him to commit a crime'

INSEGNARE: gli ha insegnato a leggere 'he taught him to read'; *gli ha insegnato l'alfabeto* 'he taught him the alphabet'

INSISTERE: insiste a or *nel dire che non è colpa sua* 'he insists it is not his fault', and colloquially *insiste* may correspond to *insiste a dire* as in *insiste di non averne colpa* 'he insists he is not to blame'; *insiste nelle sue richieste* 'he persists with his requests'

INTENDER(SI): intende (di) venirci a trovare 'he intends to come and see us'; *non s'intende di pittura* 'he doesn't know anything about painting'

INTERESSAR(SI): non gli interessa (di) vincere 'winning does not interest him', *non s'interessa di riuscire* 'success does not interest him', *s'interessa solo a guadagnare di più* 'he is only interested in earning more'; *questo libro non lo interessa* 'he doesn't find this book interesting', *questo libro non gli interessa* 'he is not interested in this book', *non s'interessa di matematica* 'mathematics is not his subject', *non s'interessa alla matematica* 'he is not interested in mathematics', *non s'interessa di lui* 'he takes no interest in him', *non s'interessa a lui* 'he is not interested in him', *si è interessato per lui* 'he concerned himself with his affairs'

INVITARE: ha invitato Ada a ballare 'he invited Ada to dance'; *li ha invitati a una festa* 'he invited them to a party'

LASCIAR(SI): lo ha lasciato bere 'he let him drink', *lo ha lasciato a bere* 'he left him drinking', *gli hanno lasciato bere una birra* 'they let him drink a beer' (cf. chapter VI. 10(c)), *lascia di tormentarlo* 'stop tormenting him', *si è lasciato imbrogliare* 'he let himself be cheated'; *lo ha lasciato* 'she left him', *gli ha lasciato una bottiglia* 'she left him a bottle'

MANCARE: non mancare di andarlo a trovare 'don't fail to go and see him'; *manca di forza* 'he lacks strength', *gli manca la forza* 'his strength is failing him' or 'he hasn't the strength', *ha mancato un'occasione* 'he missed an opportunity', *manca ai suoi doveri* 'he neglects his duties'

MANDARE: lo manda a far la spesa 'she is sending him to do the shopping', *lo manda a chiamare* 'he sends for him' (with *lo* as the object of *chiamare*), *lo manda a chiamare Ugo* 'he sends him to fetch Ugo' (with *lo* as the subject of *chiamare*); *manda Ugo a scuola* 'she is sending Ugo to school'

MERAVIGLIARSI: si meraviglia di esserne capace 'he is surprised he can', *si è meravigliato a vederlo* 'he marvelled at seeing him'; *si è meravigliato a quello spettacolo* 'he marvelled at that show', *si meraviglia di te* 'he is surprised at you'

MERITAR(SI): (si) merita di esser promosso 'he deserves to pass'; *(si) merita la promozione* 'he deserves a pass'

METTERSI: mi metto a lavorare 'I start working'; *mi metto al lavoro* 'I start work'

MORIRE: fa morire dal ridere 'it's extremely funny'; *muoio dalla fame* or *muoio di fame* 'I'm dying of hunger'

OBBLIGARE: lo obbliga a partire 'she makes him leave'; *lo obbliga al silenzio* 'she forces him to be silent'

OCCUPARSI: si occupa di ordinare la casa 'he is busy tidying the house'; *si occupa di orticultura* 'he dedicates himself to horticulture'

ODIARE: odia studiare 'he hates studying'; *odia il lavoro* 'he hates work'

OFFRIR(SI): ha offerto (or *si è offerto*) *di andare lui* 'he offered to go himself'; *ha offerto da bere, da mangiare* 'he offered something to drink, to eat', *gli ha offerto un caffè* 'he offered him a coffee'

ORDINARE: gli ordina di andarsene 'he orders him to go away'; *ordina una birra al cameriere* 'he orders a beer from the waiter'

OSTINARSI: si ostina a non credergli 'she insists on not believing him'; *si ostina nel diniego* 'he persists in his denial'

PAGARE: ha pagato da bere a tutti 'he offered everyone a drink', *ha pagato il pranzo* 'he paid for the meal', *ha pagato il cameriere* 'he paid the waiter', *ha pagato il pranzo al cameriere* 'he paid the waiter for the meal' or 'he bought the waiter a meal'

PARERE: mi pare di soffocare 'I feel I am stifling', *pare di soffocare* 'one feels one is stifling', *mi pare soffocare* 'he seems to me to be stifling', *pareva dormire* 'he seemed to be sleeping'; *gli pare un buon lavoro* 'it seems a good job to him'

PARLARE: parla di cambiare lavoro 'he talks of changing his job'; *ha parlato a Ugo di questo problema* 'he has spoken to Ugo about this problem', *parlava con Ugo* 'he was talking to Ugo', *parlava l'italiano* 'he could speak Italian', *parlava italiano* or *in italiano* 'he was speaking Italian', *parla di Dante* 'he is talking about Dante', *parla su Dante* 'he is speaking on Dante'

PENSARE: Ugo pensa a guadagnare 'Ugo is thinking about earning', *Ugo pensa di guadagnare* 'Ugo thinks he will earn'; *pensa a lui* 'she thinks of him', *lo pensa* 'she thinks of him' or 'she believes so', *cosa pensi di questo libro?* 'what do you think of this book?'

PENTIRSI: si pente di aver parlato 'he is sorry he spoke'; *si è pentito di ciò che ha detto* 'he regrets what he said'

PERMETTER(SI): mi ha permesso di dipingere 'he allowed me to paint', *non si permetta di alzare la voce* 'don't you dare raise your voice'; *permette una parola?* 'could I have a word with you?', *non mi posso permettere questa spesa* 'I cannot afford this expense', *si è permesso una domanda indiscreta* 'he took the liberty of asking an indiscreet question'

PERSISTERE: persiste a or *nel negare* 'he persists in denying', *persiste nel rifiuto* 'he persists in his refusal'

PERSUADERE: lo ha persuaso a dimettersi 'he has persuaded him to resign', *lo ha persuaso di essere brava* 'she persuaded him she was good'; *lo ha persuaso alla ribellione* 'he persuaded him to rebel', *lo ha persuaso del suo sbaglio* 'he persuaded him of his mistake'

PIACERE: *gli piace recitare* 'he likes acting', *gli piacque di ricordare quell'episodio* 'it gave him pleasure to remember that episode'; *gli piacciono le ciliegie* 'he likes cherries'

POTERE: *può scrivergli lei?* 'can she write to him?'

PREFERIRE: *preferisce camminare* 'he prefers walking'; *preferisce un gelato* 'he prefers an ice-cream', *gli fu preferito il suo rivale* 'his rival was preferred to him'

PREGARE: *lo prega di ascoltare* 'he asks him to listen'; *ti prego di un favore* 'I ask a favour of you'

PRENDERE: *prese a parlare* 'he began talking'; *prende un caffè?* 'will you have a coffee?'

PREPARAR(SI): *si prepara a partire* 'he is getting ready to leave', *si prepara per partire* or *per la partenza* 'he is getting ready for the journey'; *prepara la valigia* 'he is packing his case', *si prepara alla partenza* 'he is getting ready for his departure'

PRESTAR(SI): *si è prestato a insegnargli il greco* 'he agreed to teach him Greek'; *gli presta mille lire* 'he lends him 1000 lire', *si presta a un malinteso* 'it lends itself to a misunderstanding'

PRETENDERE: *pretende di comandare* 'he thinks he has the right to command', *pretende di essere obbedito* 'he expects to be obeyed'; *pretende l'obbedienza* 'he expects obedience'

PROIBIRE: *gli ha proibito di fumare* and *gli ha proibito il tabacco* 'he has forbidden him to smoke'

PROMETTERE: *gli ha promesso di comprarglielo* 'she promised she would buy it for him'; *mi ha promesso un regalo* 'he promised me a present'

PROPOR(SI): *gli ha proposto di collaborare* 'he suggested he could collaborate', *si propone di fare una lunga vacanza* 'he proposes to take a long holiday'

PROVARE: *ha provato a entrare* 'he tried to get in', *ha provato di essere innocente* 'he proved he was innocent'; *proviamo la macchina* 'let us try the car'

PROVVEDERE: *provvedi a spedire questa raccomandata* 'make sure you send this registered letter'; *provvede ai suoi bisogni* 'he sees to his needs', *provvede i ragazzi di scarpe* 'he provides the boys with shoes', *provvede le scarpe ai ragazzi* 'he provides shoes for the boys'

RACCOMANDARE: *ti raccomando di venire* 'do try and come'; *gli ha raccomandato Ada* 'he asked him to look after Ada', *ti raccomando la macchina* 'be careful with the car'

RALLEGRARSI: *mi rallegro di averlo fatto* 'I'm pleased I've done it'; *mi rallegro con te della* or *per la tua promozione* 'I congratulate you on your promotion'

RASSEGNARSI: *mi rassegno ad andarmene* 'I am resigned to going';

non si è rassegnato alla povertà 'he has not become resigned to poverty'

RICORDAR(SI): ricorda di esser fedele a te stesso 'remember to be true to yourself', *ricordati d'impostare* 'remember to take it to the post'; *ricorda le sconfitte subite* 'he remembers the defeats suffered', *ricordati di me* 'remember me', *ricordami ai tuoi* 'remember me to your family', *gli ricorda tuo cugino* 'he reminds him of your cousin'

RIDURRE: lo ha ridotto a tacere and *lo ha ridotto al silenzio* 'he reduced him to silence'

RIFIUTARE: rifiuto di collaborare 'I refuse to cooperate'; *rifiuto la tua offerta* 'I refuse your offer'

RINCRESCERE: gli rincresce (di) perdere 'he dislikes losing'

RINUNCIARE: rinuncia a fumare and *rinuncia al fumo* 'he is giving up smoking'

RIPRENDERE: ha ripreso a lamentarsi 'he started complaining again'; *ha ripreso il discorso* 'he went on with what he was saying'

RISOLVER(SI): ha risolto di tentare 'he decided to try', *si è risolto a tentare* 'he made up his mind to try' or 'he finally tried'; *si è risolto in nulla* 'it came to nothing'

RISPONDERE: ha risposto di essere stanco 'he replied that he was tired'; *rispondo a te* 'I am answering you', *rispondo a una lettera* 'I am answering a letter', *mi ha risposto due righe* 'he dropped me a line in answer', *non rispondo delle sue azioni* 'I do not answer for his actions'

RIUSCIRE: non sono riuscito ad aprire il baule and *non mi è riuscito di aprire il baule* 'I did not manage to open the trunk'; *questo mi è riuscito utile* 'this turned out to be useful to me'

SAPERE: sa essere duro 'he can be hard', *sa di essere duro* 'he knows he is hard'; *sa il latino* 'he knows Latin', *sa di te* 'he knows about you', *sa di tappo* 'it tastes of cork'

SBRIGAR(SI): si è sbrigato a finire 'he hurried to finish'; *ha sbrigato il lavoro* 'he got through the work quickly'

SCEGLIERE: ha scelto di tacere 'he chose to be silent'; *ha scelto il silenzio* 'he chose silence'

SCOMMETTERE: ha scommesso di batterlo 'he bet he would beat him'; *ha scommesso una forte somma* 'he bet a large sum'

SCUSAR(SI): mi scuso di essere in ritardo 'I apologize for being late'; *mi scuso del ritardo* 'I apologize for the delay', *scusa la domanda* 'excuse the question', *prega di scusarlo* 'he sends his apologies'

SEGUITARE: seguita a tormentarmi 'he goes on tormenting me'; *seguita il lavoro* 'he is going on with the work'

SEMBRARE: mi sembra di scivolare 'I feel as though I'm slipping', *sembra di scivolare* 'one feels as though one is slipping', *mi sembra scivolare* 'he seems to me to be slipping'; *mi sembra un bel libro* 'it seems a good book to me'

SENTIR(SI): sento di morire 'I feel I am dying', *mi sento morire* 'I feel I am dying' or 'the thought makes me ill', *sento gridare* 'I can hear shouting', *lo sento camminare* 'I can hear him walking', *non mi sento di far questo* 'I don't feel up to doing this'; *sento la morte che si avvicina* 'I feel death approaching', *sento un rumore* 'I hear a noise'

SENTIRSELA: non me la sento di provare 'I do not feel like trying'

SERVIR(SI): serve a (or *per*) *tagliare il pane* 'it is used for cutting bread', *non serve venire* 'it is no use coming'; *serve al governo* 'it is of use to the government', *serve il governo* 'he serves the government', *gli serve da coltello* 'he uses it as a knife', *si è servito del coltello* 'he used the knife', *gli hanno servito un vino eccellente* 'they gave him an excellent wine'

SFORZARSI: si sforzava di (or more rarely *a*) *star serio* 'he tried hard to be serious'

SMETTERE: ha smesso di lavorare 'he stopped working'; *ha smesso il lavoro* 'he stopped work'

SOFFRIRE: soffre a or *di vederla così* 'it pains him to see her like this'; *soffre il freddo* 'he feels the cold', *soffre d'insonnia* 'he suffers from insomnia'

SOGNAR(SI): sogna di esser famoso 'he dreams of being famous', *non si è sognato di partire* 'he did not dream of leaving'; *sogna la gloria* 'he dreams of glory', *sogna* (or *si sogna di*) *Ada ogni notte* 'he dreams of Ada every night'

SOPPORTARE: non sopporta di essere criticato 'he cannot bear to be criticized'; *non sopporta le critiche* 'he cannot bear criticism'

SPARARE: ha sparato una fucilata all'orso 'he fired his gun at the bear'

SPERARE: spera di dimagrire 'she hopes to slim'; *spero in lui* 'I place my hopes in him'

SPETTARE: la decisione spetta a lui or *spetta a lui* (more rarely with *di*) *decidere* 'it's for him to decide'

SPINGERE: lo spinge a tentare 'he urges him to try'; *lo spinge alla rovina* 'he drives him to ruin'

STABILIRE: ha stabilito di non bere più 'he has decided not to drink any more'; *ha stabilito la partenza* 'he has fixed his departure'

STARE: sta a sentire un concerto 'he is listening to a concert', *sta per sentire un concerto* 'he is about to listen to a concert'; *sta a te decidere* 'it is up to you to decide', *sta in te vincere* 'winning depends on you'

SUGGERIRE: gli suggerisce di non votare 'he suggests to him that he shouldn't vote'; *gli suggerisce una soluzione* 'he suggests a solution to him'

SUPPLICARE: lo ha supplicato di aiutarla 'she begged him to help her'; *lo ha supplicato di una grazia* 'he begged a favour of him'

TARDARE: tarda a venire 'he is late in coming'

TEMERE: teme di aver la febbre 'he fears he has a temperature', *non teme a* or *di dire quello che pensa* 'he is not afraid of saying what he thinks'; *teme le vespe* 'he is afraid of wasps'

TENER(CI): (ci) tengo a dichiarare che l'ho fatto io 'I want to make it clear that I did it', *ci tiene a riuscire* 'he is keen to succeed'; *ci tiene al successo* 'success means a lot to him'

TENTARE: tenterò di aiutarlo 'I shall try to help him', *mi ha tentato a provare* 'he tempted me to try'; *tenta questa soluzione* 'he tries out this solution', *questo lo tenta* 'this tempts him'

TOCCARE: cosa gli tocca (di) fare! 'the things he has to do!', *mi tocca (di) vederne delle belle* 'fine things I have to witness'; *questo non lo tocca* 'this doesn't affect him', *tocca a lui* 'it's his turn', *gli è toccata una sberla* 'he was dealt a slap across the face'

TORNARE: torna sempre a dirmi le stesse cose 'he keeps repeating the same things to me'; *torna al lavoro* 'he is going back to work', *torna dal lavoro* 'he is coming back from work', *torna alla carica* 'he is at it again'

VANTAR(SI): si vanta di essere forte 'he boasts of being strong'; *si vanta della sua forza* 'he boasts of his strength', *vanta sempre le sue ricchezze* 'he is always boasting about his wealth', *questa città vanta molti illustri pittori* 'this town boasts many famous painters'

VEDERE: li vedo giocare 'I see them play', *vedi di far presto* 'mind you are quick'; *vedo una formica* 'I can see an ant'

VENIRE: vengo a prenderti 'I'll come and collect you', *sono venuto per vederti* 'I have come in order to see you'; *viene a Firenze* 'he is coming to Florence', *viene in Italia* 'he is coming to Italy', *viene da Londra* 'he comes from London'

VERGOGNARSI: si vergogna di non saper nuotare 'he is ashamed he can't swim', *mi vergogno a ripeterlo* 'I am ashamed to repeat it'; *si vergogna della sua inefficienza* 'he is ashamed of his inefficiency', *mi vergogno a questo spettacolo* 'I feel ashamed at this display'

VIETARE: le vieta di parlare 'he forbids her to speak'; *le ha vietato l'ingresso* 'he forbade her to enter'

VOLERE: vuole far soldi 'he wants to make money'; *vuole la ricchezza* 'he wants riches'

(b) Some constructions with adjective + preposition + verb or noun. We omit past participles of verbs given in the previous list.

ALIENO: è alieno dallo spettegolare and *è alieno dai pettegolezzi* 'gossiping is alien to him'

ANSIOSO: è ansioso di ricevere tue notizie 'he is impatient to hear from you'; *è ansioso per l'esito dell'iniziativa* 'he is anxious about the outcome of the enterprise'

AVIDO: è avido di guadagnare molto 'he is greedy to earn a lot', but more commonly with a noun: *è avido di ricchezze* 'he is greedy for riches'

CONTENTO and *SCONTENTO: è contento di essere in vacanza* 'he is glad he is on holiday', *è scontento delle sue vacanze* 'he is not pleased with his holidays'

CONTRARIO: è contrario a fare il viaggio 'he is against going on the journey'; *è contrario al viaggio* 'he is against the journey'

CURIOSO: sono curioso di vedere il tuo villaggio 'I am curious to see your village'; *è curioso di tutto* 'he is curious about everything'

DECISO: è deciso ad arricchire 'he is determined to become rich'; *è deciso a tutto* 'he stops at nothing'

DESIDEROSO: è desideroso di vedere i bambini 'he desires to see the children'; *è desideroso di successo* 'he desires success'

DEGNO and *INDEGNO: è degno di essere premiato* 'he is worthy of receiving a prize'; *è indegno di un premio* 'he is unworthy of a prize'

DIFFICILE: è difficile crederlo 'it's difficult to believe it', *è difficile da fare* or *a farsi (a fare)* 'it is difficult to do'

DISPOSTO: è disposto a dirti tutto 'he is ready to tell you everything'; *è disposto alla partenza* 'he is prepared to leave'

FACILE: è facile perdersi 'it is easy to get lost', *è facile da fare* or *a farsi (a fare)* 'it is easy to do'; *è facile all'ira* 'he is quick to anger'

GIUSTO and *INGIUSTO: è giusto (di) fare così* 'it is right to do this'

GRADEVOLE and *SGRADEVOLE: è gradevole da bere* 'it's pleasant to drink' *è gradevole stare al sole* 'it's pleasant to be in the sun'; *è sgradevole al tatto* 'it's unpleasant to the touch'

IMPORTANTE: è importante (di) ottenere la sua firma and *la sua firma è importante da ottenere* 'it is important to get his signature'

LIETO: sarà lieto di accettare 'he'll be glad to accept'; *è lieto della notizia* 'he is glad of the news'

LONTANO: è lontano dal finire 'he is far from finishing'; *è lontano dalla fine* 'he is far from the end'

NECESSARIO: è necessario (di) prenotare i posti 'it is necessary to book seats'; *è necessario alla riuscita dell'impresa* 'it is necessary for the success of the undertaking'

PRONTO: è pronto a partire 'he is ready to leave', *è pronto per partire* 'he is ready for the journey', *le patate sono pronte da cuocere* 'the potatoes are ready to be cooked'; *è pronto all'ira* 'he is quick to anger', *è pronto a tutto* 'he is ready for anything', *è pronto per il viaggio* 'he is ready for the journey'

SICURO: è sicuro di venire? 'is he sure he'll come?'; *è sicuro dell'orario?* 'is he sure of the timetable?'

UTILE and *INUTILE: è utile possedere questa macchina* 'it is useful to own this car', *questa macchina è inutile da possedere* 'it's useless to own this car'

(c) One should note two other points on the use of prepositions: the first concerns the constructions noun + preposition + noun of the following type: *è una peste di bambino* 'he is a wretch of a child', *è una bestia di avvocato* 'he is a fool of a lawyer', *è stato quell'egoista del* (or *di* or *di un*) *direttore* 'it was that egoist of a director', *me l'ha detto quell'angelo di tua moglie* 'that angelic wife of yours told me', *me l'ha spiegato quel genio di Ada* 'that genius of an Ada explained it to me'. The terms introducing *di* are evaluative, either expressing a negative judgement (*bestia, egoista*, etc.), or used in an ironic or jocular way (*angelo, genio*, etc.)[5].

It will be seen that when there is *un* with the first term there is no article with the second (which cannot be a proper name), and when there is *quello* with the first term there is normally an article with the second (unless it is rejected by expressions such as *tua moglie*, etc., cf. chapter V. 9).

(d) The second point concerns some prepositions which behave differently depending on whether they are combined with nouns or pronouns: *contro il* or *al muro* 'against the wall', but *contro di me* (rarer *a me*; here and below we put the rarer form in brackets) 'against me'; *dentro la* or *alla scatola* 'in the box', but *dentro di noi (a noi)* 'within ourselves'; *dietro la* or *alla porta* 'behind the door', but *dietro di voi (a voi)* 'behind you'; *dopo la lezione* 'after the lecture', but *dopo di te* 'after you'; *fra le pagine* 'between the pages', but *fra di noi* or *fra noi* 'between ourselves', and only *fra me e te* 'between you and me', *fra me e lui* 'between him and me', etc. (the same for *tra*); *fuori* is followed by *di* or *da* both before nouns and pronouns: *fuori dalla scatola* 'out of the box', *fuori di sè* 'beside himself', but there are a few set expressions in which there is no *di* in front of a noun: *fuori città* 'out of town', *fuori casa* 'not at home'; *lungo il* or *al muro* 'along the wall', but *lungo di me* 'alongside me'; *oltre il* or *al regalo* 'as well as the present', but *oltre a noi* 'as well as us'; *presso il* or *al tavolo* 'near the table', but *presso di noi (a noi)* 'near us'; *senza i guanti* 'without gloves', but *senza di lui (senza lui)* 'without him'; *sopra il* or *al tavolo* 'on the table', but *sopra di noi (a noi)* 'above us'; *sotto il letto* or *al letto* 'under the bed', but *sotto di voi (a voi)* 'beneath you'; *sul tetto* 'on the roof', but *su di lui* 'on him'; *verso il pozzo* 'towards the well', but *verso di me* 'towards me'. Any conjunctive pronoun, in the oblique form, is naturally linked to the verb: *corrono incontro a lei* 'they run towards her' corresponds to *le corrono incontro*. It would seem that the conjunctive pronoun is only used if the preposition can be accompanied by *a*: from *corre verso di lui* 'he runs towards him' we cannot get *gli corre verso*.

9 Agreement of past participles

(a) When there is no direct object the past participle agrees with the subject if the verb is conjugated with *essere: Ada è venuta* 'Ada has come', *Ugo è venuto* 'Ugo has come'; when there is a plural subject the agreement of the past participle follows the same rule as that of adjectives: *Ada e Ugo sono venuti* 'Ada and Ugo have come', *Eva e Ada sono venute* 'Eva and Ada have come'.

The past participle has an invariable ending -*o* if the verb is conjugated with *avere*: *Ada ha dormito* 'Ada has slept', *Ugo ha dormito* 'Ugo has slept', *Ada e Ugo hanno dormito* 'Ada and Ugo have slept'.

(b) When there is a noun as direct object (or a preceding relative pronoun) the past participle usually follows the above rules, but it may agree with the object (although this is rare): *Ugo ha mangiato* or *mangiata una pesca* 'Ugo has eaten a peach', *la pesca che Ugo ha mangiato* or *mangiata era acerba* 'the peach that Ugo ate was not ripe', *Ugo si è mangiato* or *mangiata una pesca* 'Ugo has eaten a peach', *la pesca che Ugo si è mangiato* or *mangiata* 'the peach that Ugo has eaten', *Ada ha mangiato* or *mangiati due aranci* 'Ada has eaten two oranges', *i due aranci che Ada ha mangiato* or *mangiati* 'the two oranges that Ada has eaten', *Ada si è mangiata* or *mangiati due aranci* 'Ada has eaten two oranges', *i due aranci che Ada si è mangiata* or *mangiati* 'the two oranges that Ada has eaten'. (For the *si* forms see chapter VI. 11.)

(c) When there is a third person pronoun as a preceding direct object the past participle agrees with it; we give examples first with a noun and then with a pronoun: *Ugo ha mangiato la pesca* 'Ugo has eaten the peach': *Ugo l'ha mangiata; Ugo ha mangiato le pesche* 'Ugo has eaten the peaches': *Ugo le ha mangiate; Ada ha mangiato l'arancio* 'Ada has eaten the orange': *Ada lo ha mangiato; Ada ha mangiato gli aranci* 'Ada has eaten the oranges': *Ada li ha mangiati; Ugo si è mangiato una pesca* 'Ugo has eaten a peach': *Ugo se la è mangiata; Ugo e Ada si sono mangiati una pesca* 'Ugo and Ada have eaten a peach': *Ugo e Ada se la sono mangiata.*

(d) When the preceding pronouns are *mi, ti, ci, vi* and *ne,* one has to distinguish between their use with a verb taking the auxiliary *avere* and a verb taking the auxiliary *essere.* With transitive verbs and the auxiliary *avere* either

(i) there may be no agreement and the past participle will have the invariable ending in -*o*: *Ugo mi ha visto* 'Ugo has seen me', where *mi* can refer to a male or female; *Ugo vi ha visto* 'Ugo has seen you', where *vi* can refer to males or females; *hanno bevuto della birra* 'they drank some beer': *ne hanno bevuto*; or

(ii) there may be agreement: with *mi* and *ti* the past participle will end in -*o* if the pronoun refers to a man, in -*a* if it refers to a woman; with *ci* and *vi* it will end in -*i* if the pronoun refers to men, or men and women, in -*e* if it refers to women; with *ne* the ending will depend on the gender and number of the noun to which it refers: *ci ha visti* 'he has seen us', where *ci* refers to males, or males and females; *ci ha viste* 'he has seen us', where *ci* refers to females; *vi ha visti* 'he has seen you', where *vi* refers to males, or males and females; *vi ha viste* 'he has seen you', where *vi* refers to females; *hanno bevuto del vino* 'they drank some wine': *ne hanno bevuto;* *hanno bevuto della birra* 'they drank some beer': *ne hanno bevuta.*

When the verb is preceded by *ne* and followed by an object, the agreement of the past participle is compulsory if the object indicates the gender and number of *ne*: *ne hanno mangiati molti* 'they ate many' (of them, masculine plural), *ne hanno bevuta molta* 'they drank a lot' (of it, feminine singular). If the object does not indicate the gender and number of *ne* there may either be no agreement: *ne hanno mangiato la metà* 'they ate half' (of it, or of them), or there may be agreement with the object: *ne hanno mangiata la metà.*

(e) With so-called reflexive (or pronominal) verbs the auxiliary is *essere* and the past participle agrees either with the subject or with the object (as in (b) above): *ci siamo bevuti* or *bevuta una birra* 'we drank a beer'.

If with these pronominal verbs there is a direct object pronoun which precedes the verb, the past participle must agree with it (as in (c) above): *ce la siamo bevuta* 'we drank it'; with *ne* however the agreement of the past participle with the partitive pronoun is optional (as in (d) above), although in this case it is preferred; corresponding to *Ugo si è bevuto* or *bevuta della birra in abbondanza* 'Ugo drank plenty of beer', we have *Ugo se ne è bevuto* or *bevuta in abbondanza*; and, with a following object: corresponding to *Ada si è mangiata* or *mangiati molti aranci* 'Ada ate many oranges', we have *Ada se ne è mangiata* or *mangiati molti*. Note that the preceding direct object pronoun with these verbs can only be in the third person.

For agreement in the case of impersonal *si* constructions, see chapter VI. 11(c).

(f) There is no agreement with *ne* when it is not a partitive: *hanno seguito la lezione e ne hanno discusso* (invariable ending in *-o*) 'they followed the lecture and talked about it', *Ugo ha visto Ada e se ne è innamorato* (agreement with the subject) 'Ugo saw Ada and fell in love with her'.

The same rules apply to the agreement of the past participle when a modal verb is used, i.e., *potut- bere, volut- bere,* etc., instead of *bevut-*.

10 Clusters of conjunctive pronouns

(a) To begin with the simplest cases:

(i) As has been stated in chapter V. 8, when two unstressed pronouns come together the indirect object normally precedes the direct object: *ve la do* 'I'll give it to you', *glielo diciamo* 'we say it to him', *te lo impresta* 'he is lending it to you', *Ugo mi si avvicinò* 'Ugo approached me', *se li tolse subito* 'he took them off at once'.

(ii) Impersonal or passive *si* (see chapter VI. 11) always comes next to the verb, unless the accompanying pronoun is *ne: la si vede bene da qui* 'one can see it well from here', *gli si vuol bene lo stesso* 'one is fond of him all the same', *se ne parlò a lungo* 'it was discussed at length'.

(b) The examples we have given so far of indirect object followed by direct object all had a third person pronoun as direct object. The rule becomes more complicated if first and second person pronouns are used. It may be helpful to set out what seems to be the most acceptable sequence illustrating the relative order to which any combination of pronouns must conform, and then to clarify the table with examples:

mi, gli/le (datives), *vi, ti, ci, si* (reflexive), *lo/la/li/le* (accusatives), *si* (impersonal or passive), *ne*.[6]

The first person singular precedes the second person singular and plural, and the second person plural precedes the first person plural: *mi ti presento* 'I introduce myself to you', *mi ti presenti* 'you introduce yourself to me', *mi vi presento* 'I introduce myself to you (plural)', *mi vi presentate* 'you introduce yourselves to me', *vi ci presentiamo* 'we introduce ourselves to you (plural)', *vi ci presentate* 'you introduce yourselves to us'. These forms, however, tend to be avoided.

The first person singular precedes the third person direct or indirect object, but the second person singular precedes the third person direct and follows the third person indirect object: *me lo dai* 'you give it to me', *mi gli rivolgo* 'I turn to him', *te lo do* 'I give it to you', *gli ti rivolgi* 'you turn to him'.

(c) We shall examine here the behaviour of pronouns, compared with that of nouns, in certain verb + infinitive constructions. We shall first look at *fare* 'to make' followed by an infinitive (*lasciare* 'to let' behaves like *fare*), and call this the causative construction. A series of examples will be listed, based, for the sake of simplicity, only on the interpretation *faccio* + *Ada scrive una lettera a Ugo* 'I make + Ada writes a letter to Ugo'; all other interpretations are disregarded: for instance, *gliela faccio scrivere a Ada* is spontaneously interpreted as 'I make him write it to Ada', but in our list it appears, in (7.g), only with its more forced interpretation 'I make Ada write it to him'. Here, as in section (d) below, the examples are ordered as follows: seven sentences are given, numbered from (1) to (7), with nouns for the (1) subject, (2) direct object, (3) indirect object, (4) subject and direct object, (5) direct object and indirect object, (6) subject and indirect object, (7) subject, direct object and indirect object. The arabic figures in the two columns correspond to each other but the roman figures in the left hand column (I, II, III) and the letters in the right hand column (a, b, c, etc.) are only used to identify the sentences within the columns and do not correspond to each other.[7] For all sentences we substitute each noun in turn with a clitic, and list the resulting sentences in the right hand column. Forms which are felt to be grammatical but awkward are put in brackets. We use the names of the cases as follows: 'accusative' for the forms without a preposition (*lui, lei*; clitics: *lo, la*); 'dative' for the forms preceded by *a* (*a lui, a lei*; clitics: *gli, le*); 'agentive' for the forms preceded by *da* (*da lui, da lei*; no clitic counterpart).

(1) *faccio scrivere Ada*	(1.a) *la faccio scrivere*
(2) *faccio scrivere una lettera*	(2.a) *la faccio scrivere*
(3) *faccio scrivere a Ugo*	(3.a) *gli faccio scrivere*
(4.I) *faccio scrivere una lettera a Ada*	(4.a) *le faccio scrivere una lettera*
	(4.b) *la faccio scrivere a Ada*
(4.II) *faccio scrivere una lettera da Ada*	(4.c) *la faccio scrivere da Ada*
	(4.d) *gliela faccio scrivere*

(5) *faccio scrivere una lettera a Ugo*

(5.a) *la faccio scrivere a Ugo*
(5.b) *gli faccio scrivere una lettera*
(5.c) *gliela faccio scrivere*

(6.I) *faccio scrivere Ada a Ugo*
(6.II) *(faccio scrivere a Ugo, a Ada)*
(6.III) *faccio scrivere a Ugo da Ada*

(6.a) *la faccio scrivere a Ugo*
(6.b) *(le faccio scrivere a Ugo)*
(6.c) *(gli faccio scrivere Ada)*
(6.d) *(gli faccio scrivere a Ada)*
(6.e) *gli faccio scrivere da Ada*

(7.I) *faccio scrivere a Ada una lettera a Ugo*
(7.II) *faccio scrivere una lettera a Ugo da Ada*

(7.a) *le faccio scrivere una lettera a Ugo*
(7.b) *(la faccio scrivere a Ugo, a Ada)*
(7.c) *la faccio scrivere a Ugo da Ada*
(7.d) *(gli faccio scrivere una lettera a Ada)*
(7.e) *gli faccio scrivere una lettera da Ada*
(7.f) *gliela faccio scrivere a Ugo*
(7.g) *(gliela faccio scrivere a Ada)*
(7.h) *gliela faccio scrivere da Ada*

The situation can be described as follows: in the causative construction the subject of the infinitive appears

(i) as an accusative if there is no direct or indirect object;

(ii) as an accusative or agentive if there is an indirect object but no direct object expressed or understood;

(iii) as a dative or agentive if a direct object is expressed or understood; an indirect object may be present, as in (6) and (7), or absent, as in (4); in (6.II), (6.b), (6.d) the subject in the dative is acceptable if the sentences are taken as having an understood direct object, i.e., if *scrivere a Ugo* is interpreted, for instance, as 'writing a letter to Ugo'.

As for the choice of accusative, dative or agentive, where a choice is possible, it would seem to depend on conditions which will be summarized in (d)(ii) below (p. 210).

The stressed forms usually follow the infinitive in this order: accusative, dative, agentive. Two stressed forms in the same case are avoided; two accusatives (for subject and direct object) are excluded, and two datives (for subject and indirect object) are awkward; these are separated at least by an intonational break, as in (6.II), or by some other element, as in (7.I); the dative subject may go immediately after the infinitive, as in (7.I), or after the indirect object, as in *faccio scrivere una lettera a Ugo, a Ada*, or before the main verb, as in *a Ada, faccio scrivere una lettera a Ugo*. Two datives are quite acceptable if the subject is a clitic and the indirect object a stressed form, as in (7.a).

The clitics are always attached to *fare*; a clitic subject cannot be preceded by a clitic direct or indirect object; the only cluster is dative + accusative, which therefore cannot represent indirect object + subject: we find it in our list representing either subject + direct object, as in (4.d) and (7.f), or indirect object + direct object, as in (5.c), (7.g), and (7.h).

When the object of the infinitive is introduced by a preposition, as in *pensare a* 'to think of', *provvedere a* 'to take care of', *rinunciare a* 'to give up', *abusare di* 'to abuse', *sospettare di* 'to suspect', *discutere di* 'to discuss', the subject may appear as a dative (as when the verb has a direct object), as an accusative (as when the verb has no direct object), or as an agentive (as when the verb has a direct or indirect object); from *faccio + Ada parla di questo* 'I make + Ada talks of this' we get:

(8.I) *faccio parlare Ada di questo*	(8.a) *la faccio parlare di questo*
	(8.b) *le faccio parlare di questo*
(8.II) *faccio parlare di questo a Ada*	(8.c) *ne faccio parlare Ada*
	(8.d) *ne faccio parlare a Ada*
(8.III) *faccio parlare di questo da Ada*	(8.e) *ne faccio parlare da Ada*
	(8.f) *gliene faccio parlare*

(d)(i) With verbs of perception (*vedere* 'to see', *sentire* 'to hear') followed by an infinitive the situation is more varied. Using the same criteria as above, we shall list the following sentences, interpreted only on the basis of *ho visto + Ada scrive una lettera a Ugo* 'I saw + Ada writes a letter to Ugo':

(1.I) *ho visto Ada scrivere*	(1.a) *la ho vista scrivere*
(1.II) *ho visto scrivere Ada*	
(2) *ho visto scrivere una lettera*	(2.a) *la ho vista scrivere*
	(2.b) *(ho visto scriverla)*
(3) *ho visto scrivere a Ugo*	(3.a) *gli ho visto scrivere*

(4.I) *ho visto Ada scrivere una lettera*

(4.II) *(ho visto scrivere una lettera a Ada)*

(4.III) *(ho visto scrivere una lettera da Ada)*

(5) *ho visto scrivere una lettera a Ugo*

(6.I) *ho visto Ada scrivere a Ugo*

(6.II) *(ho visto scrivere a Ugo, a Ada)*

(6.III) *(ho visto scrivere a Ugo da Ada)*

(7.I) *ho visto Ada scrivere una lettera a Ugo*

(7.II) *(ho visto scrivere una lettera a Ugo, a Ada)*

(7.III) *ho visto scrivere una lettera a Ugo da Ada*

(3.b) *(ho visto scrivergli)*

(4.a) *la ho vista scrivere una lettera*

(4.b) *le ho visto scrivere una lettera*

(4.c) *(la ho vista scrivere Ada)*

(4.d) *(ho visto scriverla Ada)*

(4.e) *ho visto Ada scriverla*

(4.f) *la ho vista scrivere a Ada*

(4.g) *(ho visto scriverla a Ada)*

(4.h) *la ho vista scrivere da Ada*

(4.i) *(ho visto scriverla da Ada)*

(4.j) *(la ho vista scriverla)*

(4.k) *gliela ho vista scrivere*

(5.a) *la ho vista scrivere a Ugo*

(5.b) *(ho visto scriverla a Ugo)*

(5.c) *gli ho visto scrivere una lettera*

(5.d) *(ho visto scrivergli una lettera)*

(5.e) *gliela ho vista scrivere*

(5.f) *(ho visto scrivergliela)*

(6.a) *la ho vista scrivere a Ugo*

(6.b) *(le ho visto scrivere a Ugo)*

(6.c) *(gli ho visto scrivere Ada)*

(6.d) *(ho visto scrivergli Ada)*

(6.e) *ho visto Ada scrivergli*

(6.f) *(gli ho visto scrivere a Ada)*

(6.g) *(ho visto scrivergli a Ada)*

(6.h) *(gli ho visto scrivere da Ada)*

(6.i) *(ho visto scrivergli da Ada)*

(6.j) *(la ho vista scrivergli)*

(7.a) *la ho vista scrivere una lettera a Ugo*

(7.b) *le ho visto scrivere una lettera a Ugo*

(7.c) *(la ho vista scrivere a Ugo Ada)*

(7.d) *(ho visto scriverla a Ugo Ada)*

(7.e) *ho visto Ada scriverla a Ugo*

(7.f) *(la ho vista scrivere a Ugo, a Ada)*

(7.g) *(ho visto scriverla a Ugo, a Ada)*

(7.h) *la ho vista scrivere a Ugo da Ada*

(7.i) *(ho visto scriverla a Ugo da Ada)*

(7.j) *(gli ho visto scrivere una lettera Ada)*

(7.k) *(ho visto scrivergli una lettera Ada)*

(7.l) *ho visto Ada scrivergli una lettera*

(7.m) *(gli ho visto scrivere una lettera a Ada)*

(7.n) *(ho visto scrivergli una lettera a Ada)*

(7.o) *gli ho visto scrivere una lettera da Ada*

(7.p) *(ho visto scrivergli una lettera da Ada)*

(7.q) *(la ho vista scriverla a Ugo)*

(7.r) *gliela ho vista scrivere a Ugo*

(7.s) *(gliela ho vista scrivere Ada)*

(7.t) *(ho visto scrivergliela Ada)*

(7.u) *ho visto Ada scrivergliela*

(7.v) *(gliela ho vista scrivere a Ada)*

(7.w) *(ho visto scrivergliela a Ada)*

(7.x) *gliela ho vista scrivere da Ada*

(7.y) *(ho visto scrivergliela da Ada)*

(7.z) *la ho vista scrivergli una lettera*

(7.za)   *(la   ho   vista   scriver-gliela)*

As may be gathered from these examples, the subject of the infinitive may always appear as an accusative, not only when there are no direct and indirect objects, but even if these are present (as accusative and dative respectively). The subject may also, as in the causative construction, appear as a dative or agentive if there is a direct object (expressed or understood) and/or an indirect object; but when there is already a dative for the indirect object, one tends to avoid the dative for the subject. In (6.II), (6.b), (6.f), and (6.g) the subject in the dative is acceptable if the sentences are taken as having an understood direct object. As with the causative construction, the choice of one among these cases would seem to depend on conditions which are summarized in (d)(ii) below (p. 210).

The stressed form of the subject normally precedes the infinitive if it is in the accusative and there is a direct and/or an indirect object, as in (4), (6), and (7); otherwise it may follow or precede the infinitive, as in (1). After the infinitive the order is accusative, dative, agentive.

Two accusatives, for subject and direct object, which were excluded in the causative construction, are quite acceptable here, as in (4) and (7), and the preferred order is with the subject before and the direct object after the infinitive. Two datives, for subject and indirect object, are awkward, and tend to be separated by an intonation break; the subject may go after the indirect object, as in (6.II), (7.II), or after the infinitive, as in *ho visto scrivere, a Ada, una lettera a Ugo,* or before the main verb, as in *a Ada, ho visto scrivere una lettera a Ugo*; all these sentences are awkward, but two datives become quite acceptable if the subject is a clitic and the indirect object a stressed form, as in (7.b).

The clitics behave differently depending on their syntactic function: the subject, in the dative or accusative, must come before the direct or indirect object, and must be attached to the main verb; the direct and indirect objects, in the accusative and dative, may be attached either to the main verb, or, more awkwardly, to the infinitive; if the subject is in the accusative, as we cannot have accusative + accusative and accusative + dative clusters, the direct and indirect objects must go with the infinitive, as in (4.j), (6.j), (7.q), (7.z), and (7.za); from a different point of view one can say that if the direct object goes with the main verb, the subject must be in the dative, as in (4.k) and (7.r); and we cannot have both subject and indirect object with the main verb, because there is no dative + dative or accusative + dative cluster; the only existing cluster, i.e., dative + accusative, can be interpreted either as subject + direct object, as in (4.k) and (7.r), or as indirect object + direct object, as in (5.e), (7.s), (7.v), and (7.x), but not as indirect object + subject. Note that as an indirect object + direct object this cluster may go either with the main verb or with the infinitive, but as a subject + direct object it can only go with the main verb and not with the infinitive. The cluster cannot be split, so for (4.k) we cannot have *le ho visto scriverla*, and for (5.e) we cannot have *gli ho visto scriverla*; if we want to separate the clitics we get (4.j) and (7.q) with accusative – accusative, or (6.j) and (7.z) with accusative – dative. The only combination of three clitics is found in (7.za) with accusative – dative + accusative, representing subject – indirect object + direct object. This combination would appear to be the only one possible, considering that the subject must come first and that combinations with two datives and clusters with the order accusative + dative are excluded.

The choice of the dative for the subject is much more awkward with verbs like *guardare* 'to watch', *ascoltare* 'to listen to' than it is with *vedere, sentire*: *le ho guardato scrivere una lettera* 'I watched her write a letter', *le ho ascoltato cantare una canzone* 'I listened to her sing a song' are less acceptable than *le ho visto scrivere una lettera* 'I saw her write a letter', *le ho sentito cantare una canzone* 'I heard her sing a song'; the corresponding sentences with *la* instead of *le* would be equally acceptable with *guardare, ascoltare* and with *vedere, sentire*.

When the object of the infinitive is introduced by a preposition the situation corresponds to the one mentioned above for the causative construction; from *ho sentito + Ada parla di questo* 'I heard + Ada speaks of this' we get:

(8.I) *ho sentito Ada parlare di questo*

(8.II) *(ho sentito parlare di questo a Ada)*

(8.III) *ho sentito parlare di questo da Ada*

(8.a) *la ho sentita parlare di questo*

(8.b) *le ho sentito parlare di questo*

(8.c) *(ne ho sentito parlare Ada)*

(8.d) *(ho sentito parlarne Ada)*

(8.e) *ho sentito Ada parlarne*

(8.f) *(ne ho sentito parlare a Ada)*

(8.g) *(ho sentito parlarne a Ada)*
(8.h) *ne ho sentito parlare da Ada*
(8.i) *(ho sentito parlarne da Ada)*
(8.j) *la ho sentita parlarne*
(8.k) *gliene ho sentito parlare*

(ii) We can present the following general considerations, which apply both to causative and to perception constructions: the subject of the infinitive can be
(A) accusative, if the infinitive has no direct or indirect objects,
(B) accusative, dative, or agentive, if the infinitive has direct and/or indirect objects; the choice of one among these three cases depends on two conditions:
(I) the so-called 'like case constraint' which prevents the subject of the infinitive from appearing in a case already used with that infinitive, i.e., from being an accusative if there is a direct object of the infinitive, and from being a dative if there is an indirect object of the infinitive. Note however that the restriction against two accusatives is absolute with the causative construction, but does not apply to the perception construction; this may suggest that we identify only one predicate in the causative construction, and two in the perception construction where the subject accusative is governed by the main verb and the direct object accusative is governed by the infinitive. The restriction against two datives is relaxed in many cases, particularly if the two datives are separated at least by an intonation break, and if the subject of the infinitive is a dative clitic and the indirect object a noun;
(II) the semantic values associated with the three constructions: with an accusative subject the action is seen as a continuing process, with a dative it is seen as completed; the dative suggests also the unexpectedness of the action and the involvement of the main verb subject with the action indicated by the infinitive; with an agentive subject the attention is focussed on the object of the infinitive. We can try to convey some of these distinctions with the following English translations: *la ho vista scrivere una lettera* 'I saw her writing a letter'; *le ho visto scrivere una lettera* 'I saw her write a letter'; *la ho vista scrivere da lei* 'I saw it being written by her'.
(e) It is grammatically possible to have clusters of three and even four conjunctive pronouns, though they are unlikely to be used as

they are so clumsy. If we take *potete telefonarmi il risultato in albergo* 'you can telephone the result to me at the hotel', and we use a conjunctive pronoun for *il risultato* we get *potete telefonarmelo in albergo*; if we also use one for *in albergo* we get *potete telefonarmicelo*. If we take *uno si toglie le scarpe in giardino* 'one takes off one's shoes in the garden', use conjunctive pronouns for *le scarpe (le)*, *in giardino (vi)*, and for *uno* use the impersonal *si* (which, combined with the *si* of *si toglie* gives *ci si*, see chapter VI. 11(c)), we get *vi ce le si toglie*.

There are however simpler combinations which are excluded, for instance those of two pronouns in the same case or of two identical pronouns, as seen above for *gli* + *le* (both datives) and *si* + *si*. Other examples: we can have *mi scrivi una lettera?* in the sense of 'would you write a letter for me?', and *gli scrivi una lettera?* 'would you write him a letter?', but we cannot render 'would you write him a letter for me?' with both unstressed datives (*mi* + *gli*) in the same sentence; if we have *uno si avvicina a noi* 'someone approaches us', we cannot both use the conjunctive form *ci* for *a noi* and the impersonal *si* for *uno*, as the result would be *ci* + *ci si avvicina* which is excluded; from a sentence like *avvicinò me* (or *te, noi, voi*) *a sè stesso* 'he drew me (or you (singular), us, you (plural)) to him', according to rule (a) (i) we should get *si* followed by *mi* (or *ti, ci, vi*) *avvicinò*, but these combinations are excluded, as the table indicates.

Another combination which appears not to be available is the third person direct object pronoun (*lo, la, li, le*) + *ne*; if we take *prende il bicchiere dall'armadio* 'he takes the glass from the cupboard' and use *ne* for *dall'armadio*, we get *ne prende il bicchiere*, but if we also want to use a conjunctive pronoun for *il bicchiere* we can have neither *lo ne prende*, which is ungrammatical, nor *ne lo prende* which sounds so archaic as to be excluded from contemporary usage. Similarly, from *lo ringrazia di ciò* 'he thanks him for it' we cannot have either *lo ne ringrazia* or *ne lo ringrazia*.

The clusters cannot be split: we have *glielo dico* 'I am saying it to him', *diglielo* 'say it to him', *non dirglielo* and *non glielo dire* 'do not say it to him' but we cannot put the form of *dire* between *gli* and *lo*.

(f) In certain fixed expressions like *cavarsela* 'to cope', *sentirsela* 'to feel up to', the pronominal clusters may be treated as a unit and consequently be linked with other pronouns to form combinations which do not follow the sequence given above: *ci se la cava* 'one can cope' vs. *ce la si cava* 'one takes it off', as in *se fa caldo, ce la si cava*, *la giacca* 'if it's hot, one takes off one's jacket', and *ci se la sente* 'one feels up to it' vs. *ce la si sente* 'one feels it', as in *ce la si sente pesare addosso, la giacca, quando fa caldo* 'one feels one's jacket weighing on one, when it's hot'.

11   The use of *si*

(a) Concerning reflexives

Si is the unstressed form of the third person reflexive personal pronoun singular and plural, both direct and indirect. Like the other reflexive pronouns it can be reciprocal in the plural: *ci scriviamo spesso* 'we often write to each other', *vi scrivete spesso* 'you often write to each other', *si scrivono spesso* 'they often write to each other'.

Examples: *Ada si guarda allo specchio* (direct *si*) 'Ada looks at herself in the mirror', *Ada si guarda le unghie* (indirect *si*) 'Ada looks at her nails'.

(i) The reflexive pronoun is used in Italian when the subject performs the action on himself (or on articles of clothing he is wearing, or objects he is carrying on him or with him), treating himself as an object: *si gratta la gamba* 'he scratches his leg', *si taglia i capelli* 'he cuts his hair', *si tocca la cravatta* 'he touches his tie'. The same action can be performed on someone else with the appropriate change of pronoun: *mi gratta la gamba* 'he scratches my leg', *ti taglia i capelli* 'he cuts your hair', *gli tocca la cravatta* 'she touches his tie'. If there is no pronoun the object is presented as separate from its owner: *gratta la gamba* (which is being sculpted for a statue), *taglia i capelli* (a barber does this, to hair in general), *tocca la cravatta* (which is on the table).

There is consequently a difference between the ethic dative of *si fa il caffè* 'he is making himself some coffee' and the reflexive dative of *si tocca la cravatta*. A sentence like *si pulisce le scarpe* 'he cleans his shoes' is from this point of view ambiguous: he may be cleaning his shoes before putting them on (ethic dative), or he may be cleaning the shoes he has on (reflexive dative). This becomes apparent in cases where the ethic dative is not likely to be used like *si tocca una scarpa* 'he touches his shoe' (if he has it on), but *tocca una scarpa* 'he touches a shoe' (even if it is his own, when it is not on his foot).

(ii) The presence vs. absence of the reflexive may have another function, as in *Ada si guarda le unghie* 'Ada looks at her nails' vs. *Ada apre gli occhi* 'Ada opens her eyes'. In both cases the English equivalent introduces the possessive: 'her nails', 'her eyes'. In Italian however the reflexive is not used when the subject performs an action in which he alone is involved but does not treat himself as an object; the action is accomplished, so to speak, from within: *apre gli occhi* 'he opens his eyes', *muove la testa* 'he moves his head', *alza un piede* 'he lifts his foot'. Here again in English the possessive is used; in Italian the use of the reflexive (*si apre gli occhi, si muove la testa, si alza un piede*) would put these sentences within the previous category, implying that it is with his hands that the subject is opening his eyes, moving his head, lifting his foot.

If the action concerns the subject as a whole and not only a part of him, then the reflexive pronoun is used for the same kind of action 'from within': *mi sveglio* 'I wake up', *mi alzo* 'I get up', *mi muovo* 'I move'. If the object is a different person, the action becomes 'from without', as in *ti sveglio* 'I wake you'. Consequently one has the same type of action from within in *apre gli occhi, mi sveglio*, the same kind of action from without in *si apre gli occhi* (i.e., with his hands), *ti sveglio*. The difference between the two kinds of action is apparent in *mi alzo, ti alzi* (action from within) 'I get up', 'you get up', and *ti alzo, mi alzi* (action from without) 'I lift you up', 'you lift me up'.

(iii) When reflexive verbs are constructed with *fare* 'to make', *lasciare* 'to let', the reflexive pronoun is eliminated even in cases in which the verb is never otherwise used without it: *ho visto Ugo alzarsi* 'I saw Ugo get up': *l'ho visto alzarsi*, but *ho fatto pentire Ugo* 'I made Ugo repent': *l'ho fatto pentire*. Consequently *ho fatto alzare Ugo, l'ho fatto alzare*, are ambiguous: they may mean 'I made Ugo get up' (out of context the most likely interpretation), or 'I had Ugo lifted up' (cf. chapter V. 8(d)).

There are two other constructions with *si* in Italian: the impersonal one as in *si parte alle dieci* 'one leaves at ten', and the passive one as in *questo giornale si legge con piacere* 'this paper is read with pleasure', which is normally used when the agent is not expressed (but in rare cases the agent may be present: *questo giornale si legge ogni mattina da moltissima gente* 'this paper is read every morning by lots of people').[8]

(b) **Passive** *si*

The passive without *si* is expressed by the auxiliary *essere* and a past participle: active *vede* 'he sees', passive *è visto* 'he is seen' (see chapter V. 15(p)). The passive, especially when the agent is not expressed, can be conveyed by *si* and the active form of the verb: *si vede* 'he is seen'. This applies to third persons singular and plural, to the gerund, to the past participle (used on its own), and to the infinitive: *si vedono, vedendosi, vedutosi, vedersi.*

There is agreement in number between the verb and the subject of the passive: *si vede una stella* 'a star is seen', *si vedono due stelle* 'two stars are seen'.

In compound tenses the auxiliary *avere* is changed to *essere*, following the general rule that all pronominal verbs take the auxiliary *essere*, whatever the function of the pronoun: auxiliary *avere* in *ho bevuto una birra,* but auxiliary *essere* in *mi sono bevuto una birra* 'I drank a beer'. Examples: active *ha visto Ugo* 'he has seen Ugo', passive *si è visto Ugo* 'Ugo has been seen'; active *avrà visto Ugo* 'he will have seen Ugo', passive *si sarà visto Ugo* 'Ugo will have been seen'.

In compound tenses there is also agreement in gender and number in the past participle: *si è vista una stella* 'a star has been seen', *si sono viste due stelle* 'two stars have been seen'.

(c) **Impersonal** *si*

Si is also used in impersonal constructions, when the agent is indefinite. For practical purposes it may be useful to think of this *si* as corresponding to English *one* and to French *on* (a reduced form from Latin *homo*, parallel to Old Italian *uom* which was often similarly used as an indefinite subject): *si va* 'one goes', French *'on va'*. But unlike *one* and *on* this impersonal *si* is historically connected with the *si* of the reflexive and passive constructions.

It must be remembered that *si* corresponds to 'one' used as subject, but, unlike 'one', it cannot be used as direct or indirect object; *ci* 'us', *ti* 'you', *uno* 'one', *qualcuno* 'someone' are used instead: *se ti prendono è finita* may mean 'if they catch one, it's all over'. If in the same sentence there is an impersonal *si*, then *ci* is used as the object: *si è contenti se ci scrivono* 'one is pleased if they write to one'.

A *si* construction can often be interpreted either as passive or as impersonal: *si vede* may correspond to a passive *è visto* 'is seen' or to an impersonal *uno vede* 'one sees'. With the impersonal construction one finds an unexpected agreement in number between the verb and the object: *si compra una penna* 'one buys a pen', *si comprano due penne* 'one buys two pens'.

In compound tenses the past participle has a masculine singular ending when the verb takes the auxiliary *avere* in a non-*si* construction and a masculine plural ending when the verb takes the auxiliary *essere* in a non-*si* construction. The auxiliary actually used with a *si* construction is always *essere*, conforming with the rule mentioned above: *si è lavorato* 'one has worked' (*lavorato* because *lavorare* otherwise takes the auxiliary *avere: uno ha lavorato*), *si è partiti* 'one has left' (*partiti* because *partire* always takes the auxiliary *essere: uno è partito*). The masculine plural ending is compulsory for adjectives appearing as a predicate in a *si* construction: *si è allegri* 'one is merry'. Note that *si è allegri* is present whilst *si è partiti* is past.

The -*i* ending may be used even by women speakers, but when a feminine noun is introduced there is agreement with it: *si è sfruttati* 'one is exploited', but *quando si è donne si è sfruttate* 'when one is a woman one is exploited'. Normally the noun is in the plural; it can be in the singular, however, when it refers to a position unique in the context, and in this case an adjective or past participle would end in -*i: quando si è la prima attrice si è privilegiati* 'when one is the leading lady one has privileges'.

The impersonal *si* construction can be used with passive verbs which, as they take the auxiliary *essere*, have an -*i* in the past participle: *si è lodati* 'one is praised'.

The difference between the endings of the past participles may be the only element which distinguishes sentences with different meanings: *si è capiti* 'one is understood' (impersonal of the present passive) vs. *si è capito* 'one has understood' (impersonal of the perfect active).

The agreement mentioned above between verb and object is extended in compound tenses to gender as well as number: *si è comprata una penna* 'one has bought a pen', *si sono comprate due penne* 'one has bought two pens'.

Some grammars present only one indefinite construction with *si*, without distinguishing an impersonal and a passive construction. The superficial identity of the two constructions should not however obscure their difference at a deeper level: whilst *si compra una penna* may have the same origin at a deeper level as *uno compra una penna* or as *una penna è comprata*, and is therefore ambiguous as to its passive or impersonal interpretation, in other cases there is no ambiguity and only one of the two interpretations is possible.

With intransitives there can obviously not be a passive interpretation: *si va* 'one goes' must be impersonal; when the agent preceded by *da* is expressed (as is possible, although very rare) a *si* construction cannot be impersonal and must be interpreted as passive: *quest'opera si accoglie con entusiasmo da tutti* 'this work is enthusiastically acclaimed by all'.

In constructions with modals, as in *questo si può capire facilmente* the passive interpretation 'this can easily be understood' allows the *si* to be shifted after the infinitive: *questo può capirsi facilmente*, where *capirsi* has the meaning of *essere capito*; but this shift cannot occur with the impersonal interpretation 'one can easily understand this'.

The respective position of the noun phrase and the verb phrase may also make one of the interpretations preferable though not compulsory: *non si può sempre dire la verità* is more readily interpreted as impersonal 'one cannot always tell the truth', whereas *la verità non si può sempre dire* is more readily interpreted as passive 'the truth cannot always be told'.

The sentences already quoted *si comprano due penne, si è comprata una penna, si sono comprate due penne* can be expressed in their impersonal interpretation only, and not in their passive interpretation, in the (admittedly far less common) forms *si compra due penne, si è comprato una penna, si è comprato due penne* respectively, without agreement of gender or number between the verb and the object. Also possible, but not common, is the form with the agreement of the past participle, but not of the auxiliary, with the object: *si è comprate due penne.*

With pronominal verbs such as *pentirsi* 'to repent', *comprarsi* 'to buy (for oneself)', *lavarsi* 'to wash (oneself)', the impersonal *si* should be added to the third person singular *si* of *si pente, si compra, si lava.* However, instead of *si si*, the form used is *ci si: ci si pente* 'one repents', *ci si compra* 'one buys for oneself', *ci si lava* 'one washes oneself'. Constructions in which an impersonal *si* should be added to a *ci si* are avoided; we saw in chapter VI. 10(e) that in *uno si avvicina a noi* 'one approaches us' the *uno* cannot be changed into *si* and at the same time the *a noi* into *ci*; one either has to say *uno ci si avvicina* or *ci si avvicina a noi.* In *uno si avvicina a quel posto* 'one approaches that place', *uno* can be changed into the impersonal *si* and *a quel posto* into a locative unstressed pronoun only if it is *vi* and not *ci: vi ci si avvicina* 'one approaches it'.

When there is an object, pronominal verbs behave like non-pronominal ones: *si compra una penna, si comprano due penne,* from *comprare,* and *ci si compra una penna, ci si comprano due penne,* from *comprarsi.*

With compound tenses the ending of the past participle is in *-i,* because, as we have seen above, the auxiliary used with these pronominal verbs is *essere: ci si è pentiti* 'one has repented', *ci si è comprati* 'one has bought (for oneself)', *ci si è lavati* 'one has washed (oneself)', *ci si è cominciati a render conto di questo* 'one has begun to realize this'; but *si è cominciato a rendersi conto di questo* with *cominciato* and not *cominciati* because it corresponds to *uno ha cominciato a rendersi conto di questo* (with auxiliary *avere*) and not to *uno si è cominciato a render conto di questo* (with auxiliary *essere*).

If there is an object, there may

(i) not be agreement between past participle and object: *ci si è comprati una penna, ci si è comprati due penne;*

(ii) be agreement between past participle and object: *ci si è comprata una penna, ci si è comprate due penne;*

(iii) be agreement between the whole of the verb form (including the auxiliary) and the object: *ci si è comprata una penna, ci si sono comprate due penne* (cf. *si sono comprate due penne,* quoted above).

Note that both in the passive and in the impersonal constructions the agreement may work across complex verbal structures: *si correggono le bozze* 'one corrects proofs', *si devono correggere le bozze* 'one must correct proofs', *si devono poter correggere le bozze* 'one must be able to correct proofs', *si devono poter cominciare a correggere le bozze* 'one must be able to begin to correct proofs'.

(d) *Si* as first person plural

The impersonal construction with *si* may be used with the value of first person plural (a usage which has a Tuscan flavour), with or without a preceding *noi: (noi) si compra una penna* corresponds to *(noi) compriamo una penna.* There are circumstances in which the impersonal *si* construction and the first person plural *si* construction are not identical:

(i) in the first person plural *si* construction there is a tendency to introduce agreement between the past participle and the subject; female speakers, whilst using *ci si è comprati un libro* 'one has bought oneself a book', *ci si è comprati due penne* as impersonal forms, will use *ci si è comprate una penna, ci si è comprate due libri* 'we bought ourselves two books' as first person plural forms;

(ii) whilst, as we have seen above, with an impersonal interpretation *si comprano due penne, si sono comprate due penne* are more common than *si compra due penne, si è comprato due penne*, with the meaning of first person plural the latter two are more common.

There are two further ways in which the impersonal and the first person plural constructions differ, which we will see in our discussion of pronominalization in the *si* constructions below.

(e) **Pronominalization**

When a conjunctive pronoun is used for the object in the impersonal *si* construction *si compra una penna* gives *la si compra, si comprano due penne* gives *le si compra*, or less commonly *le si comprano, si è comprata una penna* gives *la si è comprata, si sono comprate due penne* gives *le si è comprate*, or less commonly *le si sono comprate*.

In modern Italian in a sentence like *la si compra* the pronoun *la* is interpreted as an object, not as a subject, and *si compra* can only be interpreted as an impersonal and not a passive form. There is little doubt that this is the contemporary value of such sentences, notwithstanding the efforts of grammarians who during the last century tried to prove that they had to be interpreted as passives, *la* being the unstressed form of the feminine subject pronoun (as in the obsolete or dialectal *la dice* 'she says'); sentences like *mi si vede* 'one sees me', *ti si vede* 'one sees you', *lo si vede* 'one sees him' were considered ungrammatical because *mi, ti, lo* (unlike *la*) could not be interpreted as forms of the subject pronouns. In modern Italian they are perfectly grammatical, with *mi, ti, lo,* etc., as objects.

With pronominal verbs, from *ci si compra una penna* we get *ce la si compra*, from *ci si comprano due penne* we get *ce le si compra*, and less commonly *ce le si comprano*, from *ci si è comprati una penna* we get *ce la si è comprata*, from *ci si sono comprate due penne* we get *ce le si è comprate*, and less commonly *ce le si sono comprate*.

The order of pronouns in impersonal constructions differs from the order in personal constructions: *la si compra* 'one buys it' vs. *se la compra* 'he buys it for himself', *le si compra* or *le si comprano* 'one

buys them', vs. *se le compra* 'he buys them for himself', *se le comprano* 'they buy them for themselves', *la si è comprata* 'one bought
it' vs. *se la è comprata* 'he bought it for himself', *le si è comprate* or *le
si sono comprate* 'one bought them' vs. *se le è comprate* 'he bought
them for himself', *se le sono comprate* 'they bought them for themselves'.

The same contrast applies when *ci* precedes; in personal
constructions *ci* is most naturally interpreted as a locative: *ce la si
compra* 'one buys it for oneself' vs. *ci se la compra* 'he buys it for
himself there'.

As mentioned above, when there is pronominalization we find
two further cases of distinction between the impersonal and the first
person plural *si* constructions:

(i) When *ci si* is used, the agreement between the object pronoun
and the past participle is compulsory in impersonal *si* constructions,
but it is optional in first person plural *si* constructions.

The following two sentences (with agreement of past participle
and object pronoun) can be interpreted both as impersonal and as
first person plural: (A) *ce la si è comprata*, (B) *ce le si è comprate*.

The following four sentences (with agreement of past participle
with subject) can only be interpreted as first person plural: (C) *ce la
si è comprati*, (D) *ce le si è comprati*, (E) *ce la si è comprate*, (F) *ce le si
è comprate* (in (C) and (D) a masculine *noi*, and in (E) and (F) a
feminine *noi* is understood).

Although (B) and (F) are the same on the surface, in (B) *comprate*
is interpreted as agreeing with the object *le*, and in (F) with a
feminine plural subject, as we have indicated.

(ii) With *ci si* constructions too, in the case of the first person plural,
but not in the case of the impersonal, the order of the pronouns can
be the one typical of personal constructions: (A) *ci se la è comprati*
'we (masculine) bought it for ourselves', (B) *ci se le è comprati* 'we
(masculine) bought them for ourselves', (C) *ci se la è comprate* 'we
(feminine) bought it for ourselves', (D) *ci se le è comprate* 'we
(feminine) bought them for ourselves'.

In these examples one can have an agreement between past
participle and object, so that (A) and (C) become *ci se la è comprata*,
and (B) and (D) *ci se le è comprate*.

12 The use of indicative past tenses: perfect (*passato prossimo*), past historic (*passato remoto*), imperfect (*imperfetto*)

(a) The use of the perfect and of the past historic varies in different parts of Italy. In the north the past historic is rarely used in spoken Italian, whilst in the south it is more widely used than the perfect. In central Italy a distinction is made in the use of the two tenses, and this distinction is observed in literary Italian. The notes that follow set out this usage.

The perfect is used to describe a completed action which is still felt to be in some way linked to the present. The rule often given that if an event happened in the last twenty-four hours the perfect should be used, is misleading. What is relevant is not so much the period of time which has elapsed as whether the event is felt to be related to the present: *mi diede un calcio* 'he gave me a kick' (but it is all forgotten) vs. *mi ha dato un calcio* 'he gave me a kick' (and I am still aching). If the question were asked *perchè sei così arrabbiato con lui?* 'why are you so angry with him?', the appropriate answer would be in the perfect (*perchè mi ha dato un calcio*) as the action is related to the present situation.

It is of course natural that the perfect should often be used for recent events: *mio fratello è partito due ore fa* 'my brother left two hours ago', *hai sentito il giornale radio delle sei?* 'did you hear the six o'clock news?', but one can also have examples like *lo vidi passare* 'I saw him go by' for an event of a short time before.

The perfect is also used to describe an action happening within a span of time which, however far back it began, is not yet concluded: *negli ultimi dieci anni abbiamo cambiato casa sette volte* 'in the last ten years we have moved house seven times' (but *in quei dieci anni cambiammo casa sette volte* 'in those ten years we moved house seven times'), *in questo secolo non sono nati grandi musicisti* 'no great musicians have been born this century'.

It is also used to describe past events the effects of which still last: *Dante ci ha dato nella 'Commedia' la maggiore opera della nostra letteratura* 'Dante with his *Comedy* has given us the greatest work in our literature'.

Note: *è nato nel 1901* 'he was born in 1901' (of someone who is still alive) vs. *nacque nel 1915* 'he was born in 1915' (of someone who is now dead).

The past historic is the past tense used for completed action which is no longer related to the present: *l'anno scorso non andai in vacanza* 'last year I did not go on holiday', *lo incontrai per caso in tram* 'I met him by chance on the tram', *visse ottantadue anni* 'he lived to the age of eighty-two', *passò tre anni a Napoli* 'he spent three years in Naples'. It is thus the tense normally used for the action in a narrative set in the past. The following passage from Pratolini shows the contrast between the perfect of conversation and the past historic of narrative:

'Il plotone dei fazzoletti rossi si schierò, fece fuoco, i tre al muro gridarono: "viva", e non si seppe viva cosa, non ebbero il tempo di finire.

'Sono cascati come burattini' disse Tosca.

Una donna, una sposa, accanto a lei si fece il segno della croce; Tosca la guardò, sorrise.

'Forse ho detto male?' le chiese, e si fece anch'essa il segno della croce.'

'The red kerchief platoon drew up and fired; the three against the wall cried "long live", one never knew long live what, they did not have time to finish. "They fell like puppets", said Tosca. A young married woman, standing by her, crossed herself. Tosca looked at her and smiled. "Perhaps I should not have said that?" she asked her, and she too crossed herself.'

(b) The imperfect is used in contrast with the perfect and the past historic for action (in the subordinate clause) during which something else goes on or happens (in the main clause). If the action in the main clause is continuous, it is expressed in the imperfect, if completed in the perfect or past historic: *lavorava a maglia mentre leggeva* 'she knitted as she read', *me l'ha raccontato mentre tornavo a casa* 'he told me as I went home', *mi venne in mente mentre facevo il bagno* 'it occurred to me while I was having a bath'.

The imperfect is used for completed action if this is habitual: *riposava ogni giorno dalle due alle tre* 'he rested every day from two to three', *per andare al lavoro partiva di casa presto* 'to go to work he left the house early'. Habitual action within a completed period of time is however in the past historic: *per un mese riposò ogni giorno dalle due alle tre* 'for a month he rested every day from two to three'; but *da un mese riposava ogni giorno dalle due alle tre quando cominciò a soffrire d'indigestione* 'he had been resting every day for a month from two to three when he began to suffer from indigestion': the same completed month in the past is here viewed as the background against which something else happens.

The imperfect is the tense normally used for descriptions: *la strada era polverosa* 'the road was dusty', *la nebbia copriva le montagne* 'mist covered the mountains'; for moods and physical states: *quando lo vidi era arrabbiato* 'when I saw him he was angry', *aveva molto sonno* 'he was very sleepy'.

There are some verbs which in the past are more frequently used in the imperfect: *sapeva bene il latino* 'he knew Latin well', *non capiva la musica* 'he did not understand music', *sembrava stanco* 'he seemed tired', *non credeva in Dio* 'he did not believe in God'. Their meaning may change if they are not used statively (referring to conditions which have a duration) but aoristically (referring to individual events): *seppe la notizia troppo tardi* 'he learnt the news too late', *capì che erano partiti* 'he realized that they had left', *sembrò stupito* 'he looked surprised', in the sense of: he took on a surprised expression, *non gli credemmo* 'we did not believe him'.

Another example from Pratolini exemplifies the contrast between the past historic and the imperfect: *'ella sollevò la testa e gli cercò le mani, gliele stringeva, e la sua voce, al contrario, tradì il turbamento ch'ella cercava di dissimulare, e il concetto da esprimere, così chiaro dentro di lei, riuscì sempre più sconclusionato, via via che essa parlava'* 'she lifted her head and sought his hands, she pressed them, but her voice betrayed the turmoil she was trying to hide, and the ideas she wanted to express, which were so clear inside her, became more and more confused as she talked'.

The imperfect can also be used:

(i) instead of a past conditional in sentences like: *dovevi venire prima* 'you should have come before', *potevi dirmelo* 'you might have told me';

(ii) instead of the present, in expressions like: *desiderava, signorina?* 'can I help you?' (literally: 'you wanted, miss?'), *volevo un vocabolario russo* 'I wanted a Russian dictionary'. But note that the present could only be used in the question: *desidera?* 'can I help you?'; in the statement of desire the present *voglio* would sound too peremptory. Here the other possible tense is the conditional: *vorrei* 'I should like';

(iii) instead of the pluperfect subjunctive, in conditional sentences: *se venivi prima* 'if you had come before' (cf. chapter VI. 13(c)(i));

(iv) instead of the past historic in narrative ('the historical imperfect'), originally to give a loftier, epic tone; but this has been so overworked in newspaper reporting that now it also has a journalese connotation: here is an example from the daily *Il Giorno* (24 August 1974): *'Il bandito si avvicinava alla Brembilla intimandole di aprire i cassetti della sua scrivania e qui rinveniva circa 800 mila lire, che infilava in un sacchetto di plastica. Subito dopo i due rapinatori uscivano di corsa balzando su una motocicletta, ma nell'andarsene ad uno degli sconosciuti sfuggiva di mano il casco ed il passamontagna.'* 'The robber went up to Miss (or Mrs) Brembilla and ordered her to open the drawers of her desk; here he found about 800 000 lire which he slipped into a plastic bag. Immediately afterwards the two robbers ran out, leaping on to a motorcycle, but as they went one of the two (unknown persons) lost hold of his helmet and balaclava'.

(v) Note that corresponding to the English past tenses in 'he has been here a week', 'he had been here a week', in Italian the present and imperfect are used with *da*: *è qui da una settimana, era qui da una settimana*. Whereas *è stato qui una settimana* and *era stato qui una settimana* correspond to 'he was here for a week'.

13 The use of the subjunctive

In a discussion of the subjunctive it seems desirable not so much to make general statements about its value (expressing doubt, or marking subordination) as to present some of the contexts in which it appears. The examples we have chosen are inevitably selective, but they should clarify the use of the subjunctive in the categories which seem to us the most relevant subdivisions for this analysis: (a) in main clauses, (b) in subordinate clauses where the subjunctive is obligatory, (c) in subordinate clauses where the choice between indicative and subjunctive is stylistic, (d) in subordinate clauses where the choice between indicative and subjunctive involves a clear-cut difference of meaning, (e) in subordinate clauses where the subjunctive indicates that the main clause has a different subject. We shall not discuss here the sequence of tenses which is dealt with in chapter VI. 14.

(a) Subjunctive in the main clause

(i) In the *lei* form of the imperative (commands and requests): *se ne vada* 'go away', *entri pure* 'do come in', *si accomodino, signori* 'please sit down, gentlemen';

(ii) in expressions of desire, hope or command: *possiate avere tutto il successo che meritate* 'may you have all the success you deserve', *Dio vi benedica* 'God bless you', *potessi venire anch'io* 'if only I could come too', *potessero vederti i tuoi genitori* 'if only your parents could see you', *purchè arrivi in tempo* 'as long as he arrives in time', *se venisse!* and *magari venisse* 'if only he'd come', *che non gli venga un raffreddore* 'if only he doesn't get a cold', *chissà che venga* 'let's hope he comes' (vs. *chissà se viene* 'I wonder if he's coming'), *che non si ripeta* 'mind it doesn't happen again';

(iii) in exclamations: *vedessi che lusso!* 'you should see how grand!', *sapessi che buffo!* 'if you knew how funny it was!';

(iv) in expressions of doubt: *che sia finito?* 'I wonder if it's finished?', *che venga qui?* 'I wonder if he'll come here?', *che sia lui?* 'I wonder if it's him?';

(v) in concessive expressions: *va bene, che venga anche lui* 'all right, let him come too', *sia pure come dici tu, ma io non vengo* 'it may well be as you say, but I'm not coming', *vada per la pizza* 'all right, let's settle for pizza'.

(b) Subordinate clauses where the subjunctive is obligatory

(i) After the following conjunctions and subordinating expressions:

affinchè: ti scrivo affinchè tu capisca la situazione 'I am writing to you so that you will understand the situation'; note that the personal pronoun is always used with the second personal singular of the present subjunctive to avoid ambiguities. If there is no pronoun it is assumed that the third person singular is being used: *spero che venga* 'I hope he comes', or 'I hope you come' (with the *lei* form);

benchè, sebbene, quantunque: le telefono benchè (or *sebbene*) *sia tardi* 'I'll ring her although (or: even though) it's late';

purchè, a condizione che, a patto che: vengo da voi, purchè mi aiutiate 'I'll come to you, as long as you help me', *le promise una bicicletta a condizione che* (or *a patto che*) *fosse promossa* 'he promised her a bicycle on condition that (or: as long as) she passed her exams'; *a meno che: stiamo a casa a meno che tu non abbia altri piani* 'we are staying at home, unless you have other plans';

per il caso che, nel caso che, caso mai, qualora: *lascio un biglietto per il caso che Ugo arrivi presto* 'I'm leaving a note in case Ugo arrives early';

prima che: *pulisce la casa prima che arrivino gli ospiti* 'he's cleaning the house before the guests arrive';

senza che: *è entrato senza che noi lo sentissimo* 'he came in without our hearing him' (vs. *è entrato senza salutarci* 'he came in without greeting us').

To these one should add some expressions, listed in (d) below, which have one meaning with the subjunctive, and another with the indicative, e.g., *perchè* (final) 'so that', with the subjunctive, and *perchè* (causal) 'because', with the indicative.

(ii) after some 'impersonal expressions' (the indicative here would be less acceptable than in (c)(ii) below): *è bene, meglio che* 'it is well, better that', *bisogna che* 'it is necessary that', *conviene che* 'one had better', *è facile, difficile che* 'it is easy, difficult that', *è necessario che* 'it is necessary that', *è probabile, improbabile che* 'it is likely, unlikely that', *può darsi che, può essere che* 'it may be that', *è raro che* 'it is rare that', *è utile, inutile che* 'it is useful, useless that', *vale la pena che* 'it is worth'. Examples: *bisogna che io lo veda* 'I must see him', *conviene che tu glielo dica* 'you had better tell him', *è necessario che lei si arrabbi?* 'does she have to get cross?', *può darsi che sia già arrivato* 'he may have already arrived', *è raro che il treno non parta in ritardo* 'it's rare for the train not to leave late', *è inutile che lui si metta a gridare* 'it's useless for him to start shouting', *vale la pena che lui lo pubblichi* 'it's worthwhile his publishing it'. We can also have a future or conditional after *è probabile, improbabile che, può darsi che, può essere che*.

(iii) after some verbs expressing desire, hope, permission, prevention: *augurarsi* 'to wish', *impedire* 'to prevent', *lasciare* 'to let', *permettere* 'to allow', *sperare* 'to hope', *volere* 'to want' (for verbs which allow the indicative, see (c)(v)). Examples: *mi auguro che tu guarisca presto* 'I hope you get well soon', *ho impedito che facesse troppi sbagli* 'I stopped him making too many mistakes' (also *gli ho impedito di fare troppi sbagli*), *lascerò che venga da solo* 'I'll let him come alone' (also *lo lascerò venire da solo*), *permetti che entrino?* 'will you allow them to come in?', *spero che Ugo ritorni sabato* 'I hope Ugo comes back on Saturday' (vs. *spero di ritornare* 'I hope to come back'). According to traditional grammars the indicative after *spero* is ungrammatical, but on a very informal level (especially with the second person) one can hear *spero che sei contento* 'I hope you're pleased', etc.; *voglio che venga* 'I want him to come' (vs. *voglio venire* 'I want to come'; and as for the previous example, very informally *non voglio che fai storie* 'I don't want you to make a fuss'.) We can also have a future or conditional after *augurarsi, sperare.*

(iv) with indefinite adjectives and pronouns: *qualunque cosa succeda, non preoccuparti* 'whatever happens, don't worry', *chiunque sia, non voglio vederlo* 'whoever he is, I don't want to see him', *compralo qualunque sia il prezzo* 'buy it whatever the cost'.

(v) in clauses of the following type juxtaposed to the main one without any conjunction: *così stanno le cose, ti piaccia o no* 'that is how things are, like it or not', *lo comprerei costasse un occhio* 'I would buy it even if it cost the earth', *lo faremo costi quel che costi* 'we will do it whatever the cost'.

(c) Subjunctive in subordinate clauses where the choice is stylistic

The subjunctive suggests either a nuance of uncertainty or a more formal level:

(i) *se tu l'avessi fatto sarebbe stato meglio* 'it would have been better if you had done it', and less formally *se lo facevi era meglio;*

(ii) with some 'impersonal' expressions: *è bello che* 'it is nice that', *è brutto che* 'it is nasty that', *è naturale che* 'it is natural that', *è peccato che* 'it is a pity that', *è strano che* 'it is strange that', *dispiace che* 'one is sorry that'. Examples: *è peccato* (or *che peccato*) *che sia già partito* 'it's a pity (or: what a pity) he has already left', and less formally *è peccato* (or *che peccato*) *che è già partito; mi dispiace che vada in Italia* 'I'm sorry he's going to Italy', and less formally *mi dispiace che va in Italia.*

The subjunctive is common with verbs used 'impersonally' if they introduce an element of uncertainty: *si dice che i soldati siano partiti* 'they say the soldiers have left': this is hearsay, as opposed to the affirmation *Ada dice che i soldati sono partiti.* Note that for hearsay or unconfirmed news the conditional is often used: *i soldati sarebbero partiti* 'it would seem that the soldiers have left', *il colpevole sarebbe stato arrestato* 'it would seem that the culprit has been arrested' (cf. chapter VI. 15(c)).

(iii) with verbs of feeling and thinking: *credere che* 'to think that', *parere che, sembrare che* 'to seem that'. Examples: *credo che tu abbia ragione* 'I think you are right', *mi pare che abbia il morbillo* 'it seems to me he has got measles' and less formally *credo che hai ragione, mi pare che ha il morbillo*. Statements of religious belief usually take the indicative: *credo che Dio esiste* 'I believe that God exists';

(iv) with some verbs of knowing and saying in the negative and in the interrogative: *dire che* 'to say that', *sapere se* 'to know whether', and after verbs of asking: *chiedere, domandare se* 'to ask whether'. Examples: *non dico che lui abbia torto* or less formally *non dico che ha torto* 'I do not say that he is wrong', *sai se sia vero?* or less formally *sai se è vero?* 'do you know whether it's true?', *non so se sia utile* or less formally *non so se è utile* 'I do not know whether it's useful', *mi chiese se fosse possibile* or less formally *mi chiese se era possibile* 'he asked me if it was possible'. Note that the conditional could be used to make the *se* clause more hypothetical: *non so se sarebbe utile* 'I do not know whether it would be useful', *mi chiese se sarebbe stato possibile* 'he asked me whether it would be possible' (for the use of the past conditional see chapter VI. 15(d));

(v) with some verbs indicating pleasure, displeasure, anger, regret, fear, surprise: *essere arrabbiato* 'to be angry', *aver paura* 'to be afraid', *essere contento, scontento* 'to be pleased, displeased', *essere felice, infelice* 'to be happy, unhappy', *rammaricarsi* 'to regret', *rincrescere* 'to be sorry', *essere sorpreso, stupito* 'to be surprised', *stupirsi* 'to be surprised', *temere* 'to fear'. Examples: *Sono arrabbiato che tu non mi abbia scritto* 'I'm cross that you have not written to me', *sono contento che venga presto* 'I'm pleased he's coming early', *mi rincresce che la lettera non sia arrivata in tempo* 'I'm sorry the letter did not arrive in time', *sono stupito che non mi abbia mandato un regalo* 'I'm surprised he has not sent me a present', *mi stupisce che non si sia fatto vivo* 'I'm surprised he did not get in touch', and less formally *sono arrabbiato che non mi hai scritto, sono contento che viene presto, mi rincresce che la lettera non è arrivata in tempo, sono stupito che non mi ha mandato un regalo, mi stupisce che non si è fatto vivo;*

(vi) in comparative, superlative and indefinite expressions: *è più grande di quanto mi aspettassi* 'he is bigger than I expected', *è la persona più gentile che io conosca* 'he is the kindest person I know', *non c'era nessuno che sapesse il russo* 'there was no one who knew Russian', *Ugo è l'unico che sia venuto* 'Ugo is the only one who came', and more informally *è più grande di quanto mi aspettavo, è la persona più gentile che conosco, non c'era nessuno che sapeva il russo, Ugo è l'unico che è venuto*;

(vii) when a clause introduced by *che* precedes instead of following the main verb: *che tu sia forte, lo so* 'that you are strong, that I do know', *che fosse studente non lo sapevo* 'that he was a student, that I didn't know', *che siano partiti è sicuro* 'that they have left, that is certain', and more informally *che sei forte, lo so; che era studente non lo sapevo; che sono partiti è sicuro*;

(viii) in indirect questions, at a formal level or conveying an element of surprise in the question: *domandai dove andasse* 'I asked where he might be going', *ho chiesto chi fosse* 'I asked who he might be', *ho domandato perchè fosse venuto* 'I asked why ever he had come', *mi ha chiesto se fosse possibile* 'he asked me whether it might be possible', and at a neutral level, reporting a straightforward question: *domandai dove andava* 'I asked where he was going', *ho chiesto chi era* 'I asked who he was', *ho domandato perchè era venuto* 'I asked why he had come', *mi ha chiesto se era possibile* 'he asked me whether it was possible'.

(d) Subjunctive in subordinate clauses where the choice involves a clear-cut difference of meaning

(i) after some verbs of thinking and believing: *si capisce che siano arrabbiati* 'it's understandable they should be cross', *si capisce che sono arrabbiati* 'it's clear that they are cross'; *penso che domani debba partire* 'I think he should be leaving tomorrow', *penso che domani deve partire* 'I am thinking of his having to leave tomorrow'; *mi sembra che volino* 'they seem to be flying', *mi sembra che volano* 'it seems to me they are flying';

(ii) after certain subordinating expressions: *aspetta che venga* 'wait until he comes', *aspetta che viene* 'wait, he's coming'; *dato che venga, possiamo star tranquilli* 'as long as he comes, we have no need to worry', *dato che viene possiamo star tranquilli* 'seeing that he's coming, we have no need to worry'; *dopo che Ugo fosse partito non restava più niente da fare* 'after Ugo had gone, there was never anything left to do', *dopo che Ugo fu partito non restava più niente da fare* 'after Ugo had gone, there was nothing to do'; *fermati finchè sia bello* 'stay here until it becomes fine', *fermati finchè è bello* 'stay here as long as it is fine';[9] *mi ha aiutato perchè avessi un buon voto* 'he helped me so that I could get a good mark', *mi ha aiutato perchè avevo un buon voto* 'he helped me because I had a good mark'; *per quanto abbia vinto non lo invidio* 'I do not envy him although he has won', *per quanto ha vinto non lo invidio* 'I do not envy him for what he has won'; *se venga non te lo chiedo* 'I am not asking you whether he is coming', *se viene non te lo chiedo* 'if he comes I will not ask you for it'; *se venisse nessuno lo sapeva* 'no one knew whether he was coming', *se veniva nessuno lo sapeva* 'if he had come no one would have known';

(iii) in relative clauses: *cerco una ragazza che sappia il cinese* 'I am looking for a girl who knows Chinese' (if there is one), *cerco una ragazza che sa il cinese* 'I am looking for a girl who knows Chinese' (a specific one whose existence I know of).

(e) In subordinate clauses introduced by *che*

The subject may not be the same as the subject of the main clause if the subjunctive is used; if the subject is the same a construction with the infinitive or the indicative must be used: *penso di poter venire*, or *penso che posso venire* 'I think I can come', but not *penso che io possa venire; penso che tu, egli,* etc., *possa venire* is of course correct. (One may however find examples like '*Ma adesso mi pare che debba dire basta*' 'but now I think I have to say enough is enough' (from an interview with an Italian minister, *Il Giorno*, 28 September 1974); their grammaticality is doubtful).

Ha detto che viene may mean that he said he was coming himself or that he said someone else was coming, whereas *ha detto che venga* can only mean that he told someone else to come.

14 Sequence of tenses

The use of tenses in subordinate clauses follows two different patterns according to whether the verb of the main clause requires a present sequence or a past sequence. A **present sequence** is found with the present, future, perfect, and future perfect of the indicative, and with the present conditional; a **past sequence** is found with the imperfect, past historic, perfect, pluperfect of the indicative, and with the past conditional. It will be noticed that the perfect can take either sequence, as it refers both to a past action and to the resulting present situation.

We give examples for the present and imperfect indicative only, and note the few differences for other tenses. The examples are classified according to whether the verb in the subordinate clause refers to an action which is contemporary, successive or anterior to that of the main clause. In the following tables we omit the conditional in subordinate clauses because this will be dealt with in chapter VI. 15.

(a) **Main clause**   **Subordinate clause**

                           contemporary

present indicative   + present indicative   *so che è qui* 'I know he is here'

                           + present subjunctive   *non so se sia qui* 'I do not know whether he is here'

                           successive

                           + present indicative   *so che viene domani* 'I know he is coming tomorrow'

                           + present subjunctive   *non so se venga domani* 'I do not know whether he is coming tomorrow'

                           + future indicative   *so che verrà domani* 'I know he will come tomorrow'

                           + future perfect   *so che fra due giorni sarà partito* 'I know he will have left in two days' time'

                           anterior

                           + imperfect indicative   *so che veniva* 'I know he was coming'

                           + imperfect subjunctive   *non so se venisse* 'I do not know whether he was coming'

+ perfect indicative	*so che è venuto* 'I know he has come'
+ perfect subjunctive	*non so se sia venuto* 'I do not know whether he has come'
+ past historic	*so che venne l'anno scorso* 'I know he came last year'
+ pluperfect indicative	*so che era venuto due giorni prima* 'I know that he had come two days before'
+ pluperfect subjunctive	*non so se fosse venuto due giorni prima* 'I do not know whether he had come two days before'

When the main clause has (i) the future, the subordinate clause may have a future for contemporary action: *quando partiremo ci vedrà* 'he will see us when we leave', and a future perfect for anterior action: *ci cercherà solo dopo che saremo partiti* 'he will look for us only after we have left'; (ii) the future perfect, the subordinate clause cannot express an anterior action; (iii) the present conditional, the subordinate clause has an imperfect subjunctive for contemporary and successive action in sentences like *vorrei che tu fossi qui* 'I wish you were here', *vorrei che tu venissi presto* 'I wish you would come soon' (see the sequence in conditional sentences in chapter VI. 15(f)).

(b) **Main clause**

Main clause	Subordinate clause contemporary	
imperfect indicative	+ imperfect indicative	*sapevo che era qui* 'I knew he was here'
	+ imperfect subjunctive	*non sapevo se fosse qui* 'I did not know whether he was here'

successive

+ imperfect indicative	*sapevo che veniva il giorno dopo* 'I knew he was coming the next day'
+ imperfect subjunctive	*non sapevo se venisse il giorno dopo* 'I did not know whether he was coming the next day'

anterior

+ pluperfect indicative	*sapevo che era già venuto* 'I knew he had already come'
+ pluperfect subjunctive	*non sapevo se fosse già venuto* 'I did not know whether he had already come'

When the main clause has the past historic the subordinate clause may have a past anterior for anterior action: *ci cercò solo dopo che fummo partiti* 'he looked for us only after we had left' (cf. chapter V. 15(m)).

The rules for the sequence of tenses given above do not take into account cases in which the subordinate clause:

(c) expresses a general statement: *mi disse che l'acqua bolle a cento gradi* 'he told me that water boils at 100°'; *affermava che le leggi fisiche hanno un carattere statistico* 'he claimed that the laws of physics have a statistical character', where a present tense follows a past;

(d) is formulated in 'semi-direct speech' (or bound direct speech: *stile diretto legato*), i.e., contains an expression used in direct speech and inserted into the reported sentence without conforming to the rules of indirect speech, as in *diceva che è contento* (instead of *era contento*, in a subordinate clause contemporary to the main one) 'he said he was happy', *diceva che Ugo ci restò male* (instead of *ci era restato male*, in a subordinate clause anterior to the main one) 'he said Ugo was upset'.[10]

15 The use of the conditional

(a) The different values of the conditional seem to have a common denominator suggesting desire, intention, or possibility: *mi piacerebbe saper cantare* 'I would like to be able to sing', *mi sarebbe piaciuto saper cantare* 'I would have liked to be able to sing' vs. *mi piace* (or *mi piaceva*) *saper cantare* 'I am (or: was) glad to be able to sing'.

(b) It can be used to suggest something less categorical than the indicative: *direi che è meglio andare* 'I think it might be better to go', *penserei di venire* 'I am planning to come', *non saprei* 'I wouldn't know', *vorrei un paio di guanti* 'I should like a pair of gloves', and also in questions: *avrebbe un paio di guanti?* 'would you have a pair of gloves?', *mi potrebbero dare un'informazione?* 'could you give me some information?', and with an imperative (tone 5) rather than an interrogative (tone 2) intonation: *mi lascerebbero in pace per favore!* 'would you please leave me in peace!', *vorrebbero andarsene!* 'would you go!'.

(c) It is frequently used in reporting unconfirmed news: *i criminali sarebbero ancora nei dintorni* 'the criminals are probably still in the neighbourhood', *sarebbero penetrati nel negozio durante la notte* 'they apparently broke into the shop during the night'.

(d) In indirect speech the following sequences are found: *dice che verrebbe* 'he says he would come' or 'he says he will come' (successive or contemporary subordinate); *dice che sarebbe venuto* 'he says he would have come' (i.e., next week, had we still been here: successive subordinate), or 'he says he would have come' (i.e., last week had we already been here: anterior subordinate); *diceva che sarebbe venuto* 'he said that he would come' (contemporary or successive subordinate, which can also be expressed as *diceva che verrebbe* in semi-direct speech), or 'he said he would have come' (i.e., the week before, had we already been there: anterior subordinate).

Some grammars suggest that in the past sequence referring to successive action the present or the past conditional can be used indifferently; other grammars suggest that the present should be used if the action did happen or is presented as sure to happen. In this case *diceva che verrebbe* (as a successive subordinate) would not be in semi-direct speech but in regular indirect speech. The past conditional is in fact generally preferred. But in sentences like: *che cosa vogliono? – Hanno detto che prenderebbero un gelato* 'what do they want? – They said they'll have an ice-cream' the present conditional is used with a present sequence of tenses which is compatible with the perfect of the main clause.

In colloquial Italian the imperfect indicative can also be used for successive action: *sapevo che veniva* 'I knew he was coming', but not with verbs that usually take the subjunctive: *speravo che non venisse* or *speravo che non sarebbe venuto* 'I hoped he would not come'; similarly with the present *spero che non venga* or *spero che non verrà* 'I hope he does not come'.

(e) Three types of conditional sentences (*periodi ipotetici*) are usually distinguished, depending on whether the condition is assumed to be (i) real, (ii) possible, or (iii) unreal. Examples:

(i) *se vinci ti danno un premio* 'if you win they give you a prize'; also with other indicative tenses: *se l'hai comprato ieri hai fatto un buon affare* 'if you bought it yesterday, it was a bargain';

(ii) *se tu vincessi ti darebbero un premio* 'if you won they would give you a prize';

(iii) (A) *se tu avessi vinto ti avrebbero dato un premio* 'if you had won, they would have given you a prize'; in type (iii) the imperfect indicative can be used colloquially: *se vincevi ti davano un premio* (this can of course have another meaning, and refer to habitual action in the past: 'whenever you won they gave you a prize'); it is also possible to have a type (iii) protasis (if-clause) with a type (ii) apodosis (main clause), and this gives (iii)(B) *se tu avessi vinto ti darebbero un premio* 'if you had won they would give you a prize'.

(f) Just as one has conditional sentences like *sarei contento se venisse* 'I would be pleased if he came', and *sarei contento se fosse venuto* 'I would be pleased if he had come', so with a subordinate clause introduced by *che* one gets *sarei contento che venisse* 'I would like him to come', *sarei contento che fosse venuto* 'I would like him to have come'. *Vorrei che venisse* 'I wish he would come' and *vorrei che fosse venuto* 'I wish he had come' (the former apparently contradicting the rules of the sequence of tenses) are produced on the above pattern (cf. chapter VI. 14 (a) (iii)).

There are two interesting uses of the conditional after *se*:

(g) when *se* corresponds to 'whether' or 'that': *non siamo sicuri se lo troverebbe* 'we are not sure that he would find it';

(h) when a past conditional in a protasis (instead of, as is usual, in an apodosis) indicates an action successive to the one of the main clause which is in the past: *perchè occorreva agitarsi se non si sarebbe ottenuto nulla?* 'what was the point of making a fuss, if one was not going to get anywhere?'; this is the use of the conditional for a successive subordinate clause in a past sequence discussed in (d) above. The *se* is here not hypothetical but has the meaning of 'seeing that', 'since'.

Notes

[1] In this section we use, with simplifications, the work done on English by HALLIDAY, M. A. K., *Intonation and Grammar in British English*, The Hague, 1967; cf. also Gruppo di Padova, 'L'ordine dei sintagmi nella frase', in *Fenomeni morfologici e sintattici nell'italiano contemporaneo* (Società di Linguistica Italiana, 7), Rome, 1974, pp. 147–161.

[2] We owe some ideas on the article to discussions with L. Renzi and to his paper *Per la storia dell'articolo romanzo*, Padua, 1974 (cyclostyled). Many of the categories we give are purely *ad hoc* and are only intended to provide practical help for the learner.

[3] G. Cinque has helped us to come to these conclusions.

[4] Cf. CONTE, M.-E., 'L'aggettivo in italiano. Problemi sintattici', in *Storia linguistica dell'Italia nel Novecento* (Società di Linguistica Italiana, 6), Rome, 1973, pp. 75–91.

[5] Cf. ALINEI, M., 'Il tipo sintagmatico "quel matto di Giorgio"', in *Grammatica trasformazionale italiana* (Società di Linguistica Italiana, 3), Rome, 1971, pp. 1–12.

[6] This table comes from RADFORD, A., *Counter-filtering rules*, Trinity College Cambridge, June, 1974 (cyclostyled), p. 4 (we use different labels).

[7] Cf. LEPSCHY, G., in *Festschrift für L. Palmer*, Innsbruck, 1976. Some of the sentences in brackets are ungrammatical for many speakers. Although they are grammatical for at least some informants (as emerges from a questionnaire of ours) they vary widely in acceptability. Foreign students would be well advised to steer clear of all the bracketed sentences.

[8] Cf. LEPSCHY, G., in *Studi Linguistici in onore di T. Bolelli*, Pisa, 1974.

[9] With *finchè* meaning 'until', a so-called pleonastic *non* is commonly used: *fermati finchè non sia bello*. The 'pleonastic' *non* must be used if the main clause is negative: *non uscire finchè non sia bello* 'don't go out until it becomes fine'. On a colloquial level the indicative is preferred to the subjunctive, so a sentence like *fermati finchè non c'è Ugo* may be interpreted as either 'stay here until Ugo arrives', or 'stay here while Ugo is out'. With *finchè* 'while' the *non* is not pleonastic, but has its normal negative value; thus it is possible to have *non uscire finchè c'è Ugo* 'don't go while Ugo is here'. A pleonastic *non* may also be used in comparative expressions, cf. chapter V. 6, and in exclamations: *quello che non le ha detto!* 'the things he told her!', *dove non è andato a cercare!* 'the places he looked in!'.

[10] We distinguish semi-direct from semi-indirect speech (or free indirect speech: *stile indiretto libero*); the latter uses the tenses of indirect speech in a main clause: *Mi rispose. Non mi credeva* for *Mi rispose che non mi credeva* 'He replied to me. He didn't believe me' for 'He replied to me that he didn't believe me' (direct: *Mi rispose: 'Non ti credo'* 'He replied to me: 'I don't believe you' ').

A Short Bibliography

For a general bibliography on Italian linguistics see the major work by HALL, R. A., JR., *Bibliografia della linguistica italiana*, Florence, 1958, with its *Primo supplemento decennale*, Florence, 1969; and the syntheses by MULJAČIĆ, Ž., *Introduzione allo studio della lingua italiana*, Turin, 1971; HALL, R. A., JR., *Bibliografia essenziale della linguistica italiana e romanza*, Florence, 1973.

Chapters I and II. On the history of Italian the basic work is MIGLIORINI, B., *Storia della lingua italiana*, Florence, 1960, which stops at 1915; an edition abridged and extended to our own day: MIGLIORINI, B., and BALDELLI, I., *Breve storia della lingua italiana*, Florence, 1964; in English, abridged and recast by GRIFFITH, T. G., *The Italian Language*, London, 1966. See also DEVOTO, G., *Profilo di storia linguistica italiana*, Florence, 1953; DEVOTO, G., *Il linguaggio d'Italia*, Milan, 1974 (which goes from the pre-Indo-European period to the present day; an outline of Italian, with full discussion of the pre-Roman and Roman periods in PULGRAM, E., *The Tongues of Italy*, Cambridge, Mass., 1958); DEVOTO, G., and ALTIERI, M. L., *La lingua italiana. Storia e problemi attuali*, Turin, 1968 (a readable synthesis); and the sketch by STUSSI, A., 'Lingua, dialetto e letteratura', in the first volume of the Einaudi *Storia d'Italia*, Turin, 1972, pp. 677–728.

Most important for the modern period: DE MAURO, T., *Storia linguistica dell'Italia unita*, Bari, 1976 (an enlarged edition of the work originally published in 1963). A sketch of modern Italian: SEGRE, C., 'Le caratteristiche della lingua italiana', in an appendix to BALLY, CH., *Linguistica generale e linguistica francese*, Milan, 1963, pp. 437–470. See also MIGLIORINI, B., *Lingua contemporanea*, Florence, 1963; MIGLIORINI, B., *La lingua italiana d'oggi*, Turin, 1967.

Chapter III. For the lexical material see JABERG, K., and JUD, J., *Sprach- und Sachatlas Italiens und der Südschweiz*, Zofingen, 1928–1940; this is used systematically in ROHLFS, G., *Grammatica storica della lingua italiana e dei suoi dialetti*, Turin, 1966–1969 (a more modern treatment of the historical grammar is offered by TEKAVČIĆ, P., *Grammatica storica dell'italiano*, Bologna, 1972); a brief synthesis: DEVOTO, G., and GIACOMELLI, G., *I dialetti delle regioni d'Italia*, Florence, 1972.

Chapter IV. Most information on local varieties is collected in De

Mauro's *Storia* quoted above; on sectional varieties see BECCARIA, G. L., ed., *I linguaggi settoriali in Italia*, Milan, 1973. On lexis see: PANZINI, A., *Dizionario moderno*, Milan, 1963, tenth edition with the appendix 'Parole nuove' by B. Migliorini. On Anglicisms: KLAJN, I., *Influssi inglesi nella lingua italiana*, Florence, 1972.

Chapters V and VI. There is no large scale and reliable grammar of modern Italian. Still useful in some respects are the antiquated works by FORNACIARI, R., *Grammatica italiana dell'uso moderno*, Florence, 1879 and *Sintassi italiana dell'uso moderno*, Florence, 1881 (the latter reprinted, with an introduction by G. Nencioni, Florence, 1974).

Among practical grammars in English: GRANDGENT, C.H., and WILKINS, E.H., *Italian Grammar*, Boston, 1915 revised edition; JONES, F.J., *A Modern Italian Grammar*, London, 1960; LENNIE, D., and GREGO, M., *Italian for You. A Practical Grammar*, London, 1960; MCCORMICK, C.A., *Basic Italian Grammar*, London, 1969; SPEIGHT, K., *Teach Yourself Italian*, London, 1943.

On a larger scale, in Italian: BATTAGLIA, S., and PERNICONE, V., *La grammatica italiana*, Turin, 1973 (new edition); REGULA, M., and JERNEJ, J., *Grammatica italiana descrittiva su basi storiche e psicologiche*, Bern, 1965; FOGARASI, M., *Grammatica italiana del Novecento*, Budapest, 1969.

A contrastive description: AGARD, F. B., and DI PIETRO, R. J., *The Sounds of English and Italian*, and *The Grammatical Structures of English and Italian*, Chicago, 1965; a structural description: HALL, R. A., JR., *La struttura dell'italiano*, Rome, 1971; on transformational lines there are the attempts by COSTABILE, N., *Le strutture della lingua italiana. Grammatica generativo-trasformativa*, Bologna, 1967 and *La flessione in italiano*, Rome, 1973; PUGLIELLI, A., *Strutture sintattiche del predicato in italiano*, Bari, 1970; LO CASCIO, V., *Strutture pronominali e verbali italiane*, Bologna, 1970; CÂRSTEA-ROMAŞCANU, M., *Corso di sintassi della lingua italiana contemporanea*, Bucharest, 1973 (cyclostyled). A new analysis is in the press: RADFORD, A., *Italian Syntax: Transformational and Relational Grammar* (Cambridge University Press). Much information will be found in the volumes published for the Società di Linguistica Italiana.

For the phonology see MULJAČIĆ, Ž., *Fonologia della lingua italiana*, Bologna, 1972.

For the lexis of modern Italian the largest and most reliable dictionary is the *Dizionario enciclopedico italiano*, Rome, 1955–1961, 12 vols. (*Appendice*, 1963, *Supplemento*, 1974) published by the Istituto della Enciclopedia Italiana. On a smaller scale the best are: MIGLIORINI, B., *Vocabolario della lingua italiana*, Turin, 1965; DEVOTO, G., and OLI, G., *Vocabolario illustrato della lingua italiana*, Milan, 1967, 2 vols (and in one volume *Dizionario della lingua italiana*, Florence, 1971); ZINGARELLI, N., *Vocabolario della lingua italiana*, Bologna, 1970, tenth revised edition. Historical dictionaries: TOMMASEO, N., and BELLINI, B., *Dizionario della lingua italiana*,

Turin, 1861–1879; BATTAGLIA, S., *Grande dizionario della lingua italiana,* Turin, 1967 foll.

Among bilingual dictionaries the best are the *Cambridge Italian Dictionary,* vol. 1 Italian-English, Cambridge, 1962, and the Sansoni-Harrap *Dizionario delle lingue italiana e inglese,* Florence, 1972–6. On a smaller scale one can recommend: HAZON, M., *Grande dizionario inglese-italiano italiano-inglese,* Milan, 1961; RAGAZZINI, G., *Dizionario inglese italiano italiano inglese,* Bologna, 1967.

Table of main symbols used

	bilabial	labiodental	dental and alveolar	retroflex	palato--alveolar	palatal	velar	uvular	glottal
plosive and affricate	p b		t d ts dz	ţ ɖ	tʃ dʒ	c ɟ	k g		ʔ
fricative	ɸ β	f v	θð s z		ʃ ʒ		x ɣ		h ɦ
nasal	m		n			ɲ	ŋ		
lateral			l			ʎ			
rolled and flapped			r	ɽ				ʀ	
semiconsonant	w					j			

	front	central	back	
close (or high)	i y		u	
	ɪ		ʊ	
half-close (or mid-high)	e ø		o	
		ə		
half open (or mid-low)		ɛ	ɔ	
		æ		
open (or low)		a		

The back vowels [u ʊ o ɔ] and, among the front ones, [y ø] have lip-rounding.

Diacritic symbols

_ under the symbol for a retracted consonant
˜ over the symbol for a nasalized vowel
: after the symbol for a long sound
· after the symbol for a longer (and more fortis) consonant
₀ under the symbol for a voiceless (and more lenis) consonant

Index

indefinites, 121–3
indiretto libero, stile, see semi-
    indirect speech
industrialization, 35
infinitive, *see* verb
    elimination in dialects, 57
informal, *see* formal
intensification, 106
internal migration, 35–6
interrogatives, 116–7
intransitive, *see* verb
-io endings, plurals, 103
irregular verbs, *see* verb
isogloss, 61
italiano popolare, see popular Italian
italiano settoriale, see sectional
    varieties

[j], Latin, 53–5
Jaberg, K., 237
Jernej, J., 238
Jones, D., 12
Jones, F. J., 238
Jud, J., 237
juxtaposed nouns, 79, 178–80

Klajn, I., 238
known, *see* given

la, neutral usage, 111
lasciare + infinitive, 142, 203–5,
    210
Latin, 19–21
    consonants, 51–2
    vowels, 42–5
Lei, form of address, 110–2
    agreement, 110–2
lenis, 71
lenition, 52
Lennie, D., 238
Lepschy, G., 150, 235–6
light syllables (in Latin), 43
linguaioli, 26–7
linguistic minorities, 11, 34, 40
literacy, 34–5
lo, neutral usage, 111
local dialect, 13
local varieties, 13–6, 37
    lexis, 74–6

morphology and syntax, 74
phonology, 15, 37, 62–74
Lo Cascio, V., 238
Luther, M., 25

Machiavelli, N., 22
main clause, 229–35
Manzoni, A., 23–6, 33, 38, 77, 172
Mass in the vernacular, 37
Matteucci, C., 35
McCormick, C. A., 238
media, 17, 37
Meneghello, L., 18, 31
Merlo, C., 52
metaphonesis, *see* metaphony
metaphony, 50–1
Meyer-Lübke, W., 52
mezzo, 125
mica, 119
Middle Ages, 19
Migliorini, B., 237–8
minimal pairs, 42
mixed vowels, 49
modals, *see* verb
Monelli, P., 29–30
Morante, E., 83
Moro, A., 32, 81
morphology, *see* adjectives
    see articles
    see contemporary Italian
    see local varieties
    see noun morphology
    see verb, morphology
movable diphthong, *see* verb
Muljačić,Ž., 237–8
Muller, H. F., 20
muta cum liquida, 43
Muzio, G., 22

narrative imperfect, *see* imperfect
nasalization, 73
national language, 13
ne, 112, 200–2, 211
negatives, 119–20, 235–6
    double negatives, 119
    negative imperative, 113
    with articles, 160
    with partitives, 101
Nencioni, G., 238